Diversity in Early Care and Education

HONORING DIFFERENCES

Fifth Edition

Janet Gonzalez-Mena

Napa Valley College

Mc
Graw
Hill

Boston   Burr Ridge, IL   Dubuque, IA   Madison, WI   New York
San Francisco   St. Louis   Bangkok   Bogotá   Caracas   Kuala Lumpur
Lisbon   London   Madrid   Mexico City   Milan   Montreal   New Delhi
Santiago   Seoul   Singapore   Sydney   Taipei   Toronto

The McGraw-Hill Companies

Mc Graw Hill Higher Education

DIVERSITY IN EARLY CARE AND EDUCATION
HONORING DIFFERENCES

Published by McGraw-Hill, a business unit of The McGraw-Hill Companies, Inc., 1221 Avenue of the Americas, New York, NY, 10020. Copyright © 2008, by The McGraw-Hill Companies, Inc. All rights reserved. No part of this publication may be reproduced or distributed in any form or by any means, or stored in a database or retrieval system, without the prior written consent of The McGraw-Hill Companies, Inc., including, but not limited to, in any network or other electronic storage or transmission, or broadcast for distance learning.

Some ancillaries, including electronic and print components, may not be available to customers outside the United States.

This book is printed on acid-free paper.

1 2 3 4 5 6 7 8 9 0 DOC/DOC 0 9 8 7

ISBN: 978-0-07-352586-0
MHID: 0-07-352586-3

Publisher: *Emily Barrosse*
Sponsoring editor: *David S. Patterson*
Developmental editor: *Emily Pecora*
Marketing manager: *Sarah Martin*
Production editor: *David Blatty*
Production supervisor: *Tandra Jorgensen*
Designer: *Kim Menning*
Photo researcher: *Alexandra Ambrose*
Cover design: *Kim Menning*
Cover image: © *The McGraw-Hill Companies/Christopher Kerrigan, Photographer*
Typeface: *10.5/12.5 Janson Text*
Compositor: *ITC*
Printer: *R. R. Donnelley and Sons Inc.*

Library of Congress Cataloging-in-Publication Data

Gonzalez-Mena, Janet.
   Diversity in early care and education: honoring differences / Janet Gonzalez-Mena—
5th ed.
      p. cm.
   Includes bibliographical references and index.
   ISBN-13: 978-0-07-352586-0
   ISBN-10: 0-07-352586-3
   1. Child care—United States. 2. Early childhood education—United States. 3. Multiculturalism—United States. 4. Multicultural education—United States. I. Title.
HQ778.63.G66 2008
362.71'20973—dc22   2007000673

www.mhhe.com

To my husband, Frank Gonzalez-Mena

What sets worlds in motion is the interplay of differences, their attractions and repulsions. Life is plurality, death is uniformity. By suppressing differences and peculiarities, by eliminating different civilizations and cultures, progress weakens life and favors death. The ideal of a single civilization for everyone, implicit in the cult of progress and technique, impoverishes and mutilates us. Every view of the world that becomes extinct, every culture that disappears, diminishes a possibility of life.

—Octavio Paz

Contents

CHAPTER THREE

Working with Diversity Issues 47

CHAPTER SEVEN

Socialization, Guidance, and Discipline 125

Preface

Though this book addresses the subject of teaching children about diversity, equity, and social justice, it goes about this sideways. The focus here is on adults, not children. To do a good job with children, and integrate these goals into the curriculum, we have to start with ourselves. Adults play a vital role in children's lives if those children are going to incorporate the attitudes and behaviors that go with honoring diversity and seeking equity and social justice. It's easy to just focus on anti-bias lessons for the children, but the children are watching us every minute. Without even knowing it, they pick up our attitudes and behaviors and see with whom we have relationships. It's so simple to do a lesson on being fair or conduct a circle time on the subject, but the message won't get through unless adults model what they teach. Teaching children to take social action in the name of equity is one thing, but doing it ourselves is another. So the goal isn't just to get along better, but to *work better together* for equitable decision making when it counts. We have to approach conversations about differences on a level playing field and become aware of how the power is distributed. By becoming more aware of who is in a superior position, we can begin to look for ways that power and privilege are more equitably shared.

We have to learn to stop criticizing differences and instead honor perspectives, attitudes, and beliefs, and the behaviors that spring from them, that are in contrast to our own. That may be easier when we work with people we feel comfortable with, but what about the people who make us uncomfortable? Maybe their ideas don't fit ours, maybe their values aren't the same as ours. It is in these situations that, through relationship building, we can experience amazing transformations. Therein lies the challenge and the benefits of diversity work. It can be hard, but it's always enriching. The rewards are worth the challenges!

One of the goals of diversity work in early childhood settings is to eliminate harmful mismatches between the family and the program through professional sensitivity and responsiveness. When we examine what we do, we may seem to be operating out of universal child development principles, but the truth is that those principles occur in a cultural context. You can't remove from a cultural framework the ways you relate to children, teach them, care for them, determine program curricula, handle daily routines, or view the landmarks of development. Children learn from their parents and teachers how to behave in culturally distinct ways. If we are of the mainstream, consciously or not, we try to make the children we work with into the kinds of people who fit our culture, with or without their parents' permission. It is vital that we become aware that we are doing this, and developing that awareness is one of the goals of this book. It is also important to understand the value of helping children become bicultural. Certainly moving easily between two or more cultures is a worthy goal. But it is also important to realize that in the name of creating bicultural individuals, we sometimes end up creating marginalized people who feel they don't fit anywhere. Everything we do in our work with young children and their families should have as a primary goal adding to what they already have and taking nothing away. Too often when children learn the dominant language of the country, in this case, English, they lose their home language. The same can happen when they take on the cultural characteristics of the dominant culture. This creates a loss—not just to the child and the family, but to our whole society as diversity begins to disappear. As it says in the opening quote from Octavio Paz, "death is uniformity. . . . Every view of the world that becomes extinct, every culture that disappears, diminishes a possibility of life."

An article about guidelines for enacting such change in the American Psychological Association's *American Psychologist* (2003) starts, "All individuals exist in social, political, historical, and economic contexts and psychologists are increasingly called upon to understand the influences of these contexts on individuals' behavior."[1] That is what this book is about.

This book, formerly named *Multicultural Issues in Child Care*, serves well as a companion to *Foundations of Early Childhood Education: Teaching Children in a Diverse Society, 3/e* by Gonzalez-Mena (McGraw-Hill, 2008); and *Infants, Toddlers, and Caregivers, 7/e* by Gonzalez-Mena and Eyer (McGraw-Hill, 2007). It also fits well as supplementary reading to any child development text because it covers the cultural aspects of development.

This book may also be viewed as a companion to Louise Derman-Sparks's *Antibias Curriculum* (NAEYC, 1989), complementing it nicely. *Diversity in Early Care and Education* picks up where Derman-Sparks stopped. Her focus is on an antibias approach to preschool curriculum; the focus in this book is on an antibias approach to cultural information, adult relations, and conflicts in goals, values, expectations, and child-rearing practices.

This book can be used by anyone involved in teacher training or early childhood education. It serves as a text or supplement for infant-toddler courses; child care and early education classes; supervision and administration classes; social service classes for child care workers; child development and child psychology classes; and Head Start, preschool, child care, and family day care training. The text is also useful to social workers, medical personnel, and mental health workers—in fact anyone who wants to understand more about diverse views related to children, child rearing, education, and development.

The material in this book is designed to be practical rather than theoretical; however, theory abounds in the notes following each chapter. Readers who choose to skip the endnotes and go with the flow of the reading still receive a good grounding in the subject matter because the chapters are complete in themselves, without the notes. Suggestions have been made to incorporate the information in the notes into the text. I have resisted because doing so would lengthen the book and one of the most attractive features of the book is that it is short and easy to read.

What's New in This Edition

Updated scholarship and resources as reflected in the text, notes, bibliography, and lists of further readings.

Expanded coverage of areas of diversity and culture:

- Poverty as a dimension of culture, which has to be regarded as a huge influence on beliefs, attitudes, and behavior of families.
- Sexual orientation and the ethical argument for respecting all families no matter what form they come in.
- Special needs and culture—some issues that can arise around inclusion in programs designed for typically developing children.

Additional theorists:

- Uri Bronfenbrenner. The implications of his ecological theory of human development are to always regard the context in which children and family are imbedded—another way of saying to honor diversity.
- Abraham Maslow. His focus on human potential has been an influence on individualists with his studies of self-actualization as personal fulfillment.
- Emmi Pikler who is gaining attention for her theory of infant-toddler development and its implications for infant-toddler care and education.

A deeper look into the framework of independence and interdependence:

- Added examples of how to see the difference between the two orientations and also some child-rearing approaches that integrate the two. The sample integrative approaches come from Emmi Pikler, infant-toddler theorist, and Barbara Rogoff, anthropologist.
- A look at a new and old trends in potty training from Meredith Small, anthropologist (and mother).

Differing perspectives on school readiness:

- How to understand parents who want a more academic program for their young children than appears to be developmentally appropriate.

More on differing perspectives on discipline:

- Time-out.
- "Floor time" or "time-in" for children with special needs and challenging behaviors.

Discussion of preserving home language:

- With the goal of increasing the numbers of bilingual and bicultural children from all backgrounds.
- The importance of learning English in addition to the language(s) that children bring from the home, rather than as a substitute for home language. In other words, promoting an additive process rather than a subtractive one in second- (or third-) language learning.

More on resolving differences:

- Sorting out cultural behaviors from harmful or dysfunctional ones. For example, looking more closely at the trend of childhood obesity, we have to ask if we should confront the issue as a problem, just accept that some families value fat babies and children, or decide this a cultural difference that we should be dialoguing more about.
- Figuring out how to build trusting relationships in which cross-cultural dialogues can occur—not just trusting relationships with parents, but also with colleagues and fellow staff members.
- Working on ourselves, including confronting our own biases and dealing with our discomfort, which helps us continue the dialogues around disagreements instead of turning them into arguments or running away from them.

ACKNOWLEDGMENTS

Through each edition the list of acknowledgments has grown and this edition is no exception. The list is now unwieldy and, rather than taking the chance of leaving someone out, I want to make a blanket acknowledgment to my old friends who continue to help me learn more, not only about them but also about myself as a white person. Thanks too to my new friends, participants in my workshops, and others who have shared their thoughts and ideas with me in ways that expanded my knowledge. My life has grown steadily richer thanks to the people in it.

Thanks also goes to those instructors who provided feedback on the fourth edition of the text:

Jeanne Baxter, *Tallahassee Community College*

Linda Boettcher, *Red Rocks Community College*

Johanna Hartnett, *Cortland College*

Mary Ellen McGuire-Schwartz, *Rhode Island College*

Carrie Rothstein-Fisch, *California State University—Northridge*

Last, I want to thank my family, and especially my husband, Frank, who gave me some of my early lessons on appreciating diversity.

NOTES

1. American Psychological Association, "Guidelines on Multicultural Education, Training, Research, Practice and Organizational Change for Psychologists." *American Psychologist* 58, no. 5. (May 2003), pp. 377–402.

Introduction

Often when evaluators come into early care and education programs to assess the diversity curriculum, the environment and activities become the major focus of the evaluation. Certainly adding chopsticks and kimonos to the dramatic play area and making tortillas are worthy steps to take. Further, making the environment reflect diversity is also important and can be seen by what hangs on the wall, and what kinds of books and other materials are available. But selecting materials and other physical objects or planning activities are the easy parts of honoring and respecting diversity. It is also fairly easy to expose the children to the contributions of people from groups that are underrepresented as contributors to society. Adding units or themes that relate to diversity is another way to address diversity and expand the regular curriculum. All these approaches represent forward movement, but this book goes far beyond those first steps that are fairly easy to see and evaluate.

The goal of this book is to focus on how to honor diversity in everything you do in working with children and their families. It's about interactions and attitudes. It's about appreciating differences in colleagues and coworkers as well as children and their families. It's about living with differences, gaining from them, and even celebrating them. Avoiding deficit models requires understanding ways of thinking and behaviors that deviate from what is considered the norm. This book is designed to increase your knowledge so you can begin to see some behaviors that you consider inadequate, uncomfortable, or weird in a positive light. Often behaviors that don't seem to be "normal" are really

1

competent adaptive responses that contribute to the survival and enhancement of the individual or group. In other words, this book is about regarding differences with respect as well as looking at them as sources of strength.

CHALLENGES IN HONORING DIVERSITY

Honoring diversity can be hard when ideas about right and wrong clash. Imagine this scene.

> You are an early childhood professional visiting other programs. You walk into a classroom in one center and find the adults scattered around the room, seated on low chairs or down on the floor at eye level with the children, who are all around 4 years old. The adults are fully focused on the children, talking to them, responding to them, and now and then bringing out some new materials or rearranging the environment. Once in a while, they have to help settle a conflict between two children. They aren't talking to each other. These adults are consciously doing what the literature tells them is good child development practice. They are also unconsciously reproducing the role of an old-fashioned, mainstream, nuclear-family housewife—the mythical one who was always there for her children, raising them in a fashion that kept her isolated from other adults. Part of this role is to focus on children as individuals, give them the attention they need, and to help each become his or her own person.

Now imagine yourself walking into a different setting.

> It's a similar room, but this time the adults are sitting on adult-size furniture in one area talking to each other. One holds a baby on her lap, another has a toddler standing at her knee. Most of the other younger children are playing at the adults' feet; the older ones are scattered around the room. The adults are more focused on each other than the children, yet they manage subtly to incorporate the children into their adult world without shifting their focus dramatically when they do. They seem to know what's going on in the room at every minute, although they aren't obviously supervising. They are definitely not doing "good child development practice." They are, however, reflecting an upbringing in an extended family or kinship network where children fit into adult situations. These adults are not concerned with making the children into individuals or making sure that each is his or her own person; rather they are more interested in making sure that the children get along with each other and not disturb anybody.

It's easy to guess that a trained early childhood professional would find the first situation superior to the second one and would find it difficult to honor diversity. When something doesn't match your training, style, set of goals, or beliefs about what's good for children, accepting it is a challenge.

OPERATING OUT OF UNCONSCIOUS SYSTEMS

What you saw in the previous two scenes represented diverse values, ways of doing things, beliefs about how things ought to be. The two scenes also showed how people are governed by systems that are often out of the area of their consciousness. We become conscious of our systems when they bump up against ones that are different, and we notice that we have a reaction. I'm willing to bet that one of the previous scenes triggered a reaction in you.

In early care and education programs we are lucky to be in the position of potentially discovering an enormous amount of information about ourselves and how our systems work. Even if there isn't obvious diversity in the program's population, there is bound to be at least one person or family considered weird, different, or difficult who doesn't follow what you regard as right, reasonable, sane, or normal. You can begin to see your own system working when you think about or interact with that person or family.

Learning about Your Own System

There are some wonderful things about working with people who are different from us. Of course, it's fun to have exotic experiences, but what's even more valuable is taking advantage of the chance to learn about our systems. We can achieve that awareness only by interacting with others who do not share our systems, such as members of the opposite sex; people with different sexual orientations or from different age groups; or individuals with different racial, cultural, ethnic, economic, and/or religious backgrounds. Of course, we can also learn from people with differing abilities. Or just think about a time when someone of a different sexual orientation triggered a reaction. Interacting with others who are different gives you a clue about your own system. When you can see your own system working, you can make better decisions about how to live your life. You can change your system to make it work better for you and to allow you to get along better with others who aren't like you.

What I've Learned about My System

I am only beginning to learn about my own system as a white, Anglo-American, heterosexual. I've learned that because of my ethnicity, skin color, economic level, and sexual orientation, I automatically have power and privilege. I didn't earn it and I certainly didn't ask for it; I didn't even know I had it until a few years ago. Now that I can see it in operation, other parts of my system are beginning to become visible to me as well. What I didn't realize is that many people know more about my system than I know about theirs. Those who are not of my race, ethnicity, income level, and sexual orientation know about the system under which I operate. To understand why and how that works I only need to think of myself as a woman and how much more I know about males than they know about females. I've lived all my life in a male-dominated society. I know now that my African-American friends know more about my system than I know about theirs because they have spent their lives in a racist society. If you are of a dominant group you don't need to develop the survival mechanisms that oppressed people have developed. They manage because they learn about the systems that aren't theirs, whether they like them or not. Some of us have a lot more to learn than others.

Expanding Awareness

Don't assume that because you know a system you know what an individual or a family in that system is like. People have individual values, personal inclinations, and behavior styles that influence how they think and act. Any statement about a system is a generalization and doesn't tell you much at all about an individual functioning within that system. You can see trends, themes, and probabilities by understanding something about a particular system, but be careful about generalizing that information. It doesn't apply to everybody.

A way to find out about individuals or families is to be more observant. To be a good observer you have to suspend judgments. Only then can you begin to understand someone who is different from yourself and who operates out of another system. The idea is to learn the deeper meaning of what you are seeing. Observation combined with communication helps you seek out other perspectives.

The best way to communicate is to develop dialoguing skills. What are dialoguing skills? A dialogue is a form of communication used to gather information, learn from it, and discover new ideas without seeking to convince or persuade the other person. In other words, it's not about finding holes in a person's argument so you can make a case for your side and win. The object of a dialogue is not to win, but to expand knowledge. A dialogue is not about opposite sides, or opposing views, but about understanding multiple viewpoints.

They say that we teach what we need most to learn. I am a good example. I'm working hard on my dialoguing skills. The problem is that when I have a strong reaction to something that doesn't fit my system, I usually consider it a problem. I then make a decision about whether to avoid it or address it. I almost never consider starting a dialogue with the person who bumped into my system. Instead, my natural reaction is to become defensive and start arguing if I haven't decided to turn my back on the situation. When I argue, I want to win, so I begin to make assumptions and jump to conclusions. I criticize, which makes the other person defensive too. Then I try to sell my own point of view and solutions without listening carefully to the other person. I could save a lot of emotional energy and, perhaps, some damaged relationships if I avoided the argument and focused on trying to create a dialogue. I'm making progress though. I've learned to become aware when I'm arguing by noticing my physical reactions and paying attention to my body language. When I take a defensive stance or clench my fists, I'm not dialoguing. Just changing my stance and relaxing my hands helps me move from an argument to a dialogue.

WHY I HAVE NOT USED THE WORD CULTURE UNTIL NOW

I've been asked time and again to just tell people about different cultures so they can understand the differences. People have suggested that it would be good to have a section in this book on African-Americans, Hispanics, Asians, and Native Americans. I once half-jokingly answered a white person that I'd also have to include a chapter on European-Americans, but I was met with a blank stare and then a protest: "We're not all alike," she said. These people and others have asked me to name the cultures in every example I use. I hope by now it's clear that culture is extremely complex, and people of the same culture are quite different, depending on their individuality, their family, their gender, age, race, ethnicity, abilities, religion, economic level, social status, where they live and where they came from, sexual orientation, educational level, and even appearance, size, and shape! That's why I've been using the word *system* up to this point. There's nothing wrong with the word *culture*. There are definite cultural differences that have been seen and researched, but you can't separate culture from all the different aspects of diversity. Everything is culturally embedded.

The supreme challenge of this book is to give specifics without giving misinformation. There's also the problem of good information being used to stereotype people. The issue that confronted me as I worked on this book through each edition was *truth*. I addressed this challenge by using several approaches. I spoke from my own truth by tapping into my personal experience whenever possible. My experience isn't valid for everybody, but it's true for me. I also used stories. Storytelling provides a basis for the reader to create truth and to understand a point in a different way from academic discourse. Most importantly, I used information and quotes from direct sources as much as possible. I let people talk about their own cultures. You'll see in the bibliography that I searched for books and articles by writers who belong to the culture they write about. Some are less academic than others. Some of the book publishers are small and less known.

To write this book I had to move outside my own disciplines of child development and early education to get a broader picture of diversity. I looked at postmodern views of early childhood and read a lot of books and papers. For many years I have attended the Reconceptualizing Early Childhood Education Conference (www.reconece.org). I was influenced by the anti-bias movement. I used experiences in cross-cultural exchanges, readings in anthropology, linguistics, and intercultural communication.

A FINAL WORD

If I boiled down everything I want to say in this little yellow book to only one message, here's what I want to tell you: If you continue to follow just your own ideas about what's good and right for children and their families, even if those ideas are a result of your training, you may be doing a disservice to children whose parents disagree with you.

I try to imagine a world in which people respect those who are different from themselves—a world in which oppression is a thing of the past and equity flourishes, a world that is unified not by bland sameness, but in rich diversity. I think that we can begin to reach such a world by working on ourselves and our relationships so that we provide outstanding models for children of how people can honor each other's differences and get along. My goal in writing this book is to move a small step toward that world.

Focus Questions

Here are some questions to get you thinking about what's in this chapter.

- If everyone always moves within a cultural framework, can you name the framework in which you move?

- How much are you aware of the aspects of your identity—such as race, class, gender, ability, religion—that are embedded in your cultural framework?

- Why do people of a dominant culture think their way is "regular" or "normal"?

- What does "normal" mean?

- What is cultural pluralism and why should early childhood educators be concerned about it?

- What are some examples of differences between what families believe and do and the principles, practices, and policies in early care and education programs?

- Why should early childhood educators be responsive to families' differences?

- Why wouldn't every family value independence as the ultimate goal for child rearing?

- Why is transformative education a better approach than simple parent education in the face of cultural differences?

CHAPTER ONE

Perceiving and Responding to Differences

As a white, middle-class American with mostly Anglo-Saxon and Celtic heritage (my Spanish surname comes from my husband), I was surprised to discover that I have a culture. I, like everyone else, move within a cultural framework every minute of every day. That framework is influenced by and includes what are called attributes of culture, some of which I am extremely conscious of, but some of which I am barely aware of. My life is influenced by my:

- race,
- gender,
- age,
- abilities and disabilities,
- language,
- social class, including status and economic level,
- ethnicity and national origin,
- religion and/or spiritual practice,
- original geographic location of my family, where I grew up, and present location (if different), and
- sexuality, including sexual orientation.

My framework influences the way I think and act and how I perceive, handle, and interact with people and materials. It determines my notions of time and space and even influences my behaviors related to those notions.[1]

CULTURE IS UNCONSCIOUS

I move within this cultural framework as unconsciously as I move within the physical world I live in. I don't think about putting one foot in front of the other when I walk. I don't think about my culturally determined actions, postures, or ways of dealing with people—they're automatic.

When I meet someone who obviously doesn't move in the same cultural framework that I do, I'm jarred. Because my way seems right, even normal, I tend to judge others based on my own perspective. I may consider them exotic or interesting, or I may consider them weird. But being a polite person who tries to get along with people, I do what I can not to notice. Because my way is normal to me, it seems rude to make an issue of the fact that someone else is "not normal." And because I have a whole society behind me giving me the message that "my people" are the standard by which everyone else is judged, I can afford to keep on ignoring what I choose to.

A Narrow View

But can I? What does this attitude do to me? It shields me from reality. It gives me a slanted perspective, a narrow view. I miss out on a lot because of my perspective. Besides, it gives me a false impression of importance, letting me believe that "my people" are the only ones who count in the world, when, in reality, white, middle-class Anglo-Americans like me are a small minority of the world population.

What does it do to those who are not "my people" if I continue in this narrow, slanted perspective, ignoring what I consider "not normal"? I train teachers and educate parents; therefore, I have a lot of influence over the next generation. Imagine the harm I can do both to "my people" and to those whose differences I ignore when I carry out my job with this biased attitude. Imagine what my students can do to the children they live and work with when they define "normality" in the narrow ways they learn from me. What does it do to people who are different from me to have those differences defined as abnormal? What does it do to people who are different from me to have those differences ignored?

What Are the Effects of Being Ignored?

That's an important question: What does it do to someone to ignore some integral aspect of his or her identity?

My husband was born and raised in Mexico. Every now and then someone says to him, "I never think of you as being Mexican." They mean this as a compliment. Because I'm not Mexican, I don't know how this feels. But I can imagine how I would feel if someone complimented me by saying he never thinks of me as a woman. That would shock me because being female is a vital part of who I am, and I don't want to be considered genderless. I don't want anyone to stereotype me because I'm female. I don't want anyone to hold my gender against me or treat me unequally either, but I would feel very strange if someone made a point of ignoring a vital part of my identity.

Of course, identity includes more than gender and where a person comes from. I may not be thinking of my race, class, sexual orientation, religion, and age, unless I experience being a target of oppression because of one or more of those cultural attributes. I'm probably not thinking of how all those parts of my identity are defined by culture. I may not even consider how my culture and the culture of the group in power are related. But my identity formation isn't the same as everyone else's. Everyone needs to become increasingly aware that when aspects of a person's identity make him or her a target of oppression, ignoring that aspect doesn't make oppression go away. That person is a target of oppression because of one or more of those cultural attributes.

Gay and lesbian parents may experience uncomfortable feelings when they enroll their children in early care and education programs and find themselves the target of one or more person's biased attitudes. This is an unfortunate situation for all concerned, but let's focus for a moment on the children of gay and lesbian parents. How do they feel when they get the message, spoken or unspoken, that something is wrong with their family? A basic tenet widely agreed upon in the field of early care and education is that all children need to feel that their families are acceptable to their teachers. That means they must not get the impression that their family is not normal. Also, they need to see their families reflected in materials throughout the program, and they need to be able to talk about their families and hear about families like theirs. When gay or lesbian parents enroll their children in early care and education programs it is vital that they are greeted with the same attention and respect afforded every other family. No matter what the staff's political or religious views are about marriage and families, the ethics of early childhood are clear as stated by the National Association for the Education of Young Children (NAEYC) Code of Ethical Conduct.[2] Principle 1 of the Position Statement reads: Above all, we shall not harm children." (P-1.1).

Other pertinent ethical statements from the NAEYC are included under Section II—Ethical Responsibilities to Families. Among others, the ideals are to:

- Develop relationships of mutual trust and create partnerships with families served. (I-2.2)
- Welcome all family members and encourage them to participate in the program. (I-2.3)

POINT TO PONDER 1.1

What's Normal?

What's normal? Defining "normal" involves comparing people. For some cultures, comparing individuals is inappropriate, so they never think in those terms. In the field of special education, using the term "normal" brings up its opposite—"abnormal." For a child to grow up being labeled "abnormal" can have a negative effect on his or her identity, unless someone has managed to give the term positive associations.

- To respect the dignity and preferences of each family and to make an effort to learn about its structure, culture, language, customs, and beliefs. (I-2.5)

One of the purposes of this book is to promote equity and stand up against oppression. People can do that by broadening their views. Part of broadening one's view includes exploring notions of what's considered "normal." The term is often used to mean what is typical, regular, or natural without reference to any normalizing procedure. The official definition used by human development experts relates to norms that come from research on some particular group of people. Knowing that definition of normal should bring up some questions, such as: What group? Under what circumstances and in what environment? Who were the researchers? Were they of the same language, culture, socio-economic background, race, and religious group as the subjects? Were they the same gender? How many people were in the sample? See *Point to Ponder* 1.1 for more questions about defining people by using the word *normal*.

Some years ago when women looked at norms in the medical field, they created a movement toward defining *women's* health issues and questioning the existing medical standards that, at the time, came from studying mostly men. Just as women's health was looked at from the view of male research, much classic child development research came from university laboratory schools, which had a preponderance of children from white, middle-class, educated families. See *Point to Ponder* 1.2 for something more to ponder about the subject of norms and research in the child development field.

Broadening the View

We each need to look inside and discover how often we define people and their behaviors as normal by our own standards. I, for one, am working to

POINT TO PONDER 1.2

The Five Percent Phenomenon

Child development books are sprinkled with diversity these days, yet most authors don't point out that historical research was done by Europeans on Europeans and that today, the field is heavily influenced by the United States. According to Helen Penn and Peter Moss in a paper called "The Five Percent Phenomenon" the research reported in most child development texts represents only 5 percent of the world's children, yet the implications of this research are considered universally applicable. Think about how few people in the field of child development know much about 95 percent of the world's children, many of them who live today in the United States of America.

Source: Penn, H. and Moss, P. (1998) Monograph, "The Five Percent Phenomenon."

raise my awareness so I can broaden my own perspective of what's normal and quit applying a single standard for adaptive, healthy, and competent behaviors. I have a strong desire to quit ignoring differences and begin not only to notice them but also to celebrate them. I want to look at differences as sources of strength, not abnormalities or weaknesses. I don't expect to change all at once—in fact, I've been working on this shift of perspective for a number of years. Revising one's views can be a slow process.

CULTURAL PLURALISM

In less personal terms, the ideology on which this book is based is *cultural pluralism*. Cultural pluralism is the notion that groups and individuals should be allowed, even encouraged, to hold on to what gives them their unique identities while maintaining their membership in the larger social framework. Mutual respect is the goal, though it isn't easy because, at least in the human development/education fields, we've been taught a deficit model where intellectual, family, and mental health practices that differ from the mainstream, middle-class norm are not viewed as cultural differences but as defects or inadequacies. Similarly viewed were behaviors that are competent and adaptive responses to a history of bias and misunderstanding in a society that has always had first- and second-class citizens. We have all been subjected to a good number of misunderstandings in the past. This book is an attempt to correct some of them.

A further word about cultural pluralism: It's important to understand that I am not advocating separatism. We live in this land together and we need to get along. We each can't remain behind our own closed doors as individuals

POINT TO PONDER 1.3

Should We Be a Melting Pot or a Tossed Salad?

Think about a tossed salad. If you combine several kinds of lettuce and various other ingredients like onions, tomatoes, cucumbers, mushrooms, red bell peppers, and artichoke hearts, you have a delicious dish. Each ingredient retains its identity—texture, color, flavor—and those all contribute to the unity of the whole salad. Now imagine putting that salad into a blender and pushing the liquify button so that the ingredients become one. I've done it. All the uniqueness disappears and what remains is a slimy green or gray mess, depending on the ingredients of the salad. I didn't have the guts to taste it! That's the difference between the goal of unity as uniformity compared with unity through diversity!

Gandhi said:
"Our ability to reach unity in diversity will be the beauty and test of our civilization."

or as groups. We can't automatically place individuals with differing abilities into separate programs or institutions. The point of cultural pluralism is to promote diversity. The goal of diversity is unity. Only when we can come together freely, as we are, feeling good about who we are, can we create a healthy unity among all the people of this great society. It may seem as though unity and diversity are opposites. One of the themes of this book is to look closer at opposites and see how they are really two halves of a whole. It isn't unity versus diversity. That's only the case if you define unity as uniformity. I don't! My goal is unity *through* diversity. See *Point to Ponder* 1.3 for a metaphoric example of what happens when you create unity by *blending* instead of *mixing* diverse elements.

Cultural Pluralism and Early Care and Education Programs

You can't remove from your cultural framework the ways you relate to children and guide their behavior, plan a curriculum, set up the environment, handle caregiving routines, and carry out parent education. Your behaviors are determined by your values, which are cultural, familial, and individual. They are also determined by what you consider normal, which can be influenced by your race, ability, social status, income, sexual orientation, religion, age, and/or the messages you've been given about yourself in regard to these aspects of your background and identity.

To aim for cultural pluralism in an early care and education program, you must have a clear understanding of differences. You must see where child and

POINT TO PONDER 1.4

Becoming Aware of "Images of the Child"

Although I'm using the term "needs," I hope you don't get a picture in your mind of needy children. The images that we have are powerful, and thinking of needy children is a little like thinking of developmentally disabled children or crippled children. There is a movement in early care and education to put the child first before the descriptor or label to emphasize humanity. A child should never become a label. In other words, a child may be physically challenged, but that doesn't mean he or she is a crippled child. Children have needs or a developmental disability. It's not a matter of being politically correct, it's a matter of the images we carry in our heads based on the terms we use. Those images influence our attitudes and thus our behavior.

teacher behavior fail to mesh so that you can make adjustments. You must know and respond to the parents' goals, values, and beliefs related to the care and education of their children. You must know how to meet their needs in culturally appropriate ways.

It may seem that cultural differences have little to do with the nitty-gritty of meeting children's needs. After all, how many different ways can there be to feed, clean, carry, dress, and touch children and provide for rest and warmth? Where do the cultural differences come in?

The differences show up in *the way* the needs are met—in how teachers and caregivers interact and relate to children, in the issue of body language and nonverbal communication. Culture is learned very early, and early childhood theoreticians and practitioners can't afford to ignore this fact. The term "needs" appears three times in the three preceding paragraphs. Look at *Point to Ponder* 1.4 and consider the terminology and the difference between children who have needs and "needy children."

Babies Are Raised to Be Members of Their Cultures

Look at an example of how differently two cultures relate to their babies. The difference reflects what the adults in each culture believe is good for babies, which in turn reflects their varying value systems. Here's the example. In a classic piece of research, when comparing three- to four-month-old infants in middle-class homes in Japan and America, Caudill and Frost found that American mothers (they mean white, European-American mothers) talked to their babies more, and Japanese mothers spent a good deal of time lulling and soothing their babies. The Americans were stimulating their babies. The Japanese were doing the opposite.[3]

So what? What does it matter if some parents spend more time stimulating their babies and others spend more time calming them? It matters a lot because how the adults treat babies affects those babies' behavior and personality development.

As Caudill and Frost found, the result of the differential treatment was that the American babies were more physically and vocally active, and the Japanese babies were less so. Caudill and Frost concluded, *"Thus, because of the different styles of caretaking in the two cultures, it appears that by three to four months of age infants have already learned (or have been conditioned) to behave in culturally distinctive ways and that this has happened outside awareness and well before the development of language"* (emphasis added).[4] In other words, the European-American mothers were making their babies into the kinds of people who would fit their culture, and the Japanese mothers were doing the same.

Think about what might happen if the babies were handled some of the time by European-American mothers and some of the time by Japanese mothers. They might turn out to be bicultural people, compartmentalizing their differential treatment. Children do that—they know they are treated one way by this person in this setting and another way by another person in another setting. However, instead of becoming bicultural, they might become confused about how they are supposed to be. If this is the case, the environment with the "foreign mother" might be called culturally assaultive.

Babies and young children become acculturated to the distinct individual and cultural rhythms of their teachers and caregivers. They learn synchrony that in some cases seems to be culturally specific. Cultural differences are real but so is stereotyping. Read the caution in *Point to Ponder* 1.5, which says that just because you know a person's culture doesn't mean you can predict his or her behavior.

Barbara Rogoff, in her book *Apprenticeship in Thinking*, writes about "guided participation." She notes that children pick up important learnings from adults, even if there are no lessons or conscious efforts to teach. She makes a good case for much of learning happening early and being culturally specific. One example she gives from the research of Michaels and Cazden has to do with differences in the way young white children and young black children tell stories. The two styles are distinct and, interestingly enough, though white adults see the white style as superior, black adults find the other style more interesting and effective. As a result of these differing opinions, white teachers at sharing time tend to interrupt the black children and, instead of helping them, actually hinder their storytelling.[5] Difference is deficiency in their minds. We must avoid leaving children with the impression that they are wrong when they do what they have learned at home, and instead accept them as they are. Acceptance doesn't preclude teaching them other ways of doing

POINT TO PONDER 1.5

Predicting Behavior

When you read about mothers in Japan, was it similar to any ideas you already had about Japanese people or about Asian people in general? The danger of labeling cultural differences and relating them to a specific culture is in feeding preexisting stereotypes. If you think of Japanese people as calm, quiet, and passive, and you meet a Japanese mother who is outspoken and who stirs her baby up by bouncing and jiggling, what would you do with that new piece of information that didn't fit your preconception? Many people, instead of recognizing that they are stereotyping someone, would maintain their stereotype and just classify the person who doesn't fit it as "different." The next time they meet a Japanese mother, they will still have the same expectations of what this person will be like. If there is one message I want you to take away from this book, it is this: Knowing a person's culture doesn't mean you can predict their behavior.

things. That teaching should be done so that it adds to their skills and doesn't take anything away from them.

Rogoff's concern (and mine) is that children who are grounded in one system and are attempting to function in another experience numerous difficulties. The ideal is that children benefit from learning new cultural systems and still keep their home culture. Unfortunately, that isn't always the case. More often, the dominant culture competes with the home culture and the home culture loses. This happens especially when the program's goal (whether conscious or unconscious) is to eradicate the home culture. When children encounter such "subtractive processes," they fail to grow up with bicultural skills and identities. Huge identity issues arise when children grow older and become disconnected from their families. The beginnings of losing home culture can start early, even in infancy. The child care profession has an enormous responsibility to keep children and families together and to promote healthy development of cultural identity for all children.

Synchrony Is Important

An interesting analysis of a videotape of a small group of nursery school children was done by Byers and Byers. The tape showed an African-American child who consistently failed to get her teacher's attention because she was out of synch with the white teacher's "scanning behavior."[6] Although it seems like a small thing, failing to get a teacher's attention can eventually impact how a child feels about herself. She may wonder why she never gets to talk in a group situation or answer the teacher's questions. Does the teacher dislike her? Is the teacher discounting her? Is she not as smart as the other children? Let's assume that the problem was simply a mismatch between the teacher's scanning behavior and the child's attention-getting behavior. It would be important for the teacher to learn to get more in synch with this child. It would also be important to empower the child in the teacher's culture. Cultural learning is a two-way street. However, it's important that a child not lose her own culture while becoming empowered in the mainstream culture. Cultural identity and family connectedness are vital for emotional health.

You may be thinking that the teacher is ignoring the child on purpose. There's no denying that racism can be a factor in teacher–child interactions. Classism could also be a factor if the teacher perceives this child to be from a low-income family. Of course, it could be a combination of racism and classism. It could also be sexism if further research showed that the teacher pays more attention to boys than girls. Or it could be the child's ability, if the teacher thinks the child has intellectual or other kinds of challenges and ignores her (consciously or unconsciously) because her contribution might not be up to par in the teacher's mind or because the other children might laugh at her. It's always possible that conscious or unconscious bias plays a role in the teacher's scanning behavior. Sometimes a teacher's behavior is simply a lack of understanding or skills; other times, deeply held attitudes are the problem.

Attitudes are harder to change than is a lack of skills. However, knowledge and awareness can help. That's where training comes in.

Misunderstandings

For years I have been teaching about three parenting styles called (among other things) permissive, authoritarian, and authoritative. The research behind this way of looking at parenting made perfect sense to me.[7] I have seen the problems that occur when children have authoritarian parents. I know that controlling and restrictive child-rearing practices predict poor school achievement. What I didn't see was the fact that I was looking at European-American children. Then I read an article by Ruth Chao describing a "paradox" involving the child-rearing practices of Asian parents. Chinese parents are authoritarian, but their children don't exhibit poor school achievement! In fact, they do very well in school. Chao's article broadened my view appreciably. I never considered before that the concept of authoritarianism may have very different meanings depending on the culture. I also never thought about the historical context of authority in this country. As a nation that started with a rebellion against authority, we have a legacy of ambivalence surrounding the concept. The idea of and feelings about authority in other countries is different. When Chinese children are being "controlled" and "restricted," they see their parents' behavior differently from the way European-American children see their parents' controlling behavior. My friend and training partner, Intisar Shareef, brings up the issue of authoritarianism and African-American children as well. She says that gentle, unimpassioned, authoritative approaches of European-American teachers don't work with African-American children who are used to authority looking, acting, and sounding different.

Understanding cultural differences is a subject that goes far beyond what holidays people celebrate and what foods they eat.

More Examples of Cultural Differences

Jim Greenman provides an example of a program designed to be culturally sensitive that ran into a problem.

"There has been an influx of Hmong people from Laos and Cambodia to Minnesota. A child care center with many Hmong children was trying to improve the infant and toddler program by hiring more Hmong staff. The center believed in a language-rich environment and much personal one-to-one interaction between caregiver and baby. With Hmong staff, they got very little language and very little interaction." This situation provides a very real example of a conflict of style in relating to babies. Greenman goes on to explain. He starts by examining the customs that result in the differences in style. "What would be normal in Hmong society? Mothers strap their babies to them, and this happened at the center. They have constant bodily interaction but not the interaction we know."[8] A personal account by a workshop participant brings this point home. She was raised in South Africa and has strong memories of being carried on the back of her nanny. She brought the other workshop participants to tears with her description of what that felt like and the strong ties it created between herself and the woman who raised her. Obviously there was a good deal of communication going on between the two even though none of what she described was verbal.

But this book isn't just about people who come to this country and discover cultural conflicts. It's also about Canadians and Americans who find themselves in conflict with other Canadians and Americans over cultural differences. These conflicts are in some ways even harder to deal with because of an attitude that says "when in Canada and America, do as the Canadians and Americans do," which, of course, is a meaningless statement unless you define *which* Canadians and Americans you're talking about. It's also harder to deal with because so many believe that "American" means white, European-American, and middle class—taking the "white-is-right" attitude. A further problem is that differences among Americans aren't always defined as *cultural* differences.

Greenman gives a further example, which relates to experiences I have also had in child care. He tells the story of some African-American parents who complained about sand in their children's hair:

> I worked in a center that believed kids should get dirty and be little scientists—it had a wonderful adventure playground. Parents, particularly black parents, would say: "We don't want our kids going outside. We spend an hour and a half on their hair. Two minutes later they are covered with sand. We can't get that stuff out and we spend our whole evening cleaning it up. So we don't want our kids going outside." For awhile, our earnest and empathic response was: "Gee, that's too bad. But this really is good for the children." Of course our knowing response implied, "You poor, ignorant person, valuing appearance over good child development." Conflict continued and we learned. Now the response to these sorts of issues is: "Okay, let's figure this out. Obviously it's important to you how your child looks. And you know it's very good for children to have these sorts of experiences. Let's come up with a solution." The assumption is two legitimate points of view—let's work it out together. In this instance, the answer was shower caps for the kids.[9]

When I told this story at a workshop, two African-American women spoke up right away. "Sand cuts the hair!" one explained to me. "It's a serious problem!" the other verified.

"Let's Figure This Out"

So if you're not going to just say, "This is how we do it here in our program, and you'd better learn our ways," what do you do? You start by treating the different perspectives as equally valid. When you come from that point of view, you can do some problem solving around the issue and together come up with a solution—like the shower cap one. There's more about that in Chapter 2.

One reason I wrote this book was to help me and others become aware of and sort out these conflicts. I need help to listen. I know others do too. A quote from Lisa D. Delpit brings this point home. She quotes an African-American who is lamenting what happens in discussions about what is best for African-American children: "When you're talking to White people they still want it to be their way. You can try to talk to them and give them examples, but they're headstrong, they think they know what's best for *everybody*, for *everybody's* children. They won't listen, White folks are going to do what they want to do anyway."[10] I think back on the times when I've been one of those "White women who wouldn't listen," or maybe I listened, but I couldn't hear.

The goal is for adults to discuss potential conflicts and learn to dialogue about them so that children in early care and education programs experience fewer harmful conflicts in approach when the teacher or caregiver and parents disagree about what's good or right. It's important for teachers or caregivers

POINT TO PONDER 1.6

What Are Your Feelings about the Word Dependence?

The word *dependence* may have negative connotations for many who read this book. For that reason, the word interdependence is preferred. I purposely used the word dependence here to help you see if the word triggered a reaction. Did it? Do you consider interdependence or mutual dependence more useful terms—terms that indicate two-way dependency rather than one person simply being dependent on the other? How clear are you about the difference between interdependence and codependence? These two terms are both culturally defined and can't be judged accurately across cultures.

to clarify what they believe is good practice, as well as begin to open up to other perspectives—even those that may conflict with their own.

A CONTRAST IN VALUES

It's extremely difficult to understand the perspective of someone else—especially when it conflicts with your own. One of the reasons I can't hear or understand someone who is different from me is that I have no perception of the value system. For example, if a mother insists on spoon-feeding a child who is quite capable of feeding herself, I feel upset. Until I understand that she values dependence, we'll have a hard time talking to each other!

How someone can value dependence was a question I asked myself when I first heard of such a thing. To me, being dependent is something to be avoided whenever possible. Of course, I am dependent in many areas of my life, but I don't feel good about it. If you had a reaction to the word *dependence*, which occurs many times on this page, check out the ideas in *Point to Ponder* 1.6.

Differing Perspectives on Dependence

It has been hard for me to understand that dependence is something desired and even sought after by some cultures. In fact, some families *train* their children in dependence as well as independence. Joe Tobin, coauthor of *Preschool in Three Cultures*, told me about lessons in dependence he discovered in Japan. These lessons begin about the time babies start trying to do things for themselves. The idea is to teach children to "graciously receive help." A friend of mine from Taiwan, Rose Chou, explained the concept again to me. Whenever she visits her grandmother, Rose lets her grandmother care for her and do things for her because it makes her grandmother happy.

According to Edward Stewart, cultures other than Asian see dependence differently from the way American and Canadian mainstream cultures do: "Dependence is not deplored by the Latin as it is by Americans."

He also explains why dependence is valued: "Dependence on others is desirable, for it strengthens the relationship among people." Stewart broadens the example Rose Chou gave me by reversing it: "Chinese parents take pride in being dependent on their children and supported by them in a manner to which they are unaccustomed."[11]

By giving cultural information such as this, and by putting cultural labels on people and behavior, I run the risk of promoting stereotypes that already exist and perhaps even creating some new ones. Upon looking at the literature, I've discovered biased ways of reporting research results that compare cultures in negative ways. It's easy for me to do that too, without even realizing it. When I lift facts out of their context or behaviors out of their cultures or environments, I'm in danger of confusing the issues. And if I speculate where certain practices came from, I'm in danger of being wrong. After all, very few parents can explain why they do what they do with their children, if they even recognize they are doing it at all. Many child care and education practices are handed down generation after generation and aren't explained in terms of adaptation for survival of the species and the culture.

Cultural labels are necessarily generalizations. As soon as I mention a reference that talks about the Chinese, for example, a good number of people who identify themselves as Chinese will say, "I'm not like that" or "I don't have that value." If "Mexicans" are compared with "Americans," that's a gross generalization. Which "Mexicans"? Which "Americans"? You have to consider age, income level, geographic location, ethnicity, family origins, history, dynamics, and a whole lot more. Then, even after you find two families who are the same in all these factors, individuals in that family may differ drastically from each other. My sister and I are nearly the same age, from the same culture, and were raised in the same family, yet we don't agree about what's good for children. How do you feel about the cultural labels I've used so far? Look at *Point to Ponder* 1.7 for ideas to ponder about labels.

Even when you are supersensitive to all the problems of understanding cultural differences I've mentioned, the job is still hard because cultures are constantly changing, especially as they come in contact with other cultures. It's important to recognize that the culture of a first-generation Vietnamese or Hmong immigrant, for example, is different from that of a second- or third-generation member. The culture changes when it comes to another country, even in families trying hard to preserve it. Someone who is Puerto Rican from New York is different from a Puerto Rican from Puerto Rico.

POINT TO PONDER 1.7

Labeling People

Did you react to any labels I have used so far? I've used the terms "Canadians" and "Mexicans" for the people who live above and below the United States. I called the people who live in the United States "Americans." Though those terms are common usage, the truth is that all of those people on the two continents that extend from the Tierra del Fuego to the polar ice cap live in a place called America. Why should the United States have exclusive right to the term "American"? It's a question worth thinking about.

Some differences that can cause misunderstandings and difficulties stem from social class issues. Adrie Kusserow[12] (2004) studied three different neighborhoods of white people. She chose all white people to eliminate race as a factor in her study. Kusserow came up with some interesting information about class differences in the socialization of individualism in America. These differences influence the way families raise their children. Middle-class parents and teachers embody what she called soft individualism—that is, they have a particular concept of the "self" at the core of each child. They see the self as delicate and full of promise, like a flower. Protecting self-esteem is important. They tend to teach children that the world is safe and welcoming—open to uniqueness—and that the future holds promise for success and personal achievement. They do all this by giving praise and encouragement, fostering creativity, and respecting and encouraging emotional expression.

Middle-class people with their ideas about soft individualism often work with children whose parents have a very different idea about what their children need to grow up in the world where they live. According to Kusserow, low-income people see the world as dangerous and regard their job as toughening up their children to face an uncertain future. They may hold expectations that their children will achieve success, but it won't come easy. Parents do this toughening up through such devices as teasing and criticizing. They tend to use strict discipline and avoid soft nurturing techniques. They neither spoil nor indulge their children. They don't see the self as delicate but hard and protective. They appreciate when their children are strong and determined. These may also be cultural differences, but even members of the same culture have different perspectives, expectations, and child-rearing practices by living in different contexts.

Ruby Payne (2003) came up with similar differences as she explored how people in poverty think, live, and raise their children. Context matters, regardless of what culture you come from. See *Point to Ponder* 1.8 for more issues related to poverty that educators and educational reformers face.

POINT TO PONDER 1.8

Class Differences

In a now classic study, Darla Ferris Miller[13] (1989) focused on the influence that income level has on the way adults socialize infants and toddlers. Using social reproduction theory, Miller pointed out that adults treat children in ways that make them continue to fit in with the family and the neighborhood (social class). That kind of socialization keeps systems in place so that with few exceptions, low-income people tend to remain low-income generation after generation, and middle-income people to do the same. As a result, class creates educational differences as well as economic ones. Miller's observations and conclusions show that cultural differences are influenced by the economic context of the family and the community and those differences can survive countless generations. What can be thought of as class differences are instituted early and last a lifetime. People who move from one income level to another can experience a good deal of pain and difficulty as family and friends get left behind. At the same time, if educators don't recognize how social reproduction works, we can't do much toward making the world a more equitable place. The dilemma is about how to work for change and still accept people just as they are. When we work for change, we must always ask ourselves if we are trying to put our values on somebody else.

The theorist who demanded that educators regard context as important is Uri Bronfenbrenner[14] who gave us the idea of the ecology of human development and urged us to move our focus from the child alone to the child in the context of the family and community. He says that we *must* regard the context as an important factor in child growth and development. Children come to our programs nested in ever-larger contexts, which influence them and upon which they also have some influence. Bronfenbrenner's work has contributed to our understanding of diversity. A growing trend, as a result of Bronfenbrenner's work, is that some programs are beginning to move from calling themselves "child-centered" to calling themselves "family-centered" programs. As one of the founders of Head Start, Bronfenbrenner helped ensure that the program is comprehensive and family focused.

So what do you do when you discover that diversity is much more complex than just learning about cultural differences and finding labels that fit them? You may throw up your hands and decide to eliminate cultural differences as a valid concept and instead just look at people as individuals. My advice is not to give up on understanding cultural differences, but remember that the way to approach that challenge is to develop relationships with people who are different from yourself. Knowing people personally, communicating with them, and treating them with respect creates deeper understanding and can solve many complex dilemmas. When you do that, you take the risk of making mistakes, but that's how we learn.

Focus on Themes and Trends

I've tried to minimize the mistakes by dealing whenever possible with conflicts in themes and trends. My original intention was to describe only conflicts, not cultures, so I tried to contrast cultures without naming them. I didn't want to categorize and label. I was trying to avoid a tendency of my culture: to analyze everything and put it into boxes. My goal was to raise questions rather than provide answers. But as I used the various drafts of this book in my classes and workshops, I got so much pressure to be more specific that I gave in and decided to provide references and examples. By doing that, I know I will offend those who find their culture pictured in what seems to them an unflattering way. I know sensitive people will find bias in what I've chosen to include and eliminate. I know some won't relate to what I say here about their culture. I'm sorry. I know I will step on toes, but my hope is that more good will come out of it than harm.

This chapter has looked at cultural differences to promote a particular message. Adults working with children and parents in child care and education settings need to regard sensitivity, respect, communication, and problem solving as keys to providing what children need. I propose we each work hard to reconcile differences in beliefs while tuning in to the individual needs of each child in our care in ways that promote his or her own culture.

Transformative Education

Transformative education occurs when two people or groups come together and interact in such a way that both are transformed. Even though one may be the official teacher and the other the designated learner, those roles become less differentiated when education is transformative. Transformative education is a desired effect in the presence of diversity. Transformative education comes from respectful interactions and ongoing dialogues. When we acknowledge that our experiences with one another are important, when we stretch to understand different points of view, we become transformed by each other's life experiences to a different level of knowledge and sensitive multiethnic care. **That's good for children!**

If we are continually open and sensitive, we will encounter dilemmas. Most of the time there is no one answer, only a continual process of dialogue. See *Point to Ponder* 1.9 for additional comments about what's good for children and how dialogues aid interactions.

POINT TO PONDER 1.9

What's Good for Children: A Multiethnic View

It's good for children to receive **culturally competent care** that is **sensitive** and has a **global, multiethnic view.**

Culturally competent care **requires** that:

- Adults in children's lives respect each other.
- Adults in children's lives work to understand each other's perspectives.
- Caregivers and parents understand how program and family values may differ and work together toward blending differing value systems.
- Adults in children's lives create **ongoing dialogues.**

Dialogues

- Dialogues ensure that information is exchanged so that good judgment can result from the blending of shared points of view.
- Dialogues require that everyone who works with children is both a teacher and a learner. Professionals must be willing to understand each other and to view parents as the experts who know what's good for their children.
- Dialogues occur when the people involved begin by listening to each other instead of judging each other.

My newest dilemma concerns babies and sleeping positions. To be both culturally sensitive and wise, you must be aware that research shows that SIDS (Sudden Infant Death Syndrome or "crib death") risk increases when babies are put to sleep on their stomachs.[15] Yet how many parents, for individual and cultural reasons, prefer that their babies sleep in a prone position? You have to talk about it!

SUMMARY

Everyone moves within a cultural framework; it is important for those working with young children to recognize this fact. Culture is mostly unconscious and many people of the dominant culture in any country may be unaware that they even have a culture. They may think their way of doing things is just normal or regular. This chapter questions the idea of "normal" and asks the reader to expand his or her definition to include a greater variety of people, ideas, and behaviors. The idea of cultural pluralism is introduced as a goal for society, and much of the rest of the chapter looks at how to reach that goal in early care and education programs. Children are raised to be members of their culture starting in infancy. This chapter presents examples of differences between what families believe and do and the principles, practices, and policies in early care and education programs. Because synchrony is important in the lives of young children, early childhood educators are urged to be responsive to families' differences. Perceiving those differences without judging them to be inferior or wrong is a challenge to early care and education professionals, and trying to do this can result in misunderstandings. "Let's figure this out together" should be the theme song of teachers in the face of disagreements over what children need. One area of disagreement may be over the value of interdependence in programs designed to move children ever increasingly toward independence. The answer is not simple parent education where the teacher transmits information to the families to increase their knowledge and effectiveness. In the face of disagreements, the parent education approach is inadequate. A better strategy is to focus on transformative education, where two people or groups come together and everyone is changed by the encounter.

FOR FURTHER READING

Barrera, I. and R. Corso. *Skilled Dialogue*. Baltimore: Brookes, 2003. A must-read for early childhood educators and special educators. Provides useful ideas about how to create successful interactions with diverse young children and their families.

Casper, V. *Very Young Children in Lesbian- and Gay-Headed Families: Moving Beyond Acceptance*. Washington, DC: Zero to Three, January, 18–26, 2003. Reminds the reader that theories that have shaped thinking in the field of early childhood education have been extremely gender and class biased. The author challenges the reader to understand that 1.9 million children in the United States have at least one gay parent and these children and families deserve the same attention and respect as any other family.

Clay, J. "Creating safe, just places to learn for children of lesbian and gay parents: The NAEYC Code of Ethics in Action." *Young Children* 59(6):34–38, 2004. A director of a Quaker preschool surveyed the seven lesbian- and gay-headed families enrolled to find out their experience in the school. He also surveyed his staff and discovered from the two sets of interviews how to work more effectively with families.

Darling-Hammon, L.; J. French; and S. P. Garcia-Lopez. *Learning to Teach for Social Justice*. New York: Teachers College Press, 2002. A group of student teachers learns how to teach for social justice and change, exploring such questions as What is diversity?

Ellison, S. *Don't Be So Defensive!* Kansas City, MO: Andrews McMeel, 1998. Explains how defensiveness gets in the way of communication and how to communicate nondefensively.

Garner, A. *Families Like Mine: Children of Gay Parents Tell It Like It Is*. New York: HarperCollins Publishers, 2004. About the challenges and gifts of being raised by gay parents. Debunks the anti-gay myth that children of gay parents grow up damaged and confused. They do have some unique pressures, not due to their parents' sexuality, but to homophobia and prejudice.

Gelnaw, A.; M. Brickley; H. Marsh; and D. Ryan. *Opening Doors: Lesbian and Gay Parents and Schools*. Washington, DC: Family Pride Coalition, 2004. A handbook for parents and educators that explores the relationship between parents, their children, child care, and school personnel to create a more inclusive educational environment for children of lesbian, gay, bisexual, or transgender parents.

Gonzalez-Mena, J. "Dialog to Understanding Across Cultures." in *The Art of Leadership*, eds. B. Neugebauer and R. Neugebauer. Redmond, WA: Child Care Information Exchange, 2003. Examines issues in early care and education programs that go beyond simple cultural misunderstandings.

Gonzalez-Mena, J. and I. Shareef. "Discussing Diverse Perspectives on Guidance." *Young Children* 60(6), 34–38, 2005. Looks at a variety of differences when it comes to discipline and guidance. Discusses how to work out the differences in a care and education setting.

Hall, E. T. *Beyond Culture*. Garden City, NY: Anchor Books, 1977. An eye-opening book about hidden culture and differences.

Kusserow, A. S. *American Individualisms: Child Rearing and Social Class in Three Neighborhoods*. New York: Palgrave McMillan, 2004. Looks at the differences in the way low-income white people and middle-income white people socialize their children into one of two types of individualism. Contrasts what Kusserow calls "soft individualism" with "hard individualism."

Payne, R. *A Framework for Understanding Poverty*. Highlands, TX: Aha! Process, Inc, 2003. A comprehensive look at the hidden rules of economic class and strategies for overcoming them. Distinguishes between situational poverty and generational poverty. The book is loaded with information gathered over the years by the author about poverty, middle class, and wealth.

Shareef, I. and J. Gonzalez-Mena. "Beneath the Veneers of Resistance and Professionalism." *Exchange*, May 1997, pp. 6–8. Looks at how racism affects attitudes of early childhood educators and how attitudes affect communication.

NOTES

1. E. T. Hall, *Beyond Culture*, (Garden City, NY: Anchor Books, 1977), p. 42.

2. From NAEYC Code of Ethical Conduct. Position Statement of the National Association for the Education of Young Children. Washington, DC: National Association for the Education of Young Children, 2005, p. 119.

3. W. Caudill, and L. Frost, "A Comparison of Maternal Care and Infant Behavior in Japanese-American, American, and Japanese Families," in W. P. Lebra, ed., *Youth, Socialization, and Mental Health*, vol. 3 of *Mental Health Research in Asia and the Pacific*. (Honolulu: University Press of Hawaii, 1974), p. 3.

4. Ibid.

5. B. Rogoff, *Apprenticeship in Thinking*, New York: Oxford University Press, 1990.

6. P. Byers, and H. Byers, 1974, in S. Lubeck, *The Sandbox Society: Early Education in Black and White America.* (Philadelphia: Falmer Press, 1985), p. 36.

7. D. Baumrind, "Current Patterns of Parental Authority," *Developmental Psychology* 4(1), 1971, pp. 1–103.

8. J. Greenman, "Living in the Real World: Diversity and Conflict," *Exchange,* October 1989, p. 11.

9. Ibid., p. 13.

10. L. D. Delpit, "The Silenced Dialogue: Power and Pedagogy in Educating Other People's Children," *Harvard Educational Review* 58, no. 3 (August 1988), pp. 280–297.

11. E. C. Stewart, *American Cultural Patterns: A Cross-Cultural Perspective.* (Yarmouth, ME: Intercultural Press, 1972), p. 72.

12. A. S. Kusserow, *American Individualisms: Child Rearing and Social Class in Three Neighborhoods.* New York: Palgrave McMillan, 2004.

13. D. F. Miller, *First Steps Toward Cultural Difference: Socialization in Infant/Toddler Day Care.* Washington, DC: Child Welfare League of America, 1989.

14. U. Bronfenbrenner, *The Ecology of Human Development: Experiments by Nature and Design.* Cambridge, MA: Harvard University Press, 1979.

15. S. M. Beal, and C.F. Finch, "An Overview of Retrospective Case Control Slides Investigating the Relationship Between Prone Sleeping Positions and SIDS," *Journal of Pediatrics and Child Health* 27, 1993, pp. 334–339.

Focus Questions

Here are some questions to get you thinking about what's in this chapter.

- If someone does something that offends, upsets, or frightens you, why is it important to know the meaning behind the behavior?

- Honoring cultural differences is one thing and responding with cultural consistency is another. If you have a particular philosophy and families come to your program because of it, do you have to change it for every family?

- How close can someone come to you before you become uncomfortable? Do you think that is your culture or your personality?

- How are touching, smiling, and eye contact cultural behaviors?

- How can silence be cultural? Isn't silence just the absence of sound?

- How can time be a language? Isn't time just what is measured by clocks and calendars?

CHAPTER TWO

Communicating across Cultures

 once sat by a window looking out across the street at a man who was acting very strange. I could see him only from the waist up, but that was
enough for me to know he was making extraordinary gestures and facial
expressions. I opened the window so I could hear his words. I was even more
mystified. The words coming out of his mouth were in a language I didn't
understand, and they sounded very strange indeed. I watched this man for
some time, trying to figure out what he was doing walking back and forth on
the sidewalk making weird gestures and sounds. I had decided he was crazy
and had begun to feel afraid when finally I stood up and saw the whole picture. There at the man's heels was a dog. Immediately everything made sense.
Aha, he's training a dog, I said to myself. I would have figured it out sooner if
this man had been of my culture and used the command facial expressions,
gestures, and, especially, the words I was familiar with. I learned two lessons
from this experience: (1) You have to see the whole picture to understand.
(2) It's important to know the meanings attached to the behavior.

INTERPRETING THE MEANING OF BEHAVIOR

This man-training-dog incident was a simple cross-cultural experience. It
wasn't even an encounter—I was a mere observer. Once I saw the whole picture, I could deduce the meaning of the behavior. In most cross-cultural
encounters, it isn't that simple. The meaning you attach to the behavior may
not be even remotely related to the meaning the person you're encountering

puts on it. A smile may not mean friendliness or even happiness; it may mean embarrassment. When you combine words, gestures, facial expressions, timing, proximity, and all the other parts of an exchange, the meanings become even more complex.

In any cross-cultural exchange, it is vital that you find out what meanings the behaviors have to the person performing them rather than doing what is natural—assigning meanings and values to the behavior of others based on your own culture. It is also vital to understand that your behavior doesn't necessarily convey your own meanings and values to the other person.

THE IMPORTANCE OF TEACHERS UNDERSTANDING CROSS-CULTURAL COMMUNICATION

Hedy Chang used the following opener in her diversity workshops when she worked for California Tomorrow, a research and training agency devoted to change. She asked participants to go back to their own childhoods and think about where they spent their early years. She asked everyone who spent those years at home with a parent or close relative as their caregiver to raise their hands. Almost always a majority of hands would go up. Then she asked how many people spent their early years in child care. A few hands would go up. Usually very few. Then she asked when the participants first encountered diversity; that is, when they met someone who was different from themselves or their people. A sprinkling of hands would go up for the years before age 5; a few more for when they reached school age. More would go up for around age 9 or 10. There would still be hands left to go up for the teen years and adult years. Then she asked participants to think of a young child they know—a specific child—and she asked how many of those children were spending their early years at home with a parent or close relative as their caregiver? Very few hands would go up. How many were in child care? Many hands would go up. How many encountered diversity in their early years? A forest of hands always would go up. Without a lot of charts and demographic statistics, it was immediately apparent to everyone in the room that times have changed for the new generation. Their parents' experience is different from theirs. Today children are out in the world in child care learning about diversity firsthand. They are learning from experience. They are also learning from us, the early childhood professionals. What we model for them about accepting and honoring differences will make a big difference in their lives.

In this wonderfully diverse continent of ours, teachers encounter cross-cultural exchanges every day as they care for and educate children whose cultures are different from their own. If this isn't true for you at present, there is every likelihood that it will be true in the future. You will encounter not only immigrant children from, say, Bosnia, Russia, the Pacific Islands, Africa, the Middle East, Mexico, Central or South America, or Southeast Asia, but also children of past immigrants who have been arriving in this country for the last 250 years from all over the world. I'm also talking about the original Canadians and Americans who were here first. Though all are Canadians and Americans, they don't share a single culture. The rich variety of cultures in North America makes us who we are. It also complicates and enriches the job of teachers as they strive to learn to communicate, understand, and respect the values and practices of parents from cultures different from their own.

Early care and education is a rapidly growing institution, and infant care is the fastest-growing aspect of it. The children in these programs are increasingly from ethnic minority groups as the Canadian and American populations move toward becoming a minority.

The fact that more and more infants are being cared for outside their own homes is significant considering the trend of increasing cultural diversity. Infants are still developing their identities. They have little sense of self or cultural identity and few cultural skills. They develop their identities and learn their cultural skills from those around them. They are different from the 4- or 5-year-olds who arrive in child care already knowing who they are and what culture they belong to and who already have cultural skills. Their developing sense of identity is already beginning to form. The main concern in caring for preschoolers is to keep from harming their self-esteem and cultural connections.

It's important for all children to have strong positive models from their own cultures. It's especially important for infants.[1]

Child-rearing practices and the beliefs, goals, and values behind them are deeply tied to culture. As long as parents can find people to care for their children who agree with them about child-rearing practice, there's no problem. Cross-cultural issues don't come into play when child-rearing and education practices are similar or if people choose to give their children a cross-cultural or multicultural experience. If a program has a particular approach or philosophy and families enroll because of that philosophy, it is different than if families have no choice. Or if families are looking for a cross-cultural or multicultural experience, they may not be interested in consistency with their home culture. They may not want the teacher to be culturally responsive. Often, however, parents have no choice. They must take the only slot available in the program near their home or for which they qualify. If this is the case and the value systems are very different, or the staff's ideas about best practices conflict with the families', it is imperative that the program figure out ways to be culturally responsive.

So it is important for teachers who work with families whose culture differs from their own to take a good long look at where the parents are coming from when differences arise over issues of dependence and independence, feeding, toileting, "spoiling," discipline, play, and various other aspects of the teaching-learning process. Perhaps the teachers' attitudes will not change, but if they can at least hear what the parents have to say and be open to some negotiation, everyone is bound to benefit.[2] Of course, there will be some practices a particular teacher won't bend on, but there may be others on which he or she will, after discussion. Other practices may conflict with program standards, policies, or licensing requirements, and that makes for even more discussion. Listen, look, be open, and try to understand.

It's important to note that communication issues don't just stem from cultural differences, but also from class differences. People of the same race and culture may have very different ways of behaving, outlooks on life, and ways of rearing children. Adrie Kusserow's study of class differences mentioned in Chapter 1 showed that middle-class parents and teachers often take a different view of child rearing than do low-income families. The soft style can be, in part, attributed to the work of theorist and leader in the humanistic psychology movement Abraham Maslow, who focused on individual potential, personal growth, and fulfillment. His concern was not toughening up people, but meeting their needs. In his view, only when needs are met can self-actualization occur—the ultimate goal of human development. Maslow wrote *Toward a Psychology of Being*, an influential book in its time which still affects the fields of education and psychology today. The middle-class person may find his theory relevant, but in the difficult world of a low-income family, having a positive outlook on human nature and developmental outcomes may be much harder. Fulfilling each person's unique potential has to take a backseat to survival issues in many low-income families. The differences in perspective and worldview can show up in communication styles. The soft style of the middle-class teacher may be like a foreign tongue in the ears of her low-income student.

LEARNING TO COMMUNICATE ACROSS CULTURES

I can't emphasize enough the importance of educating yourself when dealing with a person different from yourself. I don't mean read books, though that may help. I do mean observe closely. You need to learn to communicate, even when you share a common language. Cross-cultural communication skills can be learned. Listed below are six areas of nonverbal communication where miscommunication can occur easily.

Personal Space

The place to start when learning to communicate across cultures is to become aware of proxemics, how close to stand or sit when communicating. We each have an invisible circle that surrounds us called "personal space." The size of the circle is to a great extent culturally determined. White Anglo- or European-Americans usually have about an arm's length of personal space surrounding them. That means when another mainstream-culture American who is not an intimate approaches to talk, he or she automatically stops at the edge of the invisible circle. Some cultures have less personal space—smaller invisible circles; therefore, some people stand closer to talk. They invade the white Anglo- or European-American's space without realizing it. In this situation, the invaded person feels uncomfortable and reacts by backing away, perhaps without even realizing it. The invader (who, of course, doesn't realize he or she is invading) sees this retreating person as being distant or cold and is in turn seen as a "pushy" person, or perhaps just weird and suspect.

I once directed a workshop on cultural differences in which I conducted an exercise involving personal space. I had people walk around the room, stopping only to talk with each other—like at a cocktail party. It didn't take long to see that most of the people in the room stood at arm's length when talking to each other. One woman stood closer. Afterwards, we talked about personal space. This woman explained that she's a very friendly person who feels unfriendly if she stands at arm's length from someone. As it turned out, she was the only one in the room from another country. However, she didn't think her habit of standing close was culturally connected. That's how invisible culture can be.

Smiling

Smiling, touch, and eye contact are other communication skills specific to each culture. For example, Russians are reported to smile only when they are happy, not to be friendly. The friendly smile of some Canadians and Americans makes Russians feel as if those individuals are either fake or not too intelligent, whereas the Canadian and American interpret the nonsmiling behavior of the Russian as unfriendly. The Russian, who may be feeling very friendly indeed, would be shocked to know that he or she is being labeled the opposite.

For the Vietnamese, smiling has a variety of meanings.

> Almost anyone who has visited Vietnam or come in contact with the Vietnamese has noticed . . . a perpetual and enigmatic smile in all circumstances, unhappy as well as happy. . . . Many foreign teachers in Vietnam have been irritated and frustrated when Vietnamese students smile in what appears to be the wrong time and place. They cannot understand how the students can smile when reprimanded, when not understanding the lessons being explained, and especially when they

POINT TO PONDER 2.1

"The Look."

Giving a child "the look" says that the adult means business. "The look" is usually demonstrated as an intense stare accompanied by a stern and often frowning face. When Intisar Shareef, who often does trainings with me, mentions "the look" usually every African-American in the place (and sometimes an individual from another culture as well) nods in recognition. Children who are used to "the look" may completely ignore an adult who is trying to warn or reprimand a child in an unemotional way without making the same kind of eye contact.

should have given an answer to the question instead of sitting still and smiling quietly. These teachers often thought the students were not only stupid and disobedient, but insolent as well. One thing they did not understand was that the students often smiled to show their teachers that they did not mind being reprimanded, or that they were indeed stupid for not being able to understand the lesson. Smiling at all times and places is a common characteristic of Vietnamese. There are, however, no guidelines to tell foreigners what meaning each smile represents in each situation . . . the Vietnamese smile may mean almost anything.[3]

Eye Contact

Find out about eye contact and respect. Is it important to look people in the eye or to look away when you talk to them? When cultures have the same patterns of eye contact, people feel comfortable with each other. But sometimes a person of one culture thinks a person who converses while looking away is shifty and dishonest, even though that person may think he or she is conveying respect. According to Root, Ho, and Sue, "Eye contact in the western culture is considered as an indication of attentiveness, although in the Asian culture, it may be viewed as a sign of lack of respect or deference."[4]

Some people feel uncomfortable under a steady gaze. Staring at someone, even while listening to him or her speak, may be considered rude. Lou Matheson says of Native Americans, "in most tribes staring is considered rude, and in some, prolonged eye contact is extremely disrespectful."[5]

Young discusses eye contact among black people and between blacks and whites. She says that many black families communicate better in ways other than words, one of which is deep eye contact.

When parents want to impress something on a child, they give a deep long look. Black people often avoid eye contact with white people, giving the appearance of rudeness, since they don't seem to be paying attention. It may be, however, that they consider it disrespectful to look an authority figure in the eye. Or perhaps

✎ POINT TO PONDER 2.2

Consequences of Different Touching Patterns

Sometimes touch that is considered appropriate in one culture can have disastrous consequences when interpreted by another culture to be harmful or sexual. More than one family has been accused of child abuse when they saw absolutely nothing wrong with the way they were touching. For example, "coining," a health measure in some Asian cultures, leaves lasting red marks on the skin that are often interpreted as abusive, when in fact they relate to a healing procedure.

the eye contact that goes with the words in white cultures brings too strong a communication to the black who regards it as more important than words.[6]

See *Point to Ponder* 2.1 for the use of eye contact when disciplining children in some African-American groups.

Staring at someone may even be considered harmful. Some cultures have the concept of "evil eye" in which prolonged intense staring can hurt the person being stared at.

Touch

Find out about touch, too. Is touching a sign of warmth and friendliness, is it an insult, or is it dangerous? In Vietnamese culture, touching people on the head robs them of their souls.[7]

Sometimes touching is a means of establishing or reflecting status. For example, in mainstream Canadian and American culture, bosses touch their secretaries much more often than secretaries touch their bosses.

When minor cultural rules about touch are broken, something just doesn't feel right. If a person is touched by the wrong person or in the wrong place, it can give misleading messages or feel uncomfortable. Consider the unwritten rules that white, mainstream, Canadian and American cultures have about touching on the head. Anyone who touches someone else on the head is superior in some way—only inferiors (or intimates) are touched on the head. See *Point to Ponder* 2.2 for more on touching and the sometimes disastrous consequences when one culture doesn't understand the touching patterns of another.

Silence

Silence has different meanings for different groups. An interesting experiment is, as a speaker, to just stop talking and watch how long it takes your listener(s) to become uncomfortable. Of course, if you announce a period of silence, it will be different. But if you just stop talking, the average European-American will fill in the gap. When members of an audience are faced with silence, they begin to squirm in short order. Other cultures tolerate or appreciate silence more than those of the European-American culture.

How soon to speak in response to another is another interesting cultural difference. A Japanese-American woman told me that if you speak up right away without a pause, it seems as if you haven't really listened to the person. A pause between the end of what that person says and when you respond indicates respect. You've given your response some thought after considering what was said. That's very different from a fast-moving conversation where two people continually interrupt each other and neither takes it as a sign of rudeness.

Elena Alderete-Baker, who wrote her Ph.D. dissertation on "Internalized Achievement-Related Motives of Native American Women," talks about the meaning of silence to Native Americans. "We choose to remain silent when questioned about ourselves. It is considered 'bragging' when we speak about ourselves. Only others can speak about us. As a result the topic that a person chooses to discuss and the respect Native children show to their elders can become the basis for the silence." She says that in many Native American cultures silence is used as a response to ambiguity so a child in a new situation or facing a new teacher may keep quiet. The silence is taken to mean that the child doesn't know anything.

Time Concepts

You'll get along with staff and parents of different cultures better if you find out the concept each has of time. Some cultures are more "now" oriented than others. White European- or Anglo-Americans are famous for being future oriented. In practical terms, this means differences in the concept of being "on time" as well as *planning* activities versus living in the moment.[8] Some parents consistently arrive late for scheduled meetings. This habit may be a personal idiosyncrasy, but it can also mean that the parents have a different view of time. What does a deadline represent to them? The meaning can be related to cultural differences.

According to Edward T. Hall:

> Time is treated as a language, as a primary organizer for all activities, a synthesizer and integrator, a way of handling priorities and categorizing experience, a feedback mechanism for how things are going. . . . Time is a core system of cultural, social, and personal life. In fact, nothing occurs except in some kind of time frame. A complicating factor in intercultural relations is that each culture has its own time frames in which the patterns are unique.[9]

POINT TO PONDER 2.3

A Place Where Everybody Has Enough Time

Jonathan Rowe in *Yes!* magazine writes about his experience of time in his wife's village in the Philippines where he never saw a single clock. He reports there was an absence of time; instead he experienced a rhythm as the villagers went about their daily life. Because the concept of time was absent, nobody ever seemed to lack it. Contrary to Rowe's previous experience as an American in the United States where time is a commodity and always scarce, here in the village there was an abundance of time. Nobody tried to measure, manage, or save time—they didn't need to. He concludes that by trying to conquer time, we end up in worse shape than those who don't even acknowledge the concept of time. Imagine the difference in interactions and communication among the people of that village from what we experience in our lives and care and education systems.[11]

If time is a language, as Hall says, timing is important to communication. For example, some people often talk around the subject—that's culturally appropriate. Others are more apt to regard "getting to the point" an immediate priority. It's not just a difference in personalities; it's a difference in cultures.[10] If you're trying to communicate with a parent, this piece of information could be vital. It may seem like the parent never gets to the point. He or she may spend precious minutes in greetings, asking about your health, your family, your life. Whether in person or on the phone, some people always include some social chitchat before stating the purpose of the visit or call. For the efficient-minded person who never goes beyond a quick hello, these social niceties may be annoying. Even more annoying can be the person who never speaks directly about a problem but seems to constantly beat around the bush. It's important to understand that indirectness is a cultural style and, to such a person, direct communication about a problem would be insulting, rude, or confrontive. See *Point to Ponder* 2.3 for more about contrasting perspectives on time.

THE INFLUENCE OF TEACHERS' ATTITUDES ON THEIR LEARNING

It is beyond the scope of this book to give you the details of every culture you might encounter as a teacher. However, the For Further Reading sections and the bibliography will direct you where to get more information. Still, it is asking a lot of someone who works long hours at caregiving to spend more long hours doing homework.

POINT TO PONDER 2.4

Intake Forms and Interview Questions

One program has a seven-page form full of questions designed to understand the cultures of their families. For families who are anxious to share cultural information with their children's teachers, the form is welcome. For those who hate forms, who don't write well, whose first language is not English, or who have had unfortunate previous experiences with social service agencies in the past, those questions may seem uncomfortable. Some families may be suspicious about what the information will be used for. Others may wish to keep cultural information to themselves. It's always wise to be sensitive and responsive to each individual family. Another note on forms—try to put yourself in the shoes of the person filling out the form. For example, if you use gender-neutral terms you're more likely to fit everybody. You don't have to label the blanks for the parents' names as "mother" and "father." The term "parent" is gender neutral.

I suggest that teachers learn about each culture from the parents in their program. Start by creating an intake questionnaire that asks for cultural information. Ask questions such as, What is the primary language spoken at home by the father? By the mother? Ask how the parents describe their child's ethnicity. Find out who else lives in the home. See if you can open up some doors to communication by showing interest in cultural matters. Be careful to be sensitive though. Some families may find questions intrusive, especially those who have had bad experiences in the past with someone in authority who asked them a lot of questions. Check out *Point to Ponder* 2.4 for some things to consider about intake forms and interviews.

You can also study on the spot, learning culture by observing yourself and the people you interact with in your program. Become aware of your discomforts and discuss them when appropriate.

Working through personal biases can be painful. Tamar Jacobson wrote a book about that very subject called *Confronting Our Discomfort*. If you are dealing with issues of social justice, your own biases, your own blind spots, you can feel extremely uncomfortable, angry, guilty, fearful even. Tune in on these feelings and encourage others to develop this same awareness. When you begin to share, you'll learn more than you could learn from any book. You gain the most meaningful information from real people of the culture you are learning about.

In a book called *New Possibilities for Early Childhood Education: Stories from Nontraditional Students*, Susan Bernheimer tells about how sharing stories gives insight into how culture, class, and gender impact lives. When we begin to hear the stories of others, we get to know them better.

Dealing with feelings can be hard, and is something many people want to avoid, but there are things you can do about those feelings. First of all, recognize and allow the feelings. Don't try to ignore them or distract yourself from them. Don't try to make those feelings go away—you need to stay with them, not suppress them. Tamar Jacobson suggests journaling, doing self-awareness activities, and organizing support groups. You don't have to be alone. Acquire knowledge, become more aware, and make personal, deliberate choices. And remember we are all works in progress. We'll never be perfect. Love yourself! Forgive yourself.

When you begin to share, you'll learn more than you could learn from any book. You gain the most meaningful information from real people of the culture you are learning about.

You learn about cultural conflicts best by being aware of what you are feeling and trying to put yourself in the shoes of the other person to understand what he or she might be feeling. You learn about true differences in caregiving and child-rearing practices best from people who practice them rather than secondhand through lectures and readings.

Many teachers and caregivers can do this firsthand learning easily because of the cultural diversity of the parents in their programs. To what extent they seize the opportunity depends on their attitudes and openness. I see a progression of attitudes toward cultural differences from awareness, tolerance, and acceptance to respect and appreciation. Beyond that lies celebration, support, and finally, using differences as resources to expand and enrich your own life.

SUMMARY

When a teacher is offended, upset, or disturbed by a family's behavior or practice, that's a clue for the teacher to look at the bigger picture to understand the meaning behind the behavior. Keeping that principle in mind is a good way to expand one's cultural knowledge. It's important both to honor cultural differences and, at the same time, to understand that some families come to a program for the particular philosophy and approach. Honoring cultural differences doesn't mean that you have to change your philosophy and practice for every family. The way to find out whether cultural consistency and responsiveness is important is by honing cross-cultural communication skills so you can find out what each family wants for its child. Communication skills include not just language but at least the six other factors that are the subject of this chapter. They are:

- Personal space—How close do you sit or stand to communicate with someone you don't know well.

- Smiling—What a smile means, when to smile, and how to interpret another's smile.
- Eye contact—Do you expect the person you're communicating with to look you in the eye? What is culturally appropriate for a family and its children?
- Touch—Touching someone can bring you closer or create barriers. Learning the cultural meanings of touch is important.
- Silence—What is the meaning of silence and how much is too much? Silence has important cultural meanings.
- The language of time—Is a person late just because you think so? What does "late" mean anyway? Is "beating around the bush" a waste of time?

Answers to all these questions vary from culture to culture. No one can know everything about every culture they may encounter. Start by finding out about the cultures in your program. How quickly you learn depends on your ability to observe, ask questions, sense your own discomfort, and be aware of that of others. Attitude is everything, and it shows in progress from awareness and tolerance to respect and appreciation.

FOR FURTHER READING

Anderson, P. "Explaining Intercultural Differences in Nonverbal Communication." In *Intercultural Communication: A Reader*, eds. L. Samovar and R. Porter. Belmont, CA: Wadsworth, 1994. Helps clarify some of the difficulty behind cross-cultural communication.

Bernheimer, S. *New Possibilities for Early Childhood Education: Stories from our Nontraditional Students*. New York: Peter Lang, 2003. Gives voice to groups of people who have traditionally remained silent in the past. Shows the value of storytelling as a way to expand one's horizons and learn about "the other."

Bruno, H. E. "Hearing Parents in Every Language: An Invitation to ECE Professionals." *Child Care Information Exchange*, no. 153 (September/October 2003), pp. 58–60. This short article says a lot about how much you can learn from families when you suspend judgments and really listen.

Delpit, L. *Other People's Children: Cultural Conflict in the Classroom*. New York: New Press, 1995. Gives a clear picture of numerous problems that occur when teachers don't understand their students or the families the students come from.

Gonzalez-Mena, J. "Cross Cultural Conferences." *Exchange*, July 1997, pp. 55–57. Outlines some skills useful for communicating in parent conferences.

Jacobson, T. *Confronting Our Discomfort: Clearing the Way for Anti-Bias in Early Childhood Education*. Portsmouth, NH: Heinemann, 2003. Jacobson uses her own experience of discomfort to show the reader how to address personal biases in order to open up to a better understanding of where issues of equity and social justice lie.

Lee, L. "Working with Non-English-Speaking Families." *Exchange*, July 1997, pp. 57–58. Tips for handling difficult communication situations.

Patterson, K.; J. Grenny; R. McMillan; and A. Switzler. *Crucial Conversations: Tools for Talking When Stakes Are High.* New York: McGraw-Hill, 2002. Contains lots of ideas about effective communication, not necessarily with a cultural slant, but provides good strategies that work across cultures.

Quiroz, B.; P. Greenfield; and M. Altchech. "Bridging Cultures with a Parent–Teacher Conference." In *Readings for Bridging Cultures*, ed. C. Rothstein-Fisch. Mahwah, NJ: Erlbaum, 2003. Provides examples of issues that can arise when communicating across cultures.

Rogoff, B. *The Cultural Nature of Human Development.* New York: Oxford University Press. 2003. A treasure-trove of information about cultural differences that can help teachers work with diversity issues.

Tobaissen, D. P. and J. Gonzalez-Mena. *A Place to Begin: Working with Parents on Issues of Diversity.* Oakland, CA: California Tomorrow, 1998. Gives ideas on how to find out about the culture and language of families in the program.

NOTES

1. J. R. Lally, "The Impact of Child Care Policies and Practices on Infant/Toddler Identity Formation," *Young Children* 51, no. 1 (November 1995): pp. 58–67.

2. There are many instances where parent and teachers come from the same culture but have differing values, ideas, beliefs, and practices. Teachers must respect these parents even though they do not share the same views on many subjects. It is sometimes easier to understand and explain differences when a cultural label can be attached to them. It's harder to accept and respect diversity when the person looks like us. It is also important not to make assumptions about people's culture based on their appearance. I learned that lesson when, as a preschool teacher, I met a red-haired, freckled child whom I assumed was Anglo-American. However, to my surprise, the child was Mexican and didn't speak a word of English. I learned this lesson again when, at a training conference in Hawaii for child care, we went around the room and stated our background and ethnicity. The ethnicity of many of the people didn't match my first assumptions. I learned that you can't determine the ethnicity of people based on how they look.

3. D. T. Binh, *A Handbook for Teachers of Vietnamese Students: Hints for Dealing with Cultural Differences in Schools,* (Arlington, VA: Center for Applied Linguistics, 1975), p. 18.

4. M. Root, C. Ho, and S. Sue, "Issues in the Training of Counselors for Asian Americans." In H. Lefley and P. Pedersen, eds., *Cross-Cultural Training for Mental Health Professionals.* Springfield, IL: Thomas, 1986, p. 202.

5. L. Matheson, "If You Are Not an Indian, How Do You Treat an Indian?" In Lefley and Pedersen, *Cross-Cultural Training*, p. 124.

According to Morrow, while talking, Vietnamese, Cambodian, and Laotian people do not look steadily at a respected person's eyes. R. D. Morrow, "Cultural Differences—Be Aware!" *Academic Therapy* 23, no. 2 (November 1987), p. 147.

6. V. H. Young, "Family and Childhood in a Southern Georgia Community," *American Anthropologist* 72, (1970), p. 270.

7. D. T. Binh, *A Handbook for Teachers of Vietnamese Students.*

8. Lefley and Pedersen, *Cross-Cultural Training.*

9. E. T. Hall, *The Dance of Life: The Other Dimension of Time.* (New York: Anchor Press, 1984), p. 3.

10. Ibid.

       According to Morrow (1987), the Vietnamese, Cambodians, and Laotians prefer to talk around a subject before coming to the point rather than talking about it directly. Morrow, "Cultural Differences," p. 148.

       According to Hall (1981), in some cultures, a person with something on his or her mind will talk all around the point instead of letting the person being addressed know what's bothering him or her. It's expected that the person will know and will make the point himself or herself. E. T. Hall, *Beyond Culture*, (Garden City, NY: Anchor Press/Doubleday, 1981), p. 112.

       According to Root, Ho, and Sue (1986), "The Western emphasis on directness in speech may alienate many Asians. Indirectness in speech is preferred since it avoids direct confrontation which may cause loss of face." Root, Ho, and Sue, "Issues in the Training of Counselors," p. 202.

11. J. Rowe, "Out of Time." *Yes!*, Winter. www.yesmagazine.org. Retrieved August 15, 2006.

Focus Questions

Here are some questions to get you thinking about what's in this chapter.

- What do you do if you see a situation when respect for elders inhibits a child's free choice?

- What do you do when you are trying to build up a child's self-esteem and the parents don't cooperate?

- What do you do when a mother wants you to toilet train her 1-year-old?

- What if parents and teachers have different goals for children?

- What's wrong with compromise as the best solution to solving problems?

- Why isn't parent education always a good approach when working with diversity?

CHAPTER THREE

Working with Diversity Issues

All human relationships are bound to bring conflicts and disagreements. Parent–teacher relationships exemplify this principle very well. When the parent is of one culture and the teacher of another, the possibility of conflict multiplies.

Although issues around diversity can create quite a challenge, in many ways they are an asset. You can gain not only strength and skills as you work your way through them, but also new knowledge. What follows is an example of a cultural conflict that is heavily laden with emotion for many people—one in which no solution is immediately obvious.

EXAMPLES OF CULTURAL CONFLICTS

This chapter is about communicating around differences. What do you do when your personal or professional view doesn't seem to be compatible with a family's view of what it wants or needs for its child? Here is an example.

A 3½-year-old child runs into the classroom excitedly, hurries past the teacher, screams happily at her good friend, and runs to join her at a table where the two work on a puzzle together. Her grandfather sternly takes her hand, pulls her back to the teacher and demands that she greet the teacher properly. The teacher brushes off the incident by saying to the grandfather, "Oh, she's just excited to see her friend." The grandfather explains that she is being rude, and the girl looks down ashamed. The teacher explains that she is too young to understand social

47

conventions and that she'll be ready for that in a year or two. The grandfather shakes his head sadly and leaves.[1]

What's the teacher's perspective on what happened? When this example was presented to a number of early childhood practitioner audiences, they came up with something like the following:

> The teacher is clear in her ideas about ages and stages of child development and what is appropriate behavior for a preschool-age child. She's also clear about her goals for the child to engage with peers and about play as a way of learning. She's glad that the child had no separation problems today, because in the past, she has been reluctant to say good-bye to whatever family member brought her. Not today. She has come in with a smile on her face and a bounce in her step. The happy scream is music to the teacher's ears. At least the grandfather left quickly without belittling the child any more. It's been a problem before when he hung around and didn't encourage her to separate. This family needs to loosen up and let go of its child, the teacher is probably thinking to herself.

What could be going on with the grandfather? When groups of trainees were asked that question, some came up with excuses for the grandfather. He's so old he wants his granddaughter raised with all those old-fashioned conventions he was raised with. He doesn't know that it's not good to shame children. Others were able to step into the grandfather's shoes and explain his behavior in ways that were less judgmental of the differences between him and the teacher. Here are some of the things they said about what was in his mind when he shook his head sadly and left the room.

> He was concerned about respect for elders. The teacher not only allowed the child to be rude to her, but also she was rude to the grandfather, a man old enough to be her father. He might have been wondering what they are teaching his granddaughter in this program. Manners are a moral mandate, not just a mere social convention. How can the child function at home when they are letting her go wild at school? What will this mean for her when she goes on to their neighborhood public school where her siblings go? Will she sit quietly and listen to the teacher? The other children are doing fine, but they didn't go to preschool and learn these wild ways.

It's easy to imagine that the teacher and the grandfather have very different views of what is appropriate behavior for a $3^1/_2$-year-old. The big question is: What can the teacher do about these differences? One approach is for the teacher to "educate" the grandfather. If she conducts training sessions for the parents, perhaps she can expand to other family members and get him to come. The chances are, though, he will resist her training. He doesn't seem to want to learn her ways. They probably don't make much sense to him.

The teacher can take an anthropology course to learn about cultural differences in general, and maybe even study his specific culture, if she knows what it is. But she doesn't really have time to pursue a new course of study. She's busy earning in-service credits and professional development points so she can raise her qualifications. She has requirements to take and none of them include expanding into another field of study.

Well, what else can the teacher do? She can set aside her judgments of the grandfather and seek to understand his point of view. She can start by observing him with an open mind. Talking to him and trying to begin developing a relationship will help. If she aims for transformative education as it was described in Chapter 1, she has a better chance of coming to see his perspective and offering hers. It may not be easy to develop that relationship after the incident this morning, but if she eventually can prove that she really wants to understand, it's possible that the two can exchange points of view in ways that will enable them to come to some agreement about what's best for the child.

Here's another example of differences in perspectives.

> A note goes home to a family saying that its 4½-year-old son is "star of the week," and the teachers are making a display about him for the bulletin board. They ask for pictures of the boy as a baby, as a toddler, and now. The family ignores the note. Another note goes home. No response. The teacher catches the father and asks if he got the note. He says yes, but they don't have any pictures to send to school.

What might be going on here? First, what is the teachers' perspective? Why are they creating this bulletin board? Here are some answers from various workshop participants presented with this example.

> This is something the teachers learned in a workshop about how to make each child feel special. They think the child and family will feel like it is a reward to put the boy in the spotlight like this. They assume that the family knows that each child will get a turn to be featured on the bulletin board. They figure that every family has pictures of their children to send to school, so they don't understand why this family isn't responding in the expected way. They think the family is either lazy, doesn't care, doesn't want to comply, or is just being difficult for some reason. They are annoyed with the lack of response.

What's the family's perspective? Here are a variety of responses from the same audience.

> The family is mystified about what is going on, but is not comfortable asking. It isn't their way to ask questions or confront issues. They think maybe their son has done something extraordinary, has performed exceptionally well on something, or is being singled out for some other reason that they don't understand. They feel uncomfortable about their ignorance. Or maybe they just dislike the idea that he is being singled out. Even if they wanted to comply, they don't have pictures, and they are embarrassed to admit it. Maybe they are a refugee family who had to leave all of their possessions behind when they

fled their country. Or maybe they don't have any pictures because images are against their religion. Or maybe in their country it's not the custom. As one workshop participant commented, "It's strange how people carry pictures of living people in their wallets. I've never carried around pictures of people who were alive, but at home I keep, in a very special place, pictures of people I cared about who have died."

So how is this situation different from the one where the grandfather and teacher misunderstood each other? In many ways it is the same. The teachers need to examine their assumptions, set aside their judgments, and seek to understand what's behind the family's behavior. The key, again, is to work on developing a relationship with at least one family member. Again, a goal of transformative education likely will result in a better outcome than just trying to convince the family that they need pictures of their son so they can feature him as star of the week. The teachers should try to understand how the family, and possibly the son, feel about being put in the spotlight. Only when the teachers and the family exchange points of view can they figure out together what is the best way to give this child the kind of attention that he needs. Conversations will help them come to some agreement about what's best for the child. See *Point to Ponder* 3.1 about what theme might link both of these situations.

The next situation involves a teacher in an infant-toddler program and a newly enrolling mother.

> A mother seeks to enroll her 1-year-old baby in an infant center and tells the teacher that the baby is toilet trained. The teacher looks skeptical and says that the mother must still bring diapers because she doesn't believe in putting a baby that age on a potty, and even if she did, she doesn't have time to do it. The mother tries to explain that it doesn't take any extra time, but the teacher is beginning to look annoyed. "You just don't understand" says the mother over her shoulder as she sweeps out the door with the baby in one arm and diaper bag on the other. "No, you're the one who doesn't understand," mutters the teacher, closing the door behind her.

Both teacher and mother are correct. Neither understands the other. They are embroiled in a cultural conflict.[2] Unfortunately, the conversation ended before they could begin to solve their misunderstandings. If they had continued to talk, they *might* eventually have begun to see each other's point of view. Somewhere down the road, they might even have reached an agreement that both could live with.

What is "cultural" about this argument? Unless your experience is otherwise, bowel and bladder control seem to be biological facts rather than cultural differences. It is hard to justify toilet training a one-year-old when research recommends starting toilet training later.[3]

POINT TO PONDER 3.1

Individualism and Collectivism

It's possible that a thread runs through both scenes. Think about your under-standing of collectivism and individualism—that is, rearing children to be more conscious of their connections to the group than of standing out as individuals. Could it be that the grandfather in the first scene and the family in the second scene are trying to downplay their children's identity as individuals and working hard to keep their children seeing themselves as first and foremost good group members? Certainly manners and respect are priorities with collectivists. Refusing the spotlight is also a characteristic of many collectivists.

CONFLICTING DEFINITIONS AND GOALS

Sometimes a conflict lies in a difference in definitions and goals. Let's look at the toilet training disagreement. If the teacher defines toilet training as teach-ing or encouraging the child independently to take care of his or her own toi-leting needs, and her goal is to accomplish this as quickly and painlessly as possible, she'll regard 12 months as too early to start. Children of 12 months need adult help. However, if toilet training is regarded as a reduction of dia-pers and the method is to form a partnership with the child to do just that, you'll start as soon as you can read the children's signals and "catch them in time." In the first case, the focus is on independence; in the second, it is on interdependence or mutual dependence.[4]

How is such a partnership between adult and child possible? you may wonder.

Start asking around and you may be surprised to find out that a number of new parents are trying what has been called infant potty training. A website called diaperfreebaby.org is dedicated to getting babies out of diapers by three weeks of age and is supported by a group of parents who have the backing of a pediatrician and some child-rearing experts. This is a new idea to many, and probably to these parents who are trying it, but of course, it isn't new at all. Around the world and throughout history babies have been raised without dia-pers. Anthropologist Meredith Small, in a 2005 article published in the *New York Times* called "Dare to Bare," explains how early training works in cultures where it is practiced. "The trick is that infants in these cultures are always physically entwined with a parent or someone else, and 'elimination commu-nication' is the norm. With bare bottoms, they ride on the hip or back and it's easy to feel when they need to go. The result is no diaper rash, no washing cloth diapers, no clogging the landfill with disposables, no frustrating struggle in the bathroom with a furious two-year-old." Small ends her article with ". . . given the opportunity, I'd certainly go the diaper-free route."[5]

Toilet training can be a hot topic because child-rearing traditions are so entrenched that many people can't see any other way. Small admits that while studying other cultures' child care activities, she never thought about potty training, though she borrowed lots of other approaches when her own daughter was born. Further, Sigmund Freud made toilet training seem like a risky business if done wrong, so many people never even considered trying their own way of doing it.

Personally, I didn't believe it would be possible to comply with a request to toilet train a baby in a child care program. Then a child care teacher told me this story. "A mother told me her year-old baby was toilet trained and didn't need to wear diapers. I was skeptical, but I didn't tell her that. Instead I asked her to show me what she did. She did; I tried it, and it was easy! It worked. It didn't involve holding the child all the time, but merely paying attention to when she likely needed to go. It wasn't coercive or negative in any way. That baby was still surprisingly young when she didn't need my attention any more. She could go on her own. I wouldn't have believed it if I hadn't seen it with my own eyes." I'm still not telling you to do anything you don't believe in. I just want to open your mind to the idea that something seemingly 100 percent impossible may not be.

AN EXAMPLE OF BETTER TEACHER–PARENT COMMUNICATION

Here's a replay of that earlier toileting scene showing the teacher trying to prolong the discussion by acknowledging the parent's strong feelings.

> "I see you have strong feelings about my continuing what you are doing at home. I'm sorry, but I just can't do what you want," says the teacher. "I don't have time with all these other children to care for. But I can see how much you want me to."
>
> "Yes, I do want you to. It's important to me that my daughter wear dry clothes all the time—and it's so easy if you just put her on the potty when she has to go. Then I won't have all those diapers at home."
>
> "I can tell this is really important to you. . . ."
>
> "It sure is! I just don't understand why you want to keep changing diapers when you don't have to."
>
> "I guess the problem is you and I have different ideas about toilet training."
>
> "Yes, it seems we do but are you willing to have me show you what I do?"
> "Okay."

The chances of the two reaching some sort of agreement in just one short conversation are slim. However, the door is open for further conversations about this subject because, instead of arguing and setting up blocks, the teacher tried to keep communication going.

It's often hard for parents to explain their points of view to knowledgeable professionals who carry an aura of expertise. It becomes even harder for parents who do not speak English fluently.

The previous dialogue got the problem out on the table, and although the two didn't reach any agreements or conclusions, they both discussed the issue in a direct way. However, some cultures avoid the direct approach. Laying out the problem in a forthright manner is an insult to the listener. Think of the family in the star-of-the-week situation. They didn't answer the notes and gave only a short, abrupt answer to the direct inquiry. It's possible that this family felt offended by being approached in the way that they were. If the teacher's next step were to say, "We have a problem here, let's talk about it," the family may have gotten even more offended. According to Hall, in some cultures, a person with something on his or her mind will "expect his interlocutor to know what's bothering him, so that he doesn't have to be specific. The result is that he will talk around and around the point, in effect putting all the pieces in place except the crucial one. Placing it properly—this keystone—is the role of his interlocutor. To do this for him is an insult."[6] This may seem very strange to those who don't communicate in this way, but it is right and normal to those who do. Direct ways of stating problems are strange, if not insulting.

Even if the parent in the toileting example had been able to convey the problem effectively, even if she had been able to make the teacher understand how important it is that her daughter be given the kind of attention needed to remain dry most of the time, that doesn't necessarily resolve the conflict. It's not just the understanding that's important, though in some exchanges that's the first and most difficult obstacle to overcome.

Once he or she understands the problem, the teacher must decide how to respond. In some situations the teacher would have a harder time agreeing to go along with the mother because what the mother wanted was so clearly against the teacher's value system.

All of the situations that have been presented so far are difficult. There are many questions to be asked and no right answers to any of them. As a professional, you must consider the child's needs, the parent's needs and values, your own needs and values, and the program's philosophy. If you are clear about your own view and that view is in tune with the program's philosophy, you stand on solid ground. People who are unclear or uncertain are more likely to be defensive and staunchly defend their own side without considering the other person's side. If you're secure, you'll have an easier time truly listening to a parent and understanding his or her child. With an awareness and understanding of the elements of this conflict, you'll be able to create a relationship and eventually an ongoing dialogue. Only then can you figure out what to do.

The need for relationship-building comes up regularly in this book. It's easy to say, but how do you do it? Sometimes relationships just happen. You meet someone and you like them. You keep on seeing them and the relationship grows. But in our work with children and their families, that isn't good enough. When relationships don't just occur naturally, you have to consciously and intentionally build them. To take the first steps toward relationship-building you must become aware that it needs to occur and you must be intentional about taking some further steps. It all starts the first time you meet and should be the focus of the intake interview. For relationship-building to begin, you may have to set aside some of the routine matters that might get in the way and put your main attention on getting to know the family and their child. You have to think about building trust, which is the foundation of relationships. Families will tell you a lot more about their child-rearing approaches and beliefs if they aren't suspicious that you'll use what they say against them. Some people have had unfortunate experiences with social workers and other kinds of authority figures and they'll be suspicious of educators too. Knowing that, you do what you can to not only be friendly, but respectful and trustworthy. Communication skills such as listening, validating, and responding are part of relationship-building. They can be learned if one doesn't naturally have them. An important part of relationship-building is staying on neutral territory if possible. Sidestep whatever conflicts you can instead of going into them head-on the first day, week, or month. The doesn't mean to avoid conflicts forever—it's just if you have built a solid, trusting relationship, it's much easier to deal with conflicts and they are more likely to result in positive outcomes.

FIVE OUTCOMES TO CULTURAL CONFLICTS

I see five possible outcomes to working toward resolving cultural conflicts. Let's look at how each outcome might play out in a particular situation. For example, an 18-month-old child, whose mother says is toilet trained, arrives in day care without diapers. She wets her pants repeatedly, using up her spare clothes and the center's extra clothes. This situation has the potential to become a conflict between parent and staff if it happens more than once. What are the possible outcomes of this conflict?

Resolution through Negotiation Resulting in Compromise

If both the parent and teacher can work together and problem solve this issue, they may find a mutually satisfying solution. Saying "Let's figure this out together," is a good way to start the discussion. If they come to a joint agreement that involves action by both, they've resolved the problem through negotiation. For example, the mother could say, "I'll continue to toilet train my child at home, but will bring her to the center in diapers." And the teacher might say, "I'll try each day to put her on the toilet when I have enough staff and it will work out." They both give a little.

Ongoing Management of the Unresolved Conflict

The teacher may disagree with the mother's idea that the child is ready for toilet training but may be unable to convince the mother that she's wrong. In this case, the conflict may continue in a negative way, with smoldering tensions and continual arguments that both will have to cope with. Or it may continue in a positive way, with both parent and teacher managing the conflict by agreeing to disagree. Trust can make a big difference as to whether the ongoing management of a conflict is negative or positive. It helps if the teacher knows that the parent loves the child. Indeed, some teachers believe that all parents love their children and that they are doing the best they can with what they know, who they are, and the circumstances they find themselves in. On the other hand, for a parent, trust comes when he or she knows that a teacher has the child's best interests at heart. This kind of trust helps adults agree to disagree.

Teacher Education

Suppose that the teacher learns from the parent how to keep the child dry. In that case, the teacher learns the parent's way, which helps broaden the teacher's view of child care practices. When teachers understand the parent's point of view, they may broaden, adjust, or fine-tune their own goals, policies, or procedures to be more like the parent's.

Parent Education

Perhaps the teacher convinces the parent that the child isn't ready to be trained because she wets all the time. She may also show how hard it is on the child to be taken away continually from what she's doing to have her wet clothes changed. Parent education is fine as long as the teacher is sensitive to parental goals and values. It's not good to alienate parents from their own cultural beliefs and practices.

Mutual Education

Sometimes conflicts can be solved through creative problem solving. When teachers can move from dualistic thinking to holistic thinking and put their heads together with parents, they may come up with solutions that neither party would have thought of on their own. The 1997 edition of the book *Developmentally Appropriate Practice* (DAP for short) from the National Association for Education of Young Children challenges professionals to move beyond dualistic thinking (which it calls either/or thinking). When we stop thinking in terms of opposites such as right or wrong, good or bad, appropriate or inappropriate, black or white, we can come up with ideas we never even dreamed of. What I am calling holistic thinking, the DAP book calls both/and thinking. That is, when viewed in a larger context, the two views may fit together and create a whole new view that encompasses both and takes them out of an oppositional stance. Isaura Barrera, a professor of special education at the University of New Mexico, uses the term "third space" to describe a way of reconciling diverse perspectives. She isn't talking about "meeting half way." Third space isn't a compromise but a whole new territory. The teacher who asked the mother to show her how she toilet trained her child entered "third space." She didn't have to give up what she believed in; she was able to expand her view to encompass something new. The mother perhaps was also able to accept that some people have a different idea of toilet training, but that other views don't diminish hers.[7]

SHOULD TEACHERS EVER CONVINCE PARENTS TO CHANGE?

This question is hard to answer because the parents' goals must be considered. Do the parents want themselves or their children to be "Americanized"? Perhaps they will return to their own country and their concern is whether their children will still fit into their own culture. This is a legitimate concern.

For families who are already Canadians or Americans but not in mainstream culture, the issue of retaining their own cultural practices is important. If we are to have a salad bowl instead of a melting pot, diversity must be honored and preserved so that each group keeps its own flavor.

However, flavors change. Culture is never static; it continues to evolve. Further, when one culture rubs up against another, both are transformed. A challenge for many parents is to maintain their cultural identity and pass it on to their children in the face of this inevitable evolution. This need for retaining cultural identity can become a tremendous source of internal conflict when members of a culture perceive that they are held back from full participation in

POINT TO PONDER 3.2

Getting Parents to Change Their Ways

It's appropriate to help parents change if they want to or are harming their children, *but* it's hard to judge what's harmful without a clear view of the parents' cultural perspective. If the teacher holds independence as a high priority, the parents' goal of life-long interdependence may look harmful. The teacher needs to know more about how interdependence works in families where it is top priority. On the other hand, if parents want their children to give up their home language and use only English, the teacher may know about the harm that can cause both the child and the family. In that case, the parents need to know more about the effects of their decision and understand that when children switch to English only, they may leave their heritage and family behind.

society because of cultural behaviors, values, or goals. If you have never experienced that conflict yourself, try to imagine the tremendous strain it would cause in you if you were faced with the problem. See *Point to Ponder* 3.2 for more things to ponder about seeking to change parents.

PARENT EDUCATION AND TEACHER EDUCATION

I do believe in parent education, even when it creates conflicts between people of diverse cultures. However, I also believe in teacher education. No matter how well versed you are in developmentally appropriate practices, you must realize that even child development information based on sound research is culturally biased. Researchers have values. They consider questions important to their cultures. They look at results through cultural spectacles. For example, researchers, recognizing that a certain kind of language background is related to school success, find deficiencies in children who come from a different kind of language background. When researchers examine the issue from the cultural perspective of these children's families, they can see strengths in the differences.

I'm not saying to throw out child development information. I am saying that we all have something to learn from taking a culturally sensitive perspective.

Most of us also need to learn not to judge other cultures with our own yardsticks. People tend to be ethnocentric; that is, they see their own culture as "normal" and other cultures as "not normal." Most feel that their own culture is superior. That's natural. Recognize and accept that fact in yourself and others. At the same time, understand that all cultures have evolved to the way they are for specific reasons. Cultures aren't superior or inferior; they just *are*.

Knowing all this, how do you manage to survive conflicts with parents? How do you come out with your own cultural beliefs intact while helping the parents feel good about themselves and their cultures? And how do you even have these discussions about issues when most of your time is taken up with the education and care of each individual in a group of children? It isn't easy. It takes a good deal of willingness and a lot of patience, communication, and relationship-building skills. It helps to be well-grounded in child development theory as well.

A PROCESS CALLED RERUN FOR WORKING WITH DIVERSITY ISSUES

I never liked the steps I learned for problem solving. Things never work out so neatly and sequentially for me. I tend to think holistically. So I came up with a scheme of my own for communicating about issues of diversity. I'm explaining it in steps, but the elements can happen simultaneously and in any order.

R = REFLECT
E = EXPLAIN
R = REASON
U = UNDERSTAND
N = NEGOTIATE

The **R** for reflect has two parts. One, reflecting the feelings or thoughts of others and two, self-reflection. Reflect what you see and hear as you do with children who are exhibiting feelings. This is called active listening and is basically a receptive mode. For example, to an upset parent you could say, "I see you are agitated about something," "It sounds like you are worried," or "You seem really hesitant." The point is to open up the doors of communication. The usual responses most of us give in the face of emotion tend to close doors rather than open them up. Being consciously aware of trying to keep the conversation going can help us find the skills to avoid arguments, accusations, criticisms, distractions, and all the other devices that close down communication. The other part of opening up communication is to look deep inside ourselves. Self-reflection can reveal deep pain, insecurities, fears, and all manner of hidden feelings and the experiences that caused them in the past. When we can recognize and acknowledge our own feelings to ourselves, we are more available to communicate honestly with others. Look at *Point to Ponder* 3.3 for a further explanation about dealing with one's own feelings.

Think of the **E** as a small **e** because we should do a lot of listening before starting to explain. Our perspective is important too, but a dialogue becomes

POINT TO PONDER 3.3

The Stories We Tell Ourselves

"You make me so angry!" is a common expression among people who don't realize that our feelings come not from the outside, but from within ourselves. It helps to recognize that our interpretations affect how we feel. Those interpretations take the form of stories we tell ourselves. Take this situation, for example. I'm standing in an elevator and someone pokes me in the back, hard. A surge of anger comes from the quick story I tell myself about the intention of the person who hurt me. I turn around and discover the person is blind. The reality changes my whole story and my feelings about it. We always tell ourselves stories in any incident that bring forth feelings. We have the power to change our stories by gaining more clarity and understanding through communication, which is primarily what this book is about.

Note: The idea of "stories we tell ourselves" comes from K. Patterson, J. Grenny, R. McMillan, and A. Switzler. *Crucial Conversations: Tools for Talking When Stakes Are High.* (New York: McGraw-Hill, 2002).

an argument if we come in too soon and too strong. We have two ears and only one mouth, so that's a good reminder that it's better to listen twice as much as we talk. Remember also that if you rearrange the letters of the word *listen*, they spell *silent*.

Think of a small **r** for reason. That is, when explaining your position, give the reason for it. You may have discovered a different reason than you first thought of after doing self-reflection. It is a lower case letter also because both explanation and reason should be less important to you than listening to what the other has to say. Make it your top priority to understand what the other person is telling you. Don't let your urge to make the other person understand your explanation and reason overshadow your top priority.

The **U** represents a vital part of this process. It stands for understand. As you listen, self-reflect, and talk, the goal is to develop a more complete understanding of the other person's perspective, feelings, ideas, and beliefs, within that person's context. History comes into play here, too. You're trying to get a bigger picture. Understanding yourself is the other half of this part of the process.

N is for negotiate, which can start only after you and the other person have managed to increase your understanding of each other. It's easy to rush into negotiations when you feel the urge to fix the problem right away. It's important to resist that urge! Leveling the playing field may be a prerequisite for the negotiation. If one or the other is feeling powerless, negotiations will be affected. Learn about self-empowerment. Learn under what conditions we empower others. When you do finally get to negotiations, remember that if

POINT TO PONDER 3.4

Using the RERUN Process

A natural tendency for many people is to start a conversation by stating directly, "We have a problem here" and then asking, "What can we do about it?" That approach is sometimes culturally inappropriate. Further, it leads to the idea that a quick fix is possible. In the examples given in this chapter, there are no easy solutions. The first step is to work on the relationship with the person, which in the best of circumstances is already firmly established. When two people who have a trusting relationship try to figure out what to do about their differences, the RERUN process works much better. The immediate focus should not be on solving a problem, but rather on clarifying differing perspectives. That way both parties may find common ground so that negotiations don't have to be about compromise. The best outcome is when nobody has to give in. A win-win resolution means that both parties feel satisfied.

they break down at any point, start reflecting again. How do you start the RERUN process? *Point to Ponder* 3.4 gives advice.

SUGGESTIONS FOR APPROACHING CULTURAL CONFLICTS

Here is a summary of hints to help you deal with the diversity issues that can arise in an early care and education setting:

1. Take it slow. Don't expect to resolve each situation immediately. Building understandings and relationships takes time. As already stated, some issues won't be resolved; they'll just be managed. You have to learn to cope with differences when there is no common meeting ground or resolution. This sounds hard, but it's possible, if you're willing to accept that resolution is not always the outcome of disagreements.

2. Understand yourself. Become clear about your own values and goals. Know what you believe in. Have a bottom line, but leave space above it to be flexible.

3. Become sensitive to your own discomfort. Tune in to what is bothering you instead of just ignoring it and hoping it will go away. Work to identify what specific behaviors of others make you uncomfortable. Try to discover exactly what in yourself creates this discomfort.

4. Learn about other cultures. Books, classes, and workshops help, but watch for stereotypes and biased information. Your best source of information comes from the parents in your program. Check out what they believe about their cultures, and see if it fits with other information you receive. However, don't ever make one person a representative of his or her culture. Listen to individuals, take in the information they give you, but don't generalize to whole cultures. Keep your mind open as you learn. Check out your point of view. There's a difference between finding and honoring diversity and explaining deficiencies.

5. Find out what the individual parents in your program want for their children. What are their goals? What are their care and education practices? What concerns do they have about their child in your program? Encourage them to talk to you. Encourage them to ask questions. You may find out about cultures this way, or you may just find out about individual or familial differences. All are important.

6. Be a risk taker. If you are secure enough, you may feel you can afford to make mistakes. Mistakes are a part of cross-cultural communication. It helps to have a good support system behind you when you take risks and make mistakes. Ask questions, investigate assumptions, confess your curiosity—but do it all as respectfully as possible.

7. Communicate, dialogue, negotiate. If you have a chance to build a relationship before getting into negotiations, you're more likely eventually to reach a mutually satisfying point. You'll find examples of the communication–dialogue–negotiation process throughout this book.

8. Share power. Empowerment is an important factor in the dialogue-negotiation process. Although some see empowerment (allowing others to experience their own personal power) as threatening, in reality, empowerment creates new forms of power. Some teachers and caregivers fear that empowerment means giving away their own power, but this is not true! No one can give personal power, and no one can take it away. We all have our personal power, though we can be discouraged or prevented from recognizing or using it. Sharing power, or empowerment, enhances everyone's power.

Hard as it may be to take the risks involved in working with diversity issues, to learn what is needed to understand culturally different people, to gain skills in communication, and to cope when conflicts arise, exposure to more than one culture is a definite asset. As you work with children from various backgrounds, everyone gains. You, the children, and the parents have the opportunity to learn more about and appreciate human diversity.

SUMMARY

This chapter showed three situations that required the teacher to work with diversity issues. It also gave examples of conflicting perspectives, definitions, and goals and showed a sample of positive teacher–parent communication. Five outcomes to cultural conflicts were named and explained. They include:

- Resolution through negotiation resulting in compromise
- Ongoing management of the unresolved conflict
- Teacher education
- Parent education
- Mutual education in which teacher and parent educate each other

A question was asked: When working with diversity, is it the teacher's job to convince the parents to change? The answer was explored from a number of perspectives. The last part of the chapter explained a process for working with diversity issues called RERUN, the elements of which are:

- Reflect, which includes both active listening and self-reflection
- Explain your perspective, but only after trying hard to understand the other's perspective
- Reason; give the reason for your perspective, if you know it
- Understand, both the other person and yourself
- Negotiate a solution only when both you and the other person feel empowered

The chapter ended with eight suggestions for approaching cultural conflicts, which included advice about being patient and taking it slow; understanding yourself and being sensitive to your own discomfort; finding out about culture differences, particularly the ones that apply to the parents in your program; taking risks and making mistakes, while working hard on communicating, dialoguing, and negotiating in ways that share power.

FOR FURTHER READING

Barrera, I. and R. Corso. *Skilled Dialogue.* Baltimore: Brookes, 2003. A must-read for early childhood educators and special educators. Useful ideas about how to create successful interactions and work around differences with diverse young children and their families.

Fadiman, A. *The Spirit Catches You and You Fall Down: A Hmong Child, Her American Doctors, and the Collision of Two Cultures.* New York: Noonday Press, 1997. The story of a child with epilepsy that provides a fascinating look at a huge cultural clash between Western medicine and Hmong ideas about disease and cures. It gives a lot of examples of not listening or understanding.

Gonzalez-Mena, J. *50 Strategies for Working and Communicating with Diverse Parents.* Columbus, OH: Merrill, 2006. Practical information on partnering with families to support, enhance, and maximize the quality of care and education of young children.

Koulouras, K.; M. L. Porter; and S. A. Senter. "Making the Most of Parent Conferences." In *The Art of Leadership*, eds. B. Neugebauer and R. Neugebauer. Redmond, WA: Child Care Information Exchange, 2003, pp. 319–322. How to conduct conferences so you build a bond of trust.

Phipps, P. A. "Working with Angry Parents—Taking a Customer Service Approach." In *The Art of Leadership*, eds. B. Neugebauer and R. Neugebauer. Redmond, WA: Child Care Information Exchange, 2003, pp. 226–228. Shows how to focus your actions and responses to achieve a win-win solution.

Quiroz, B.; P. Greenfield; and M. Altchech. "Bridging Cultures with a Parent–Teacher Conference." In *Readings for Bridging Cultures*, ed. C. Rothstein-Fisch. Mahwah, NJ: Erlbaum, 2003, pp. 27–29. Parent-teacher conferences are a prime occasion for cross-cultural communication.

Rogoff, B. *The Cultural Nature of Human Development.* New York: Oxford University Press. 2003. A treasure trove of information about cultural differences that can help teachers work with diversity issues.

Small, M. *Our Babies, Ourselves: How Biology and Culture Shape the Way We Parent.* New York: Anchor Books, 1998. Full of fascinating information by an anthropologist about beliefs and practices that conflict with the American experts' recommended practices.

Zepeda, M.; Gonzalez-Mena, J.; Rothstein-Fisch, C.; and Trumbell, E. *Bridging Cultures in Early Care and Education.* Mahwah, NJ: Erlbaum, 2006. A training manual designed to help pre-service and in-service early childhood educators and other professionals who work with children and families understand the role of culture in their programs.

NOTES

1. This example and also the next example is from a training module used in field testing by the authors. M. Zepeda, J. Gonzalez-Mena, C. Rothstein-Fisch, and E. Trumbull. *Bridging Cultures in Early Childhood*, (Mahwah, NJ: Erlbaum, 2006).

2. This particular issue doesn't have to be a cultural conflict; it can be a generational conflict. My own mother often bragged to me that I was toilet trained at a year. She used to call me a lazy mother because I was relaxed about training my own children, who were over 2 before they exhibited the signs of readiness I was looking for. But I had research and a whole pediatric and early childhood community to back me up, so I stuck to my guns. We never did see eye-to-eye on this issue. It wasn't until I ran into the same issue as a cultural conflict that I began to see it from a different perspective.

3. P. Leach, *Your Baby and Child,* (New York: Knopf, 1997).

4. "Americans, who value independence and individuality, see the baby as dependent, undifferentiated . . . the Japanese, who prize close interdependence between child and adult, regard the infant as having a small component of autonomy . . . believe they must tempt the infant into a dependent role, rush to soothe a crying infant, respond quietly to the baby's excited babbling, and sleep with the young child at night in order to encourage the mutual bonding necessary for adult life." J. Kagan, *The Nature of the Child,* (New York: Basic Books, 1984), p. 29.

5. M. Small, "Dare to Bare." *New York Times,* October 11, 2005. Also Janice Hale-Benson explains how early training works with African-American babies. "Because Black babies are held so much of the time, there is an immediate response to urination and bowel movements. Hence from an early age, there is an association in the infant's mind between these functions and action from the mother. Consequently, when the mother seeks to toilet train the child (in the early and stringent manner that has been observed in the Black community), the child is accustomed to her direct involvement in the process. In contrast, the transition is more startling for middle-class American infants whose functions typically occur alone. The mother begins to interfere with bowel and bladder activity after many months of only cursory attention. There is greater continuity, then, in the behavior of Black mothers." J. Hale-Benson, "Black Children: Their Roots, Culture, and Learning Styles," in O. N. Saracho and B. Spodek, eds., *Understanding the Multicultural Experience in Early Childhood Education,* (Washington, DC: National Association for the Education of Young Children), p. 24.

   Here's what another anthropologist, Dorothy Lee, says. Her description of Chinese toilet training has the same result, but is somewhat of a contrast to Hale-Benson's explanation. "American observers had noticed that Chinese babies had learned, by the time they were about six months old, to indicate that they wanted to micturate; yet they seemed to be treated very permissively with no attempt at toilet training. When the baby wants to urinate, his whole body participates in the preliminary process. The Chinese mother, holding the baby in her arms, learns to be sensitive to the minute details of this process, and to hold her baby away from herself at exactly the critical moment. Eventually, the infant learns to ask to be held out. The mother neither tries to control the baby, nor does she train the infant to control himself according to imposed standards. Instead, she sensitizes herself to his rhythm, and helps him to adopt social discipline with spontaneity, starting from his unique pattern. What is interesting here is that as an end result of this, the baby is "toilet-trained" at a very early age; but it has been an experience of spontaneity for him and his autonomy has remained inviolate, because his mother has had the sensitivity and the patience to 'listen' to him. D. Lee, *Freedom and Culture* (Englewood Cliffs, NY: Prentice Hall, 1959), p. 8.

6. E. T. Hall, *Beyond Culture.* (Garden City, NY: Anchor Press/Doubleday, 1981), p. 112.

7. I. Barrera and R. Corso, *Skilled Dialogue.* Baltimore: Brookes, 2003.

Focus Questions

Here are some questions to get you thinking about what's in this chapter.

- What's an individualist and what's a collectivist?

- What are some diversity issues regarding food and eating?

- How are eating and sleeping patterns that are built around natural rhythms different from those built around schedules?

- What happens to a child in child care when the family has one kind of eating and sleeping pattern and the program stresses another?

- What are the issues regarding children sleeping alone or with someone else?

- What does it mean to deal with a conflict by creating a dialogue?

- Does everybody stress self-help skills, like getting babies to feed themselves?

- Should adults take responsibility for the amount a child eats?

CHAPTER FOUR

A Framework for Understanding Differences

How could anyone possibly know everything about every different situation that might occur in an early care and education program? Just understanding simple cultural differences is a challenge because early childhood professionals aren't anthropologists! And even if they were, how many cultures could they study? Then, to further complicate things, children come into programs from bicultural and multicultural families. Maybe the families themselves aren't even in agreement at home about how to do things.

One way to become more sensitive to diversity is to understand some common patterns that relate to attitudes and behaviors. You can think of putting on a particular lens to examine a situation. Remember back at the beginning of the book, the story about a man training a dog? I became confused and frightened by his strange behavior until I saw the whole picture and then understood the meaning of his behavior. This chapter is designed to help you understand the meaning of some behaviors that you may judge as inappropriate or even harmful if you don't see the whole picture. The chapter uses a framework that came from research by Patricia Greenfield and others. This framework makes meaning of common behaviors that can cause dissention between families and teachers. Greenfield's research contrasts two perspectives—that of the individualist and that of the collectivist.

Although I am using the terms individualists and collectivists as a short cut for contrasting the differences, nobody I know calls him- or herself by those terms. And nobody is purely one or the other—but all families encompass both kinds of behaviors. The point is that families usually lean one way more than the other. Remember as you read on that these concepts have been boiled down to make them understandable, but don't reflect reality as most of us live it.[1]

Individualists tend to live in urban environments; as income levels rise, so do tendencies toward individualism. Collectivists often come from more rural areas and may have less income than individualists, although not all collectivists are from low-income groups. Many collectivists are immigrants who come to the United States from countries where collectivism was or is a tradition, necessity, or political system. Some of those immigrants arrived many generations ago (willingly or unwillingly) and have kept their collectivistic roots. Collectivism is also alive and well in the United States in indigenous groups and also in some religious or spiritual groups from a variety of cultures.

WHAT'S AN INDIVIDUALIST AND WHAT'S A COLLECTIVIST?

Most people trained in early childhood education can easily see the perspective of an individualist. They are the ones who stress self-help skills by giving babies finger food and spoon-feeding them only until they manage to feed themselves. They say to preschoolers who managed to zip their jackets, "You did it without any help!" Individualists are concerned with self-esteem and making every child feel special. They help children stand out in a crowd. They are individualists because they perceive their jobs to be to treat children as unique and special *individuals* who are on the way to gaining *independence*.

A collectivist, on the other hand, sees the child first and foremost as a member of the group, not apart and separate. Collectivists perceive their jobs to be to firmly attach the child to the group. To do that they may *de-emphasize* individuality and independence. They may downplay specialness and focus on group esteem instead of self-esteem. Collectivists are likely to spoon-feed babies much longer than individualists. They may continue spoon-feeding into the preschool years and even beyond. They are aiming for *interdependence*. They not only feed babies, but they also put coats on preschoolers—and zip them. They see such acts as solidifying connections. As one Vietnamese woman said, "My mother fed me until the second grade, but she always made me do my own homework." See *Point to Ponder* 4.1 with a point to ponder about collectivism and autonomy.

Individualists start encouraging children to do things on their own at a very young age. They are the ones who wait a bit for little babies to learn to calm themselves before they jump in and soothe them. They teach three-year-olds problem-solving skills and help the children develop "inner controls" so they don't have to depend on adults as much for guidance.

A collectivist's top priority is strengthening relationships and moving children away from their independent urges. Instead they give children the

POINT TO PONDER 4.1

How Do Interdependence and Autonomy Fit Together?

Barbara Rogoff makes the point that a family can be collectivistic and still emphasize autonomy along with interdependence. The difference between such a family and one that stresses independence and individualism is that in the collectivist family, autonomy is oriented toward the group. Children can have freedom of choice and learn to cooperate at the same time.

At the Pikler Institute, a residential nursery in Budapest, Hungary, even the casual observer can see that interdependence is a focus. The children in each room form a group and they know that they are each members of it. Babies thought by outsiders to be too young to care for and about each other exhibit empathy and helping skills. Children of such tender ages that they know nothing about the word cooperation, are cooperative. At the same time a great deal of attention is paid by their caregivers to ensure that each child comes to see him- or herself as a unique individual. During interdependence times, when the essential activities of daily living occur (like diapering and bathing), the focus of the caregivers is one-on-one. During other play periods the children show that they have had sufficient attention for themselves from adults and they are able to focus their attention on each other and being members of the group. It is hard to describe this integration because it is so solid, it almost doesn't show.

B. Rogoff. *The Cultural Nature of Human Development*, (New York: Oxford University Press, 2003), pp. 200–208.

M. David, and G. Appell. "Lóczy: An Unusual Approach to Mothering." In Jean Marie Clark; revised translation by Judit Falk (ed.), *Lóczy ou Le Maternage Insolite*. Budapest: Association Pikler-Lóczy for Young Children, 2001.

message that it's okay to depend on adults. Those children who want to do everything themselves get an even stronger message about the importance of graciously accepting help. When children are old enough to help others, collectivists encourage them to do so. Helping yourself is not considered important enough to teach because it is seen as a natural inclination that needs to be discouraged rather than encouraged.

Individualists recognize achievement and expect even the youngest child to feel good about accomplishments. "Look what a great job you did," says the individualistic adult. "And you did it all by yourself!" When the child responds with a show of pride, the individualistic adult sees evidence that self-esteem is rising. The individualistic adult thinks it's even better when children point out how strong, smart, or capable they are. "Look at me!" is encouraged.

Collectivists, on the other hand, value modesty and humbleness; they downplay expressions of pride in personal achievements. Self-praise is considered

POINT TO PONDER 4.2

The Danger of Labeling People

Individualism and collectivism are useful labels, but they are not meant to be used to put people into categories. The two perspectives are not necessarily mutually exclusive. People have elements of both. Think of a continuum and imagine that any given person or group falls somewhere along it. This chapter contrasts the extreme ends. Also realize that these two labels don't explain everything about a person or a group. The idea is to expand awareness and understanding, not to limit it by categorizing in simplistic ways. The examples in Chapter 3 provide many explanations about behavior that don't fit neatly into labeled categories. That's always true of every situation. Remember, these labels aren't reality, only a convenient framework for beginning to understand some differences in goals and perspectives. Think of it like a map. There's the map and then there's the reality of the landscape. They aren't the same, but the map is still useful.

bragging and is discouraged. Collectivists do not value individual achievement but rather group achievement.

Although I'm describing collectivists and individualists to point out the patterns, I want to repeat that no one is all one way or the other. (See *Point to Ponder* 4.2 if you're tempted to start thinking in either/or terms.) The use of those labels is deceiving. People don't call themselves collectivists or individualists. Mostly people just think the way they do and behave accordingly without analyzing why or labeling themselves. I'm using the labels as a convenient way of explaining the framework.

Imagine what happens when a collectivist's child ends up in a individualistic program or classroom. Most children experience confusion at the very least. To minimize difficulties, adults need to become aware that their actions are culturally based. Awareness of differing perspectives helps adults begin to figure out what to do about the difference so that children who are grounded in one system and end up in another one do not experience conflicts that interfere with their growth, development, and education. It's important that professionals honor differences in the families they serve and work together with those families to figure out what is best for the child.

Here's a simple example. In one situation, when lunchtime came, a group of adults got out their lunches brought from home and went into the lunch room to eat together. Each ate his or her own lunch. In another situation when the group of adults sat down with their own lunch bags and boxes, they immediately took out all the food and put it in the middle of the table to share. It isn't that the first group never shared food—they did. But when a shared meal was planned, they announced ahead of time that it would be a "potluck." For the second group every meal where people brought food was a potluck and it didn't need to be labeled as such. Is it easy to tell which group is the more focused on independence and individuality? If you aren't sure, keep reading.

Look at some other situations that can be analyzed by using the framework of individualism and collectivism. The first two come from *Bridging Cultures*, a research project conducted on Latino immigrants in Los Angeles (Rothstein-Fisch, 2003). The first situation is just a little incident, but it shows two different ways of thinking. A mentor-teacher observing the kindergarten teacher she is working with notes how the newer teacher sets out crayons for children to use. She arranges them by color, putting all the yellow ones in one paper cup, all the blue ones in another, and so forth. The effect is that the children have to inter-act with each other to get the crayons they need. The mentor-teacher suggests that it would be better to give each child a personal set with all the colors. Further, she suggests that the other teacher write each child's name on the cup.

If you use the individualistic–collectivistic framework to analyze this situation, you might say that the mentor-teacher thinks that teaching about personal property is important. She might also be thinking that it's better for each child to have a full set of crayons so the children don't need to bother each other. If she sees a need for children to learn to focus on their own work, she doesn't want them distracted by interactions. These are all individualistic concerns. The other teacher may have a collectivistic approach. She may be more concerned that the children are aware that they are part of the group sitting at the table. She may feel that interacting with the other children by passing crayons is preferred over each concentrating on his or her own drawing. The social considerations take precedent over the personal.

As it turned out in the real situation reported by Rothstein-Fisch, the teacher and children were Latino immigrants and when the teacher switched to go along with the wishes of the mentor-teacher, it didn't work very well. The children didn't respond by taking care of their personal property, which was the goal of the mentor-teacher. They didn't keep their crayons separate, so the teacher had to reorganize the cups of crayons every day. Were those children feeling caught between the way things were done at home and the way they were now being done at school?

Another situation from this same research project involves a different kindergarten teacher. She's got the children in a group and she is trying to get them to describe an egg. She wants to make them aware of the properties of the egg—it's shape, color, texture. She asks the group to think about the times they had cooked and eaten eggs. One child starts by telling about when she cooked eggs with her grandmother. The teacher ignores her story. She tries three times to tell it, but the teacher listens only to the child who says that eggs look white and yellow when they are cracked.

Can you see the collectivistic and individualistic aspects of this situation? The individualistic approach is to focus on eggs as isolated physical objects with sets of physical attributes that can be studied. People from collectivistic cultures are more likely to view objects in connection with social interactions and use them as a mediator of relationships. Objects are valuable because they connect people to each other. The one child knew what the teacher was really asking—describe an egg as a separate physical entity. The other child, the one who wanted to tell the story about her grandmother, took the teacher's question at face value. Her answer made perfect sense to her, but it was of no importance to the teacher.

Here's a different situation, this time with a baby and a home visitor. It also involves differing perceptions about the use of objects as learning tools. Whenever the home visitor comes, the mother holds the baby while the two adults talk. The home visitor notices that when the baby reaches for an object, the mother takes it away from her and brings her attention back to what's going on between the adults. The home visitor brings toys and the mother puts them out of the baby's reach. When the home visitor asks why, the mother can't seem to explain.

The mother probably can't explain because she hasn't analyzed her own behavior. The home visitor may not have analyzed hers either, but she is convinced that it is important for babies to handle objects. As in the other situations, we can't know what is *really* going on; we can analyze, but it is only speculation. Try this analysis. The mother sees objects as distracting the baby from the important learning—being part of the social scene. The mother is a collectivist. The home visitor may also be a collectivist, but she is trained in early care and education and believes in the value of playing with objects.

How do people end up as individualists and collectivists? The example of the baby shows that it all starts in infancy. Let's look at early child-rearing practices to see how the two patterns are learned from the beginning of life.

EATING AND SLEEPING: TWO CONTRASTING PATTERNS

In the beginning of life, the processes of taking in food and going to sleep are quite intertwined. As children grow older, they become separated, though to what extent and how soon depend on the adults' attitudes toward the two.

Pattern One: Schedules

Two patterns emerge when looking at adult approaches to babies eating and sleeping. One pattern is a movement toward a schedule—toward consistency.

The goal is to get the baby into a routine so that eating and sleeping become regular and predictable. This is done by regulating the feedings and keeping the baby awake at certain times during the day or in the evening.

The schedule may not start from day one, but from day one the parents or caregivers in this pattern are trying to get the baby to distinguish between day and night. The goal is to get the baby to sleep longer and longer periods at night and to be awake and to eat during the day.

The baby may be fed at first according to need; that is, whenever the adult thinks the baby is hungry. However, eventually some sort of a schedule establishes itself, and the adults concerned feel a sense of accomplishment. The baby takes a bottle or is breast-fed every three or four hours and catnaps periodically between feedings, sleeping six to eight hours at night. The next step comes when the baby settles into a schedule that includes three meals and two naps a day. As time goes on, the morning nap gets later and later until it blends with the afternoon nap, and the adult announces, "She's down to one nap a day now."

Babies who are raised by routine-loving adults usually have a specific bedtime as well as regular feeding and nap times. Things that change the routine may be upsetting to adults and babies alike, and the adult may explain fussiness as a disruption of routine: "She's fussy because she didn't get her nap today" or "He's fussy because his schedule's all off."

These adults believe that establishing a routine, a schedule, creates a daily rhythm, a sameness that is important to good health and happiness. "Easy babies" are those who adjust to routines. "Hard babies" are those who defy the adult's attempts to schedule and regulate them.

Pattern Two: Natural Rhythms

Some adults don't go by the clock; they don't have schedules. Their own lives may be in tune with their natural body rhythms, and if they can resist the clock taking over their lives, they do so. Even if they can't resist for themselves, they may be dedicated to the idea of doing it for babies.

The natural rhythm pattern of sleep is linked at the beginning to feeding rhythms. Pattern two works best with breast-feeding because the milk is always ready and the right temperature, and adults don't think in terms of ounces consumed. Mothers who sleep with their babies and breast-feed upon need are less likely to be concerned about how soon the baby sleeps through the night. True pattern-two people feed when the baby seems to be hungry without regard to how long it's been since the last feeding. (This is in contrast to pattern-one feeders, who make statements like, "He drank six ounces just two hours ago; he can't possibly be starving now.") Because the amount of breast milk consumed isn't measured, the pattern-two person is less apt to be convinced the baby isn't hungry when crying.

Children who come from pattern-one backgrounds, where schedules and routines are stressed, often fit right into early care and education programs, where schedules guide the routines. What happens when pattern-two babies (natural rhythms, ignore the clock) go into an infant care program that's structured for pattern-one schedule types?

Pattern One and Pattern Two in Child Care Programs   Usually pattern clashes don't create a problem with younger babies because they often are encouraged to follow their own schedule or natural rhythms for both feeding and sleep. However, the goal for even young babies may be to establish an individual daily schedule if pattern-one caregivers are part of the staff.

Feeding for young babies is usually an individual matter, though no one is there to breast-feed whenever the baby is hungry, so the individual natural feeding rhythms won't work in quite the same way even if the caregiver firmly believes in them. Sometimes a caregiver will try to duplicate the natural rhythms approach, using a bottle and ignoring the clock. But if the baby wants to eat very often, the caregiver who complies may meet with disapproval from those who feel constant feeding isn't good for babies and that bottles should be spaced, even if no schedule is intended. All the focus on childhood obesity may be another reason for disapproval. A difference between breast-feeding and bottle-feeding, as mentioned before, is that adults know how much bottle-fed babies have consumed.

For young babies, the most common approach in child care is to encourage an individual schedule for eating and sleeping, taking each baby's needs into consideration. As the babies grow older, some attempt is usually made to coordinate all the children's schedules until, by two or sometimes three years of age, all or most eat and sleep according to the same schedule.

The Issue of Sleeping Alone   The issue of sleeping alone in a crib sometimes arises in child care. A pattern-one parent is more likely to put her baby to sleep in another room, or at least in his own crib in her room. She is most likely to regard her baby as an individual who needs to come to see himself as separate from her.[2]

A pattern-two parent may also have a crib but may not use it as much as the pattern-one parent. Some pattern-two parents never even buy a crib, preferring that their babies not sleep alone.[3] Pattern-one and pattern-two parents may disapprove of each other. Each has strong reasons why the other is wrong.

Most programs in Canada and the United States lean more toward pattern one than pattern two and are dedicated to the idea that each child needs a crib to sleep in, and there is often a licensing regulation to back up the program's policy.

Here's what happened in one program. A refugee family enrolled its baby in an infant center program. The baby had never slept by himself before, and when he was put into a crib off in a quiet, darkened room, he got very upset. It wasn't just the ordinary upset of a child who was resisting going to sleep even though tired; it was the panicked reaction of a child who was very fearful of the situation. No matter what the staff tried to do to help this child sleep alone, nothing worked. He would sleep only near someone in the midst of the activity of the playroom. Being by himself to sleep was a fearful and foreign situation for him.

The staff wanted to accommodate the child's special need, which they perceived to be a cultural difference; however, state licensing regulations got in the way. But this story has a happy ending! The staff was able to convince the licensing authority to grant a waiver to the regulation that infants sleep alone in a crib in a room separate from the play area.

Putting Children to Sleep   Adults, even within the same culture, don't necessarily agree about ways to put children to sleep. Some feel it is important for babies to discover their own soothing devices and use them to settle down to sleep. These adults are likely to put the tired baby into a crib and let him put himself to sleep, even if he creates a fuss before he finally settles down.

Other adults use their own soothing devices to put a baby to sleep and are not willing for babies to be unhappy if they can help it. Sometimes this attitude is influenced by culture; other times it relates to living circumstances (when a crying baby disturbs others, adults may keep that baby from crying out of respect). Imagine a situation where a number of people live in a small apartment and a baby who puts himself to sleep by crying hard every night for fifteen minutes moves in. Respect for the adults' peace and quiet may have priority over the baby's method of putting himself to sleep.

Putting older children to sleep is another issue. If they don't sleep in cribs, or do sleep in cribs but climb out of them, either you have to find some way to put them down and keep them there so they can put themselves to sleep, or you have to use various means to settle them down and put them to sleep. If you're a dedicated pattern-one person, you may train them to stay on their cot or blanket or in their crib long enough so they fall asleep either on schedule or when you perceive they are tired. If you are a pattern-two person, you may be inclined to be less firm about "putting the child down," but you may expect children to "put themselves down" whenever they are tired.

Very few teachers or caregivers in my experience use this latter approach, partly because the adults need a break from the children, and they get it at nap time. Indeed, even if they wanted to let children rest whenever they wanted rather than according to schedule, they'd find various kinds of outside pressures to create a regular "nap time" in their program. They'd also get arguments about children being overtired and not able to put themselves down. A criticism of pattern-two adults is that they let the children "go until they drop from exhaustion." The answer to that criticism is that children who are taught to tune in on their own body rhythms from the beginning are aware of their needs to rest just as they are aware of their needs to eat. Pattern-two people believe that it's good training for adulthood to get in touch with one's own physical needs, especially in a society in which so many are out of touch.

MORE DIVERSITY ISSUES AROUND FEEDING AND EATING

Both the sleeping and feeding processes are highly charged with feelings and have great potential for conflicts between teachers or caregivers and parents. The following scene shows an example of a cultural conflict.

> A mother arrives to pick up her son from an infant center. She enters the room to find him seated, waving a spoon in the air with one hand while jamming mushy cereal into his already full mouth with the other one. The mother hurries over to him, frowning, and says gruffly to the caregiver sitting close by watching him, "Where's a washcloth?"
>
> She takes the cloth handed to her, and as she briskly cleans up her protesting son, she is mumbling under her breath. The gist of her mumbling concerns her dissatisfaction with the self-feeding process and the mess created.
>
> The caregiver, who is now cleaning up another child nearby, tries to talk about self-help skills and sensory experiences, but the angry mother's back is turned the whole time as she works over her son. She finally gets her child's hands and face clean, but his clothes, in spite of the bib, still show signs of the meal he has just enjoyed. Hurriedly she changes his shirt, which now clashes with the pants he has on. She looks at the outfit and shakes her head in disgust. She is still looking distressed as she bustles out the door, diaper bag and son in hand.
>
> The caregiver, angry herself by now, sits down for a minute to cool off before dealing with the children needing her attention.

With this scene in mind, look at *Point to Ponder* 4.3.

Dealing with a Conflict by Creating a Dialogue

A parent's attitude may trigger anger in the teacher or caregiver, which makes him or her less inclined to try to understand the parent's perspective. It hurts to feel attacked and criticized. However, it is vital that teachers and caregivers tune in to parents in conflicts like this and not just defensively write them off.

How can a teacher or caregiver communicate by creating a dialogue when parents leave like this one did? What do you do with angry parents who will neither talk nor listen?

POINT TO PONDER 4.3

Messy Eating

When shown a video clip of a baby eating, similar to what was described in this scene, a group of well-trained infant caregivers could easily explain all the benefits of allowing the child to eat on his own in this way. Many of their explanations related to an individualistic perspective and involved developing self-help skills, making choices, and being independent. They saw side benefits too—like fine-motor development and sensory experiences. When the same group was shown a second clip of a mother neatly spoon-feeding a four-year-old, there was silence. When asked what the benefits of this method were, no one spoke. Many of the caregivers came from relatively collectivistic backgrounds and had shown surprise or disgust at the messy eating scene. In spite of the attitudes that showed in their facial expressions, all knew the "right answers" to the question about the benefits. No one wanted to defend a mother who, according to their training, would have to be labeled as wrong.

Whatever you do, don't give up! Work hard to build a relationship. Don't be as concerned about getting your point of view across as about opening lines of communication. It helps if the parent feels you care about and respect him or her. One way to convey this caring and respect is to tune in to feelings. When you acknowledge how a parent feels, you have a better chance to get to a dialogue eventually.

Above all, try not to get defensive about your own perspective. Try hard to tune in to the parent's point of view. Start by looking at goals and priorities. Are you on the same wavelength? In a situation like the previous one, you probably aren't. Whereas your priority may be self-help skills and sensory experiences at mealtimes, the parent may have much stronger feelings about neatness for a lot of different reasons.[4] How to eat brings up a whole set of issues. *What* to eat brings up even more. See *Point to Ponder* 4.4 to look at differences in dietary practices.

Varying Perspectives on Early Self-Feeding

The experts in this country agree that it is important to encourage babies to take part in the feeding process and to hand this task over to the child completely soon after the baby can get the food from plate to mouth, no matter how much mess results. Comer and Poussaint say, "When your baby makes reasonably good attempts to feed himself, encourage it. Not only does this support a feeling of independence, but it also permits him to develop greater skill in using

POINT TO PONDER 4.4

Dietary Practices

Vegetarians and vegans have different ideas about diet than do old-fashioned farm families who don't consider it a meal unless meat is served. Knowing about healthy vegetarian or vegan diets is helpful, but it won't tell you everything about what every family wants its child to eat. It's critical to find out what a child can or cannot eat, whether for moral, religious, or cultural reasons. Staying kosher, for example involves more than just avoiding pork; it also involves reading labels of packaged foods. It is also important to understand fasting practices, as well.

his hands."[5] Other experts advise leniency about letting children *touch*, and even *play with* their food, and even see these behaviors as *sensory experiences.*[6]

In some cultures, food is revered and is never considered a plaything, not at the eating table or at the activity table. Many people frown on such things as finger painting with pudding, playing with play dough, or placing beans or rice in a "sensory table." Anyone who has experienced severe food shortages may be horrified at the thought of playing with food. Some people, even without personal starvation experience, have strong feelings about world hunger. They feel that it's wrong to use food as a plaything.

The issue of food shortages may be combined with the cleanup issue. Anyone without washers or dryers and plenty of extra clothes may have a different attitude toward letting babies play with food or have a sensory experience. A family may have plenty of everything but live in a home not set up for messy meals. In both cases, the priority is on preventing rather than cleaning up messes. Prevention means spoon-feeding the baby.

Sodetaini-Shibata says this about the Japanese approach to self-feeding:

> Children are fed until they acquire the ability to handle a spoon on their own . . . but parents often resort to the use of both self-feeding and adult-feeding. . . . As the child approaches school-age, feeding by the parents is weaned, and it is stopped when the child enters school. . . . [O]rderliness and tidiness are highly stressed in the Japanese daily life.[7]

Valuing neatness may be less of an issue than lack of time. When parents have to rush to feed their babies and clean up after them, they may find it more expedient to continue to spoon-feed until their children can eat neatly and efficiently by themselves, which may be as late as four years old.

The opposing values of independence versus interdependence often lie behind conflicts that involve self-help skills, like self-feeding. I remember some of the Hispanic parents I used to work with who spoon-fed their children far beyond the age that I considered reasonable. I was trying to make their children independent through early self-help skills; they had different ideas. They were less concerned about the children helping themselves than they were about teaching them to help others. By feeding them, they were modeling the behavior they were trying to teach. The goal was interdependence.

If you see little reason for children to stand alone (on their own two feet, as the expression goes) but lots of reasons for them to experience and value relationships, you may be very willing to let self-help skills come much later. You may see a value in one person being dependent on another. The point is mutual dependence. Now it's the small child dependent on more capable adults. Once that phase is over, other dependencies will take its place. But dependency isn't a one-way proposition as you grow up; just as you are dependent, so are you depended upon. Interdependency is a lifelong condition, one that relates to permanent attachment with your family or your people—something that is highly valued in some cultures.

Taking Responsibility for the Amount That a Child Eats

Another potential area of conflict is taking or not taking responsibility for how much children eat. Parenting experts oppose urging or forcing children to eat, citing *body wisdom* as the reason. Babies will eat when they are hungry because of the body's natural inclination to keep itself healthy. Babies have a way of getting what they need when offered a balanced diet, agree the experts. All advise not to force, coax, or bribe. When parents, teachers, and caregivers exhibit those behaviors, it may lead to eating problems in children.[8]

Getting children to eat is only an issue in families where there is an abundance of food. On a worldwide basis, urging or forcing children to eat is seldom thought about. According to Werner:

> Three-quarters of all the world's children under the age of 15 . . . live in developing countries. Every 30 seconds, 100 children are born somewhere in Asia, Africa, Latin America, or Oceania. Twenty of them will die within the year. Of the 80 who survive, 60 will suffer from malnutrition during the crucial weaning and toddler stage, with the possibility of irreversible stunting of physical and mental growth.[9]

The parents of these children don't face the problem of urging their children to eat—their worry is getting the food to offer them. Starving children need no urging.

Parents who have access to adequate amounts of food but have witnessed the starvation of others often feel it is their job to get a certain amount of food into their children. Many cultures value chubby children, perhaps because thin children tend to die. But beyond that factor, many cultures see chubby as attractive

POINT TO PONDER 4.5

The Issue of Childhood Obesity

Although I am stressing to honor and appreciate cultural and individual differences, issues often are more complex than they seem. Another lens to look at feeding issues is through that of childhood obesity, which has become a national concern and a serious health issue. To address this issue, professionals have an ethical mandate to at least begin to discuss what can be done. Some are taking steps to work with parents around changes in both the program and family eating patterns. It's a delicate issue and one to be approached with caution, but not ignored. It's also important to note that obesity is a bigger problem in low-income families than in more economically comfortable ones. Although it is easier to focus on educating parents, we all need to realize that if the society could eliminate poverty, obesity would more than likely greatly diminish.

and desirable. According to Stringfellow, Liem, and Liem, of 41 Vietnamese parents asked, all said they thought that babies should be fat.[10] See *Point to Ponder* 4.5. Some parents have a different reason for wanting to get a certain amount of food into their children. Children who have special needs or particular challenges may not be hungry in the same way that typically developing children are. If the parent or caregiver just waits until the baby wants to eat, that baby may become dehydrated and end up in the hospital attached to an IV tube.

Some of these differences in feeding practices relate to individual circumstances and others reflect conflicting values. In families where the goal is for the child to remain close to the family, not to grow up to be an independent person living apart and perhaps alone, the stress is on interdependence. Caregiving practices, including feeding routines, reflect the fact that parents do not stress individuality and independence but rather cooperation and connectedness, both in the present and as a future goal.

SUGGESTIONS FOR RESOLVING CONFLICTS OVER EATING AND SLEEPING

Here are some steps you can take when you find yourself on the opposite side from a parent in a conflict over sleeping or feeding issues:

1. Sort out whether this is an important issue or not. Is the parent's practice actually harming the child? The issue may concern whether to hold the babies to put them to sleep or to let them sleep with their parents. This issue may not be important. Talk with others as part of this sorting

process. Upon close examination, you may see that there is no potential harm and that it is just a difference of opinion. Neither of you is
right or wrong. If this is the case, perhaps you can let go of the issue.
What about the situation of a baby sleeping with a bottle? What about
the risks of "bottle mouth"? (Bottle mouth is a term for tooth decay
caused by formula, milk, or juice bathing the teeth for long hours during sleep.) In addition, as mentioned in Chapter 1, there's an issue
regarding the risks of putting young babies to sleep on their stomachs.
If you know that the baby has a higher chance of dying of sudden infant
death syndrome (SIDS), could you just go along with what the parent
says if he or she says to place the baby in a prone position?

2. If you can't let go of it, try looking at the issue from the parent's perspective. This may not be easy if you don't have experience with
changing perspectives. But if you work with young children, you probably have had experience seeing the world through a child's eyes. Try
now seeing this situation through the parent's eyes. An important prerequisite for seeing a new view is not to get angry or defensive. That's
easier said than done if this conflict has triggered strong feelings in
you. See if you can set aside those feelings and ask yourself, "Do I
understand this parent's goals for his or her child?"

3. Help the parent articulate his or her goals. This probably won't happen
overnight. It is most likely to happen as the result of a rather lengthy,
ongoing dialogue. Once you both understand what the parent wants for
his or her child, together you can examine whether or not the practice
in question reflects those goals. If the practice and the goals fit, you
should reconsider your own position in the matter. However, if the
practice and goals conflict, you have your job cut out for you.

4. The ideal situation is when, with or without your efforts, parents come
to see on their own that the practice and the goals are in conflict and
figure out what to do about that situation. They may want your advice
at this point if you haven't been too pushy about your own point of
view from the start. Now the parents may decide to change the practice to be more in accordance with personal or cultural goals.

SUMMARY

The chapter started by examining the differences between an individualist and a collectivist and provided warnings about stereotyping or putting people into boxes. It
made the point that adults teach children collectivistic or individualistic tendencies
early so the children absorb the messages (many of which are nonverbal) during eating and other caregiving routines. Two contrasting approaches to feeding babies and

putting them to sleep involve individualistic or collectivistic leanings. Pattern one involves the clock and schedules, and pattern two involves natural rhythms. Whether children should sleep alone or with someone and putting children to sleep are also issues that have differing perspectives. There are varying perspectives on whether children need to learn to feed themselves as soon as they have the skills or whether an adult should keep feeding a child beyond the toddler years. The first perspective fits the individualistic approach. The second is more collectivistic and comes from the idea that feeding a child is a way of solidifying the bonds between adult and child. Another issue is how much responsibility an adult should take for the amount a child eats. The individualist may always let the child decide, but if the child has special needs, that approach may not work. Suggestions for resolving conflicts over eating and sleeping include the following: sort out important issues from unimportant ones, look at the issue from the other person's perspective, help parents articulate their goals, and give advice only when it is appropriate.

FOR FURTHER READING

David, M. and G. Appell. "Lóczy: An Unusual Approach to Mothering." In Jean Marie Clark; revised translation by Judit Falk (ed.), *Lóczy ou Le Maternage Insolite*. Budapest: Association Pikler-Lóczy for Young Children, 2001. Written by European psychologists who studied at the Pikler Institute and captured the essence and details of the approach. One of the first books translated into English that gave the English-speaking world a view of Emmi Pikler's work in her residential nursery in Budapest.

Eggers-Pierola, C. *Connections and Commitments: Reflecting Latino Values in Early Childhood Programs*. Portsmouth, NH: Heinemann, 2005. A book that helps teachers be more responsive to Latino families by explaining four values on which to build teaching practices: family, belonging, education, and commitment.

Gonzalez, N.; Moll, L. C.; and Amanti, C. *Funds of Knowledge: Theorizing Practices in Households, Communities, and Classrooms*. Mahwah, NJ: Erlbaum, 2005. Families have strengths that sometimes teachers don't recognize. Recognizing, acknowledging, and building on those strengths helps families and teachers alike.

Greenfield, P. M. "Independence and Interdependence as Developmental Scripts: Implications for Theory, Research, and Practice," in P. M. Greenfield and R. R. Cocking, eds., *Cross-Cultural Roots of Minority Child Development*. (Mahwah, NJ: Lawrence Erlbaum, 1994) pp. 1–37. Discusses the effects of cultural scripts on development.

Greenspan, S. I. and S. Wieder. *The Child with Special Needs*. Reading, MA: Perseus Books, 1998. Although this book doesn't focus on cultural differences, someone with the collectivist/individualist framework can use the information as a basis for examining cultural differences.

Kagitcibasi, C. *Family and Human Development Across Cultures*. Mahwah, NJ: Lawrence Erlbaum, 1996. This cross-cultural psychologist from Turkey looks at human development assumptions and conclusions from a non-Western viewpoint.

Phillips, C. Brunson, and R. M. Cooper, "Cultural Dimensions of Feeding Relationships." *Zero to Three* 12(5), June 1992, pp. 10–13. More about culture and infant feeding.

Rothstein-Fisch, C. *Bridging Cultures: Teacher Education Module*. Mahwah, NJ: Lawrence Erlbaum, 2003. Provides good examples of individualism and collectivism in children in early elementary grades.

Sandall, S. R. and I. S. Schwartz. *Building Blocks for Teaching Preschoolers with Special Needs*. Baltimore, MD: Brookes Publishing, 2002. The building-block model includes three practical methods teachers can use to include young children with disabilities in the classroom.

Trumbull, E.; C. Rothstein-Fisch; and P. Greenfield. *Bridging Cultures in Our Schools: New Approaches that Work*. San Francisco: WestEd, 2000. Describes a project that trained teachers to understand the concepts of individualism and collectivism and work effectively with parents.

Zepeda, M.; Gonzalez-Mena, J.; Rothstein-Fisch, C.; and Trumbell, E. *Bridging Cultures in Early Care and Education*. Mahwah, NJ: Erlbaum, 2006. A training manual designed to help pre-service and in-service early childhood educators and other professionals who work with children and families understand the role of culture in their programs.

NOTES

1. Remember from Chapters 1 and 2, there are two kinds of individualism—soft and hard. What is described here is soft individualism. Hard individualism, which is more common among low-income families, doesn't look the same. The goals are similar in that both kinds of families are preparing their children to live as individuals who can take care of themselves in the world their families know and live in. It's just that those worlds are different from each other. A. S. Kusserow, *American Individualisms: Child Rearing and Social Class in Three Neighborhoods*, (New York: Palgrave McMillan, 2004).

2. Dorothy Lee describes the pattern-one person, going beyond the issue of separate sleeping arrangements to the larger issue of separation. She says not only do babies sleep separately in cribs, but also individuals are kept apart in many other ways even when they are mothers and babies. "In our society, clothing separates mother and child; is it to protect each from the hazards of a sudden draft? It was 102°F in my hospital room when I was first allowed to hold my baby; yet both baby and mother were carefully swathed in cloth which kept them to that degree distinct. Clothing, in fact, guards everyone against cutaneous contact with others, except perhaps, at the beach. We have divided our benches into individual units, our seats in school, on the train, on the bus. Even our solid sofas, planned for social grouping, have demarcating lines or separate pillows to help individuals keep apart." Obviously, a separate crib makes sense to a culture where individuals are kept apart from each other. D. Lee, *Freedom and Culture*, (Englewood Cliffs, NJ: Prentice Hall, 1959), p. 31.

3. The following references describe pattern-two cultures. Meredith Small said in the introduction to her book, *Our Babies Ourselves,* "I discovered that babies in other cultures lead lives very different from those I was used to seeing and hearing about here in the United States. Babies in some other societies, I learned, are carried in slings all day, sleep with their parents in the same bed, and are often integrated into the social fabric early on. I also heard that in other cultures, babies do not cry very often and never develop colic. This was an entirely different view of raising children than the one espoused by Dr. Spock." Small has a whole chapter on sleep in this book. M. F. Small, *Our Babies Ourselves,* (New York: Anchor Books, 1999), p xii.

Young writes of African-American families: "In many cases, the physical closeness between infants and adults is reinforced by the fact that they are often observed to sleep with their parents or either parent alone. There is a kind of rhythm found between eating and napping with short periods of each activity found with frequent repetition. This rhythm is very different from the disciplined long span of attention cultivated in middle-class child-rearing and expected in schools." Virginia Young, 1970, quoted in J. E. Hale-Benson, *Black Children: Their Roots, Culture, and Learning Styles,* (Baltimore, MD: Johns Hopkins University Press, 1986), p. 70.

Morrow says that Vietnamese, Cambodian, and Laotian children often sleep with their parents—Cambodian children sometimes up to ten years of age. R. D. Morrow, "Cultural Differences—Be Aware!" *Academic Therapy,* 23 no. 2 (November 1987), p. 147.

Caudill and Plath looked at sleeping arrangements in Japanese families. They found that the father and mother often slept in separate rooms, each with a child or children. The grandmother was also likely to sleep with a child. W. Caudill, and D. Plath, "Who Sleeps by Whom? Parent–Child Involvement in Urban Japanese Families." *Psychiatry* 29, no. 4 (1966), pp. 344–366.

According to Werner, "in a great majority of societies infants sleep in the same bed with their mothers during the time they are nursing—the first 2 to 3 years. In less than 10 of the world's societies whose ethnographies were surveyed did infants sleep in a crib or cradle of their own. Even where infants have a cradle or cot of their own, it is generally placed near the mother's bed within easy reach. Only in Western societies, notably middle-class United States, do infants have a bedroom of their own. In slightly less than one-half of the societies under consideration, the father also shared the bed with mother and infant. In slightly over half of the societies of the world, the husband slept in a bed in the same room but at some distance from his wife, or in another room." E. Werner, *Cross-Cultural Child Development: A View from the Planet Earth.* (Monterey, CA: Brooks/Cole, 1979), p. 270.

In describing a pattern-two culture, the Tikopia, Lee discusses sleeping arrangements and their relationship to individuals: "the Tikopia help the self to be continuous with its society through their physical arrangements. They find it good to sleep side by side crowding each other, next to their children or their parents or their brothers and sisters, mixing sexes and generations." Lee, *Freedom and Culture,* p. 31.

4. According to Shinnamon, "Hand feeding of children, sometimes through age four, is fairly common throughout the world. When this practice is analyzed objectively

we can see that it is a logical adaptation that mothers and caretakers make in environments where (1) mothers are essential workers in the economy and have a short amount of time each day to devote to children's feeding; (2) water, which is necessary for washing baby's hands, face and clothes, may be scarce; (3) food is in short supply and cannot be wasted by allowing a baby or young child to feed itself . . . the ability to allow a baby freedom to feed itself, with all the mess and waste that goes with it, is a definite luxury which few people in the world can afford." F. Shinnamon, "Childhood: A Multicultural Perspective," Unpublished manuscript, p. 6.

5. J. P. Comer, and A. F. Poussaint, *Black Child Care*, (New York: Simon & Schuster), 1975.

6. P. Leach, *Your Baby and Child from Birth to Age Five*, (New York: Knopf, 1997). B. Spock and M. Rothenberg, *Dr. Spock's Baby and Child Care*, 8th ed. (New York: Pocket Books, 2004). Shelov, S., ed. *Your Baby's First Year* (New York: Random House, 2005). Sears, W. and M. Sears. *The Baby Book* (New York: Little Brown, 2003).

7. A. E. Sodetaini-Shibata, "The Japanese American," in A. L. Clark, ed., *Culture and Childrearing*, (Philadelphia: F. A. Davis, 1981), p. 98.

8. B. M. Beebe, *Best Bets for Babies*, (New York: Dell, 1981). See also Comer and Poussaint, *Black Child Care*; Leach, *Your Baby and Child*; and Spock and Rothenberg, *Dr. Spock's Baby and Child Care*.

9. Werner, *Cross-Cultural Child Development*, p. 1.

10. L. Stringfellow, N. D. Liem, and L. Liem, "The Vietnamese in America," in A. L. Clark, ed., *Culture and Childrearing*, (Philadelphia: F. A. Davis, 1981), p. 235.

Focus Questions

Here are some questions to get you thinking about what's in this chapter.

- What differences in adult attachment behaviors can you observe in an individualistic family compared to a collectivistic one?

- How can what a family does in a child's infancy affect the child's lifelong close attachments?

- What does it mean when a family focuses more on a child's embeddedness than his or her individuality?

- What clues in a parent's behavior tell you that they are a family that values "cutting the apron strings"?

- Are survival practices always related to cultural values?

- What is one possible effect that a high infant mortality rate can have on a family's attachment behavior?

CHAPTER FIVE

Attachment and Separation

A ttachment and separation may not seem important to a teacher except when he or she is working with those few children who have trouble leaving their parents at the classroom door. However, understanding differing views of and practices for handling attachment and separation can shed further light on diversity issues and how to best serve each and every family.

COMPARING BABIES IN TWO FAMILIES

Again, the collectivistic and individualistic framework can be used to explore the subject of attachment. Consider the following two scenarios, each depicting a three-month-old baby at home with her mother.

Baby A

Baby A is on her back on a blanket in the middle of the floor. Her mother, also on the floor, sits in front of her and is leaning over looking into her eyes. They are playing a little game. Baby goes "agggg" and laughs. Mother imitates her. Baby repeats the sound. Then her mother goes "agggg" and clicks her tongue three times. Baby imitates her sound exactly, waving her arms toward her mother's face. The only sound in the house is of the two voices.

The phone rings, shattering the stillness and interrupting their play. The mother says to her baby, "There's the phone. I have to go answer it. I'll be right back." She gets up as she speaks, picking up a toy as she does so. She shakes the toy, which has a bell in it, and when the baby's eyes grasp the toy, she sets it down by the baby's face within easy reach. She moves quickly away and out the door. The baby's face clouds up as she watches her mother's retreating back. When she disappears, the baby lets out a loud howl. "Yes, yes, I know you don't want me to leave. I'm right here in the other room. I'll be back." The sound of her mother's voice temporarily reassures the baby, and she turns her attention to the toy by her ear.

If we follow this mother around for a whole Saturday (she works during the week), we find that she and her baby spend periods together and periods apart. The mother values "time to herself" and feels the baby needs privacy and "alone time" as well, so she arranges the day that way.

Here are the ways the baby gets alone time: she sleeps in her crib in her room during her two naps, and she spends time by herself on the floor and is sometimes in a playpen while her mother is occupied elsewhere in the house. She's also away from her parents periodically in the evening. They get a babysitter and go out fairly often because they need "couple time."

Although Baby A is apart from her mother regularly, when they are together, her mother often gives her full attention to her daughter, as in the previous scene. She talks to her, plays little games with her, shows her toys, and responds to what the baby initiates. She spends "quality time" with her.

This mother thinks about attachment. She's aware of the term and of its importance. She knows that attachment comes from being sensitive to her daughter. She understands the importance of interactions in promoting attachment. She knows that she is her daughter's primary attachment. The baby's father is also part of the picture, and the baby is attached to him, too, but prefers her mother when both parents are together.

The mother feels confident that putting her daughter into child care has not hurt their attachment. She knows that her daughter recognizes her, and she has noticed that the child responds to her differently than she responds to the caregivers in the program. Once in a while she worries that her daughter will become too attached to one of the caregivers, but then she recognizes that this is just normal jealousy on her part—mothers are supposed to be possessive. She is able to reassure herself that in the long run, she's the one who really counts.

Baby B

Now look at Baby B. She is on her grandmother's lap, sitting up, looking outward. She slumps over and contentedly sucks and nibbles on her grandmother's arm, glancing up occasionally to look at the people in the room. Her grandmother is having a conversation with her mother, who is sitting on the other end of the couch. The baby's aunt is sewing in one corner of the room, and two cousins are watching TV in another corner. Now and then the baby makes a fussing sound, and the grandmother jiggles her or strokes her back without taking her attention away from the conversation she's deeply engrossed in.

The TV watchers leave the room, and the grandmother gets up and turns down the volume, taking the baby with her on her arm. As the grandmother walks back toward her seat, the baby's mother holds out her arms, and the grandmother deposits the baby in her lap. The children come back in and turn up the volume of the TV again. The mother rocks the baby, matching the rhythm of a commercial on the TV.

The phone rings. The mother gets up and answers it. She holds the baby while she's talking on the phone, but when the baby starts to fuss, the aunt gets up from her sewing machine and comes to take the baby out of her arms, walking her around the room, bouncing her gently.

The baby quickly falls asleep in her aunt's arms. The woman carefully puts her down on the couch beside the grandmother. She goes back to her sewing machine and in a few minutes announces to one of the TV watchers, "Well, your dress is done—just in time for the party tonight. Go try it on." That rouses the rest of the group, who get up and leave the room, presumably to start getting ready. Only the grandmother is left in the room, sitting by the baby on the couch until the mother comes to relieve her. The mother arrives from the other room, bringing the special outfit the baby will wear to the party.

This baby is never alone. She is always in someone's arms or near them. When the family goes somewhere, she goes too—like to the party they're all getting ready for.

The family thinks very little about this baby's attachment. There's always been a baby or two in the house and always plenty of people to take care of them. The concept of infant attachment isn't something this family worries about.

This baby has multiple caregivers, and the mother sees it as an asset, wondering what she'd ever do if she were the only one responsible for her baby. She shudders at the thought.

In this family, the attachment issues (though they don't call them that) lie beyond infancy. The concern of the older family members is not about whether the babies are attached or not, but how to keep the generation that has just reached adulthood tied to the family when so many forces pull it away. It's a special worry for the grandmother, who has one son in college in another city. Will he come back when he becomes a lawyer? And her youngest daughter recently married a man who is in the service. So far she is still at home, but when her husband is stationed someplace where she can join him, what will happen? If you had to describe Baby A's family and compare it to Baby B's family, what would you say? Look at *Point to Ponder* 5.1 to see what a class of community college students said when given that assignment.

POINT TO PONDER 5.1

Who Are the Families of Babies A and B?

A community college teacher asked her class of future early childhood teachers to further describe the two families they read about in this chapter. Almost without exception they described Baby A's family as middle- to upper-income and Baby B's family as low-income. Do you think that is always the case? Can a collectivistic family like Baby B's be in the middle- or upper-income bracket? Could the differences between the two families be based on culture rather than on income?

A THEME IN ATTACHMENT: CUTTING OR NOT CUTTING THE APRON STRINGS

Edward T. Hall, in his book *Beyond Culture*, says: "The world is divided into those cultures who cut the apron strings and those who do not."[1]

Baby B lives in a family where growing up has not traditionally been a matter of cutting apron strings. In the past, the adults in the family have not had to establish their own identities independent of their parents. They became mature adults while remaining part of their extended family. They didn't consider alternatives.[2] Do you have questions about families that don't cut the apron strings? Look at *Point to Ponder* 5.2 for something to think about concerning this subject.

According to Francis Hsu, in his culture, "the parent-child ties are permanent rather than transitory. It is taken for granted that they are immutable, and so are not subject to individual acceptance or rejection."[3]

Baby A's mother is from a culture that cuts the apron strings. Ironically, her concern is about tying her baby to the apron strings in the first place. Because her child is in care outside the home, attachment is an issue for her. But she also has begun the process of making her baby into a separate individual in anticipation of cutting the strings eventually. For her, the two processes of attachment and separation are an intertwining theme to be played out together throughout the child's life. She expects someday her daughter will move away from home, from parents, and make her own life elsewhere, just as she did.

Baby A, in contrast to Baby B, is being encouraged to attach to one person—her mother. Although she has secondary attachments—her father and perhaps a caregiver at the program where she goes—her mother is the most important person in her life. Their interactions, especially when coupled with caregiving routines such as feeding, tend to produce the kind of infant attachment valued by Baby A's mother's culture. She is already showing differentiated reactions by demonstrating her attachment to her mother. In a few more months, she may

POINT TO PONDER 5.2

Boundary Issues

When some people reflect on their own lives, either by themselves or with the help of counseling, they discover that they have boundary issues—that is they don't know exactly where they stop and other people begin. This seems to be more of an issue for those who have individualistic tendencies than for those who are strong collectivists. It also can occur when a new generation moves away from collectivistic roots and begins embracing individualism. If you are an individualist, the idea of adults not establishing their own identities independent of their parents may make you feel uncomfortable. Identity issues and relationships are culturally bound, and what is right for one culture can feel wrong from another culture's perspective.

also begin to show fear of people she doesn't know and may begin to protest mightily at being separated from her mother. Many children with this kind of attachment begin to exhibit what is called "separation anxiety" at about nine months of age, crying when the parent leaves, even though they have been in child care for some time and have never protested before.

Baby B is used to multiple caregivers, which brings various personalities into her life. She probably won't experience the pulls of the exclusive relationship that Baby A has or the feelings of jealousy among the adults in her life.[4] Both Baby B and Baby A are too young to show separation anxiety. But because Baby B is always with at least one of her caregivers, she probably won't show it when she is older either. However, if she were to be left with a stranger, she'd probably protest even louder than Baby A and at an earlier age as well.[5] Some babies with a strong group connection get very upset when they are away from the group they identify with.

Baby A and Baby B illustrate a set of priorities rather than two absolutes. Although the goal of Baby A's parents is to produce an individual who can stand on her own feet, they aren't excluding the social needs of their daughter. Of course they want her to feel close to people and to get along with them. They want her to be able to commit to relationships, both inside and outside the family. They don't intend that their daughter will eventually move away and shun her parents. And, of course, Baby B's family wants her to be able to function in the world beyond the family and to attain a measure of individuality.

The difference in the goals for Baby A and Baby B is the degree of separateness. Another difference is that Baby A's parents expect their daughter to be able to move in and out of relationships and to break off any relationship that takes away her freedom to be an individual. Baby B's family doesn't have this same goal of breaking off relationships when they begin to pinch. They expect their daughter to work out things *within* the relationship, not leave it behind and move on.

THE INFLUENCE OF LIFE THREATS ON THE ATTACHMENT PROCESS

Life-threatening situations may influence the nature of early attachment. A premature or very sick baby may not have the kinds of behaviors that promote attachment, automatically endearing parents and others to him or her. Some adults become attached in spite of the baby's lack of ability to promote the attachment. However, in other cases, family members distance themselves either consciously or unconsciously because they fear the pain of the potential loss.

It's not that preemies or sick newborns never develop attachment; it's just that the patterns can differ from those of healthy newborns. This may not be a permanent disruption. The attachment may well occur when the crisis is past or later even with the life-threatening situation still present.

This relates to my experience of life-threatening situations as they occur among middle-class Americans. It's not a major theme of many U.S. families; it's an individual situation—isolated incidents. However, some families experience infant death as a theme in their lives. I'm not talking about long, long ago; high mortality rates in the first year are still an issue in some populations. Seven out of 1,000 babies do not survive their first year in the United States, which ranks 21st on a scale of developed countries according to a March of Dimes report. That number is deceiving because, if you look at the race of the mother, you find that there is a wide discrepancy between the death rates of African-American and European-American babies, according to a Children's Defense Fund report. For example in California, for every 1,000 white babies born, 5.3 of them die, while out of 1,000 African-American babies born, 13.7 of them die. These numbers are similar for the rest of the 50 states. They reflect the same rate as in developing nations such as Trinidad. Of course, in both the United States and Trinidad, poverty is an important factor behind the dismal figures.[6]

When I first started working in an early childhood program, I worked with low-income Mexican immigrant parents and their children. I remember, now and then, asking the parents how many brothers and sisters they had. Each gave me two answers—the number born and the number left alive. That was a different experience for me because until then, I didn't know anyone in my generation who had lost brothers or sisters.

If you've always lived in a population where infant survival seems assured, you may have a hard time understanding the possible effect of a high infant mortality rate on child-rearing practices. Imagine what it must be like to live in a family where babies have died—not only recently, but for generations. Experiences with the constant threat of infant death influence the way parents behave.

Parent Behaviors

Parents in these circumstances or with this background concentrate on ways to save the baby rather than on ways to develop physical or intellectual skills, as do parents who have little or no experience of infant mortality. But "saving the baby" is so ingrained into the child-rearing practices that it isn't thought of in those terms. Those in this situation would probably not explain to you in those particular terms why they are doing what they do. They accept what they are doing as normal child-rearing practices. It's what they're used to, what they were raised with. Outsiders call them cultural practices.

Here are some common patterns of infant care in Africa, Latin America, and Indonesia in populations with high infant mortality rates:

1. The infant is on or near a caretaker's body at all times, day and night.
2. Crying is quickly attended to and becomes rare relative to Western infants.
3. Feeding is a very frequent response to crying.
4. There is, by Western standards, little organized concern about the infants' behavioral development and relatively little treatment of them as emotionally responsive individuals (as in eye contact, smile elicitation, or chatting).[7]

What do these characteristics have to do with promoting survival? LeVine says:

> The infant is kept on or near a caretaker at all times so his condition can be monitored. His cries are immediately attended to so that the caretaker can receive immediate feedback concerning whether they are easily reduced by shaking or feeding; if not, perhaps he is ill. Minimizing his crying from other causes heightens the value of crying as a signal of organic upset, i.e., disease. Frequent feeding, particularly breast-feeding, serves to replace fluids and alleviate the dehydration from diarrhea that is probably the most frequent precipitant of infant death in the tropics. Keeping the infant on someone's body or otherwise restricted prevents the accidental injuries that can lead to death if not properly treated. All in all, though not a highly effective medical system, it is an adaptive response to extreme environmental hazard and probably has more efficacy than is readily apparent. . . . In this pattern of infant care adapted to the risks of disease and death in the earliest years, there is no place for an organized concern about the development of the child's behavioral characteristics and social and emotional relationships; such

POINT TO PONDER 5.3

Survival Issues or Cultural Values?

If you look at the list of common patterns of infant care described by LeVine, you may notice that they are very similar to the patterns collectivistic parents value for creating close relationships with their babies. The collectivist priority is to make the connections strong so they last a lifetime. It's quite possible that survival and collectivism are linked for many people. Chances of surviving are stronger when they are bound to a group than when they operate as an individual. This is just one more example of how difficult it is to tease out and explain the roots of diversity.

concerns are postponed until later in his life, when custom provides a basis for confidence in his continued survival.[8]

Separating Survival Practices from Cultural Values

Now the question is what happens to the infant care practices after the circumstances change. Suppose the family moves to a new country, finds relative economic security and good medical care, and the risks to their babies drop drastically. Perhaps no baby dies in this family for several generations. Do the infant care practices change?

LeVine's theory is that they continue on after the threat is passed, perhaps for generations. These customs become ingrained in the cultural approach to infant care. My theory is that it is hard to separate these survival practices from cultural values and attachment patterns. Look at *Point to Ponder* 5.3 to see a point to consider about this subject of separating survival practices from cultural values.

The issue is whether you have to. If you're in the position of doing parent education or find yourself working with a child for whom you have some concerns, you're going to have a dilemma about what to do with a family that, for example, doesn't seem sensitive to its baby's emotional signals, seldom speaks to its baby, or never holds the baby in a face-to-face position so adult and baby can make eye contact. What if the baby is never called by name, but rather by a variety of nicknames, some of which may be derogatory, or even called nothing at all? See *Point to Ponder* 5.4 for more discussion about naming babies. How do these behavior patterns fit into the family's cultural values? Are they leftover survival practices, or do they relate to the family's goals for their baby? What about language? Will the baby learn by just hearing language but not being spoken to directly? Is the family using nonverbal communication that the outsider isn't aware of, or is there a lack of communication? Is there an attachment problem or just a cultural difference?

POINT TO PONDER 5.4

Naming Newborns

Not calling a baby by its name may be a self-protection measure when a baby isn't expected to live. My last baby, born 3 months early, hovered between life and death for 109 days in intensive care. We gave him a nickname that had nothing to do with his given name. It wasn't something we thought about—just something we did. After experiencing this situation, I became sensitive to parents and the way they handle names. I remember one child in the intensive care nursery who never even received a name from her parents. It's easy to criticize someone like that until you experience the prospect of losing a baby yourself. Every instinct tells you not to get attached. A further note about names. No one in my husband's family is called by his or her given name—they all have nicknames. So now that I've linked the nickname of my son to his drastic start, it's possible his nickname came from a family tradition. Except I'm the one who gave him the nickname and my family has no such tradition.

These are not easy questions, and your answers will depend on how well you, while being supersensitive to cultural differences, judge how well the behaviors are serving the child and the family. Of course, you don't have to judge unless you're in a position that makes you an interventionist. Then you have to ask whether intervening with this family is appropriate or not. This kind of judgment is best made by a skilled and trained person of the same culture as the family, but that's not always possible. See *Point to Ponder* 5.5 for further points about differentiating cultural differences from dysfunctional behavior.

There's also the issue of parents being overprotective. How can you tell if a behavior is appropriately protective or not? It's hard for an outsider to make that judgment because behaviors that may make sense culturally may look extreme to someone who is not of the culture. Goals for the child can enter in here too. For one family the birth of a child with special needs feels like a tragedy and they set out to make sure their child develops to the fullest extent possible—teaching self-help skills and challenging him right up to his limits. This family is less likely to be judged overprotective. Another family sees the birth of their child with special needs as a blessing. As one mother told me, "I'm so happy because this child really needs me and won't grow up and leave home like his older brothers and sisters." She wasn't pushing him to become independent, but rather letting him develop at his own rate to the extent he could. Some would consider her actions overprotective, but not someone of her culture who understood her attitude toward her baby. When you are working across cultures, it can be very hard to sort out cultural behaviors from dysfunctional ones.

POINT TO PONDER 5.5

Differentiating Culture from Dysfunction

How do you differentiate between cultural differences and dysfunctional behavior, especially in the area of attachment? It's not easy unless you are able to look at a family through its cultural eyes. If you are not careful, you may look at a dysfunctional family in a culture different from yours and accept harmful behaviors as cultural without seeing how they hurt the members of that family. It's also possible to look at a well-functioning family and decide they need intervention because you don't understand that their differences are cultural. That's why understanding diversity issues is so important!

Here's an example of a cultural practice that was complicated by other factors. The issue was infant mobility. The setting was a child-care center for migrant farm workers. The director of the program, who was of the same culture as the parents, insisted that babies be given freedom to move around by being put on the floor. She felt that holding the babies all the time or keeping them restricted in other ways shortchanged their development. The parents protested that it wasn't their way. Babies shouldn't be on the floor. And indeed, in their homes, the floor was dangerous. With a number of people who work outdoors living in a small space, there was no telling what might be on the floor in addition to dirt (no matter how often it was swept) and possibly splinters. Besides, you don't leave babies to be stepped on in small, crowded rooms. Being on the floor in the clean, spacious center was very different from being on the floor at home; yet the parents still resisted the idea.

The director understood the parents' perspective, why they held their babies all the time and why, in the center, they expected someone to hold their babies or at least keep them in cribs or infant swings. She wanted to respect the parents' wishes, but at the same time, she had seen with her own eyes the way unrestricted infants develop, moving their bodies freely. She wanted the best for the babies in her center, and she knew the parents did too. They just didn't know any way other than the one they were used to. The director was finally able to convince the parents that she wasn't taking the children's culture from them by carrying out a practice different from what they were used to at home.

SUMMARY

The attachment patterns illustrated in the first part of this chapter show the difference between independence and interdependence as goals. Baby A is being trained in an independence mode; Baby B's family values interdependence. Both goals aim at producing fully functioning, competent individuals. The difference between the two patterns is in the outcome. Baby B's family values lifelong attachment to the group; Baby A's family aims to produce a separate and unique individual who can stand alone. But the comparison demands highlighting the differences—looking at extremes. In reality, it's a matter of balance. Baby A's family wants her to relate to the group, gain social competencies. They emphasize the individuality within a group context. Baby B's family needs a fully functioning individual who knows who she is and what she can do. They focus on her embeddedness rather than on her individuality.

The descriptions of Babies A and B relate to the theme of cutting or not cutting the apron strings. Baby A's family expects her to cut them eventually; Baby B's family does not. When we think about attachment behaviors and patterns, sometimes we fail to separate survival practices from cultural values. Some patterns of attachment behavior are related to a high infant mortality rate. One such pattern is keeping the baby on the caregiver's body, or at least very near by, 24 hours a day. This pattern can persist even after life circumstances change and several generations go by without a baby dying. If that is the case, it is hard to know whether the behaviors are left over from earlier times, whether the family is exhibiting collectivistic behaviors, or both. A related issue is determining which behaviors are cultural and serve the family and which are dysfunctional. Early childhood educators, and especially early interventionists, must learn to distinguish the difference.

FOR FURTHER READING

Bowlby, J. *Attachment and Loss: Vol. 1: Attachment.* New York: Basic Books, 1969. A classic book on attachment theory.

Brazelton, T. B., and S. I. Greenspan. *The Irreducible Needs of Children.* Cambridge, MA: Perseus, 2000. Discusses the most basic needs and the kinds of experiences and types of nurturing to which every child has a right and without which a child can't grow, learn, and thrive.

Eggers-Pierola, C. *Connections and Commitments: A Latino-Based Framework for Early Childhood Educators.* Portsmouth, NH: Heinemann, 2005. With the aim of improving culturally and linguistically responsive practices in early childhood practice, this book examines the impact on practitioners of four values in Latino culture: *familia* (family), *pertenencia* (belonging), *educación* (education), and *compromiso* (commitment).

Fernandez, M. T., and K. Marfo. "Enhancing infant-toddler adjustment during transitions to care." *Zero to Three* 26(6), July, 2005, pp. 41–48. A tool for caregivers and teachers to use to identify adjustment difficulties in young children who are entering or transitioning in child care settings and to create a plan for intervention.

Gonzalez-Mena, J. "Making Meaning of Separation: Contrasting Pictures of the First Good-bye." *The First Years, Nga TauTuatahi (New Zealand Journal of Infant and Toddler Education)* 3, no. 2 (September 2001), pp. 4–5. Looks at separation in a collectivist child.

Gonzalez-Mena, J., and D. Eyer. *Infants, Toddlers, and Caregivers.* New York: McGraw-Hill, 2007. An introduction to curriculum and care for infants and toddlers integrating the approach of Magda Gerber, Emmi Pikler, and the Program for Infant Toddler Caregivers. Applies this approach in a practical, meaningful way for students and faculty in introductory early childhood courses.

Hall, E. T. *Beyond Culture.* Garden City, NY: Anchor Books, 1977. Does not specifically discuss attachment, but does mention attachment among other subjects.

Harwood, R. L.; J. G. Miller; and N. L. Irizarry. *Culture and Attachment: Perceptions of the Child in Context.* New York: Guilford Press, 1995. Delves deeply into attachment theory and cultural variations.

Howes, C., and S. Ritchie. *A Matter of Trust.* New York: Teachers College Press, 2002. Applies attachment theory to child-teacher relationships and explores ways teachers can foster positive child behavior and build successful classroom communities.

Miller, K. *Simple Transitions for Infants and Toddlers.* Beltsville, MD: Gryphon House, 2005. Offers tips, ideas and easy activities and includes ideas to help parents deal with the bigger transitions in their child's life, such as separation anxiety and potty training.

Raeff, C.; P. M. Greenfield; and B. Quiroz. "Conceptualizing Interpersonal Relationships in the Cultural Contexts Of Individualism And Collectivism." In *New Directions For Child and Adolescent Development* 87, pp. 59–74, eds. S. Harkness, C. Raeff, and C. M. Super. San Francisco: Jossey-Bass. 2000. How individualism and collectivism affect attachment.

Sears, W., and Sears, M. *The Attachment Parenting Book.* New York: Little Brown, 2001. Encourages early, strong, and sustained attention to the new baby's needs and outlines the steps that will create lasting bonds between parents and their children.

Tan, A. L. *Chinese American Children and Families: A Guide for Educators and Service Providers.* Olney, MD: Association for Childhood Education International, 2004. Presents educators and service professionals with critical relevant, pertinent, and comprehensive information about Chinese Americans, with relevant applications to East Asian Americans and Southeast Asian Americans. Can be seen in terms of its broader application to all cultures.

NOTES

1. E. T. Hall, *Beyond Culture*, (Garden City, NY: Anchor Press/Doubleday, 1981), p. 226. Hall also says, "In many cultures, the bonds with the parents, grandparents, and even ancestors are not severed but are maintained and reinforced. I am thinking of China, Japan, the traditional Jewish family of central Europe, the Arab villagers, the Spanish of North and South America, and the Pueblo Indians of New Mexico, to mention only a few." Children move from childhood to adulthood, but they do not establish lives of their own, identities separate from their parents—their people.

2. Other writers and researchers discuss this view of lifelong attachment found in Baby B's family. Dorothy Lee says of the Hopi: "Loyalties are to the group; they are not person-to-person loyalties. And parents have been known deliberately to try to shift a child's affection from concentration upon one family member, to diffusion among the group." D. Lee, *Freedom and Culture*, (Englewood Cliffs, NJ: Prentice Hall, 1959), p. 20.

   Sally Lubeck says of African-American families: "From an early age, a Black child is likely to live in an extended family, with grandparents, aunts, uncles or cousins, as well as siblings, likely, as people move in and out with changing circumstances, to have a broadened sense of 'family.' A Black child is far more likely to sleep with others, to experience less privacy (and also less loneliness) than a White American child. A child will frequently be nurtured and supervised by more than one primary adult." S. Lubeck, *The Sandbox Society: Early Education in Black and White America*, (Philadelphia: Falmer Press, 1985), p. 110.

   Lubeck also talks of two patterns, which she calls a collective orientation versus an individualistic orientation. "A collective orientation is apparent when enculturation occurs in a shared function environment where the focus is on social relations, stressing 'kinship,' interdependency, and cooperation, a holistic world view, relational thinking, and the importance of non-verbal communication. An individualistic orientation predominates when enculturation occurs in a nucleated family structure, focusing on manipulator experience and stressing self-achievement, competition, the ability to abstract parts from wholes, abstract thinking and the importance of verbal communication." Lubeck, *Sandbox Society*, p. 40.

   Matthiessen says of the Hmong: "Hmong households are usually composed of several generations, including married sons and their families. It is expected that children, especially the youngest of the family, will care for their parents as they grow old." N. Matthiessen, *The Hmong: A Multicultural Study*, (Fairfield, CA: Fairfield-Suisun Unified School District, 1987), p. 7.

   Dung Trinh Ngoc says of the Vietnamese: "Traditionally, a Vietnamese family may consist of three or perhaps four generations. Daughters, when married, join their husbands' families." D. T. Ngoc, "Understanding Asian Families: A Vietnamese Perspective." *Children Today*, March–April 1984, p. 11.

   Duong Thanh Binh says of the Vietnamese: "The majority of Vietnamese are deeply attached to their families. Feelings of family honor, duty, and responsibility are very strong, even in the very young." D. T. Binh. *A Handbook for Teachers of Vietnamese Students: Hints for Dealing with Cultural Differences in Schools*, (Arlington, VA: Center for Applied Linguistics, 1975), p. 13.

3. F. L. K. Hsu, *Americans and Chinese: Purpose and Fulfillment in Great Civilizations*, (Garden City, NY: Natural History Press, 1970), p. 110.

4. Werner writes of families where "the responsibility for child care is shared among members of a homogeneous family group. Although the child may have a number of caretakers, they will all have a common set of socialization goals and a common set of practices in relation to child rearing. Child rearing is thus a collective rather than an individual responsibility. . . . [T]he more people . . . there are in the house, the less exclusively attached to the mother is the infant. Intensity of affect, thus,

may vary inversely with the number of caretakers, as Mead suggested . . . in her comparison of the Samoan extended family with the American nuclear family. Also fitting the Mead interpretation is the pattern reported for Israeli kibbutzim. In terms of the infant's development, several stable caretakers are seen as providing more stability than a single one, by lessening the stress of separation from the mother, for instance through the possibility of replacement by a second familiar caretaker." E. E. Werner, *Cross-Culture Child Development,* (Monterey, CA: Brooks/Cole, 1979), pp. 271, 275–276.

5. According to Mary Ainsworth, 1967, Ganda babies who grow up in an extended family exhibit separation protest as early as six months. Reported in Werner, *Cross-Culture Child Development,* p. 274.

6. *The State of America's Children: Yearbook 2001.* Washington, DC: Children's Defense Fund, pp. 34, 35, 131.

7. R. A. LeVine, "Child Rearing as Cultural Adaptation," in P. H. Leiderman, S. R. Tulkin, and A. Rosenfeld, eds., *Culture and Infancy: Variations in the Human Experience,* (New York: Academic Press, 1977), p. 23.

8. Ibid., p. 25.

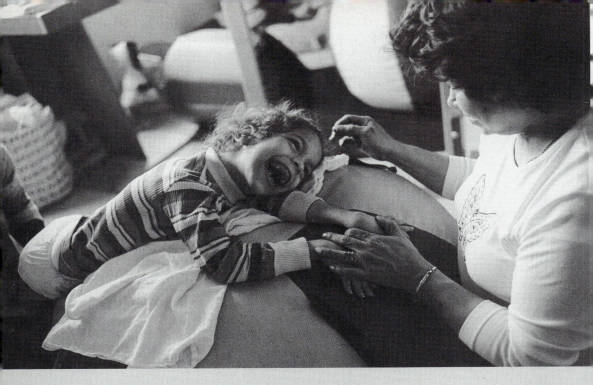

Focus Questions

Here are some questions to get you thinking about what's in this chapter.

- How are adults' ideas about play influenced by their cultures?

- Why do adults react differently to watching the same scene of babies playing?

- Why doesn't everyone agree on the amount of stimulation that babies need?

- What are some of the disagreements around preschoolers playing?

- Why wouldn't everybody think that children need to learn to make choices?

- What are some adult behaviors that show they are more interested in children's social relations than in having them play with toys?

- What are some ways to defuse a cross-cultural encounter?

CHAPTER SIX

Differing Perspectives on Learning through Play

Children, from infancy on, learn through everything that happens to them (as well as the things they cause to happen). They learn as teachers and caregivers interact with them during caregiving times and daily routines and even when they don't interact with them. They learn when they play. Play is highly regarded by most early childhood education professionals.

ADULT ATTITUDES TOWARD PLAY ARE INFLUENCED BY CULTURE

How an adult regards play, facilitates it, plans for it, sets up the environment, and interacts with the child are all influenced by that adult's culture. Play may be valued or not. Culture helps determine whether play is seen more as something that children do on their own with little or no adult involvement or whether adult involvement is valuable. Culture also may determine whether children spend most of their time in a child-centered environment—one set up for them with child-size furniture, equipment, and toys. Some adults prefer children to be in an adult-centered environment and some prefer a combination.

Even when two adults agree that young children should spend at least some of their time in a child-centered environment, they may differ about how the children should use this environment. See *Point to Ponder* 6.1 for different ways that adults see play.

POINT TO PONDER 6.1

Different Ways That Adults See Play

One adult may see play as an opportunity for individual involvement with the physical environment, as in self-motivated, solitary play. Another adult may regard play as an opportunity for learning to get along with others. If solitary play is valued, interruptions by others will be discouraged (like the kind of protection for the individual seen in some Montessori programs). If play is regarded primarily as socialization, the adult will encourage children to interact.

BABIES PLAYING

Look at the following scenario of babies playing and pay attention to your reactions to what you are reading.

Two eighteen-month-olds are rolling around and tussling over a partially deflated beach ball. Their squeals of laughter are the main sounds heard in the room containing two caregivers and eight children from six months to twenty months of age. These two frolickers continually bump up against a low, carpet-covered divider that is part of an enclosure containing a six-month-old and a seven-month-old who are lying side-by-side on a rug looking at each other through a forest of toys. The two gurgle and coo periodically, their voices intermingling with the squeals coming from the other side of the divider.

A fourteen-month-old toddles over to the divider. She pushes a toy on a stick. She abandons her stick and climbs over the divider, plops herself down between the two babies, and touches the younger one gently on the face. An adult immediately appears and sits down with the three children inside the enclosure. She doesn't do anything but says, "You like to touch Ana's face." It is obvious that she is ready to protect the immobile child if the need arises. The girl starts playing with the toys scattered around the floor, and the baby starts to fuss with the attention gone. The girl gets up and leaves, and the caregiver says, "You liked her to play with you." Then she hands the baby a plastic toy, which she waves and bangs contentedly. The caregiver turns to the seven-month-old, who has been rolling back and forth, pulling at her, and producing a series of sounds accompanied by bubbles. The two begin a "conversation." The caregiver imitates the baby at first, then turns her own sounds into words, saying things like, "That's a funny noise you're making," "Oh look at your bubbles," and "I see what you're doing with your fingers!" She's teaching what is called "turn taking"— waiting each time for a response from the child before she takes the next turn at "conversation."

A scene such as this one produces a variety of reactions from observers.

Across the room a fifteen-month-old climbs the stairs to a small slide and delights in going down head first, catching himself with his hands as he reaches the bottom. His laughter mingles with the squeals of the other two. He is watched by a nineteen-month-old who is tucked away in a small cubby under the slide.

The nineteen-month-old crawls out of the cubby and walks over to some two-piece puzzles laid out attractively on a very low wooden table. He picks up a piece in each hand and bangs them together. He turns to look at another child, who has pulled a hat down over his eyes and is prancing blindly up and down in front of a mirror giggling.

The room is quiet except for the periodic noises from the children. Even those are subdued because of the thick carpets, soft furniture, cloth wall hangings, and other sound absorbers.

The colors of the room are as subdued as the sounds. The walls and furnishings are natural tones—earthy, with just a touch of peach and quiet country blue accents here and there to liven them up. The toys, however, are bright primary colors, so they announce themselves, making splashes of color against the neutral background.

An adult is sitting quietly beside the child who is now trying on different hats from an assortment in a basket conveniently located beside the mirror. The caregiver gets up unobtrusively and walks over to a record player. He announces to the child in the hat that he is going to play some "dancing" music. He puts on a classical piece, carefully adjusts the volume so the music is soft, and goes back to sit down by the child.

The two children with the beach ball have now begun to fight over it. The squeals are no longer happy as they tug and pull on the ball. The other caregiver comes over to the two and holds out a second ball. "Here, you can each have one," she says pleasantly. But they ignore her. One pulls harder and the ball comes out of the other's hands. He takes the ball and runs off to hide under the slide. The other follows and grabs the ball back; then the first child crawls out and slaps the child, who immediately looks for an adult to help. He's not disappointed. She's right there. She squats down between both boys, talking in soft, soothing tones. "Gently, gently," she demonstrates gentle touching. "Jason hurt you," she says to the boy who is now crying. She continues talking in an even, calm voice, describing what she thinks is going on within each child and discussing the interaction that just occurred. She doesn't criticize or judge. She just keeps talking in the same quiet vein. The crying stops. The energy gone from their conflict, both wander away, abandoning the caregiver and the beach ball.

"Snack time," announces the other caregiver cheerily, showing a tray of banana slices and raisins to the children. Several follow him to a little table. Others continue playing and ignore the interruption as if it never occurred.

Adult Reactions to the Amount of Stimulation in the Scene

Here's how some adult observers reacted to this scene. "B-O-R-I-N-G!" says the first observer. "Not enough happening. It was so quiet and toned down I thought I'd go to sleep watching. If I was a baby there, I'd stir things up a bit," she says, winking. "And the music. . . ." She wrinkles her nose in distaste. "It was much too quiet. Music with a good beat makes a place *alive.* I'd have the music going all the time, and I'd add some more activity and some color too!"

"I liked it," says another observer. "I thought it was just right. There was plenty happening. Any more and it would be chaos. If you have too much going on, children can't concentrate on any one thing. They lose their focus. The way this environment was set up was good; the quiet background allowed some aspects of the environment to claim the children's attention. For example, the muted colors let the toys be seen; and the muted sounds allowed the children to hear each other's voices clearly."

"I thought it was too noisy and busy," remarks still another observer. "I prefer a quieter setting for babies. All that wild screaming and laughing would disturb some children and stir others up to be wild themselves. The teachers should have tried to calm those wild kids down."

These are three different reactions to the amount of stimulation the scene provided. What one person feels is the optimum amount of sensory input—sights, sounds, and movement—another feels bombards the children, and a third feels is boring. To some extent, this variation in sensory needs relates to individual preference and style, but it also connects to culture.

Cultural Differences Related to Stimulation

Some cultures wish to promote calm, placid styles of interaction and temperament, so they prefer less stimulating environments. They worry that the babies will get overstimulated in the exciting play and intense interactions if they aren't toned down. Some cultures value activity; others value stillness.[1] Active cultures promote exploration and movement for infants because these activities help develop problem-solving skills. However, there is another view. Meaningful inactivity is a concept that many adults have never heard of. Yet, in some cultures, being inactive is a valuable use of time. Dr. A. C. Ross (whose Lakota name is Ehanamani) points out that meditation can be a problem-solving method. Instead of actively engaging the environment or trying to reason out an answer through logic, one sits in silence. According to Ross's way of thinking, answers to problems come from the collective unconscious in moments of silence.

PRESCHOOLERS PLAYING

Consider a typical classroom of three- to five-year-olds. It is set up in areas where children are free to play. A group is busy putting on dresses and scarves, getting ready to cook up a big meal for "company" in the dramatic play area. Big wads of play dough sit on a little table waiting for the children to finish dressing so they can start cooking. Three children are painting at easels. One uses big armstrokes, splattering the paint. Another one is attending to some minute details in her picture. The third is covering the whole paper with paint, including the corner where the teacher wrote her name. The one working on details complains when splatters hit her painting. A teacher glances over, but is immediately distracted by a child who is crying, so the painters continue to work on their own. One child stands at a table full of puzzles with a piece in his hand and looks perplexed. He tries to fit it into several places, but it just won't work. Next to him, three children are nestled in cushions reading from a big pile of books. More books are displayed in a case behind them. A teacher holds a boy on her lap and reads to him. She stops, looks at her watch, and announces to the whole room, "It's five minutes to ten, almost snack time." Over in another corner a boy and a girl are playing with blocks and farm animals, making lots of noise. Nearby is a table with small plastic toys for children to manipulate. Two boys are building weapons, until a teacher comes over to them. They quickly change to building "machines" until the teacher moves on. The teacher puts a tape into a tape recorder, and then, keeping time to the music, he walks over to a closet and takes out a box of musical instruments. Immediately, four children come over to him begging to have first choice. When two children start tugging on the same tambourine and screaming at each other, the teacher gets down on their level and talks them through their conflict. He doesn't tell them what to do; he helps them sort it out themselves.

A water table just outside the door engages a group of children who are pouring from containers and beating with egg beaters. A teacher adds liquid soap and the egg beaters create suds. One little girl squeals with delight. Just beyond is a slide where a boy and a girl are having a contest to see who can run up without sliding back. They've been told by the teacher that it's okay until somebody wants to come down. Then they have to stop and all go the same way or somebody may get hurt. Three children are racing around the play yard on tricycles, making whooping noises. Four are digging in the sand and talking loudly. Three teachers are scattered around the yard supervising the children. They mostly stand up and scan the yard. Every now and then one will stoop or squat to talk to a child.

Adult Reactions to This Scene

Observers of this scene said, "I think there should be fewer toys. The children had too much to do—too many choices. The world isn't like that. Children need to learn to adapt and adjust to what's there, not be presented with a whole bunch of choices. We all need to learn to play the hand we're dealt, not act as if we could deal ourselves any hand we wanted."

"More teaching. Those teachers weren't doing anything! I would have some learning objectives and have the adults work on them with the children."

"A fake world. Why put children in a place where the whole focus is them? I think children learn more when they tag along after adults who are doing real things in the real world. They can learn to help from an early age if they are part of adult life, not tucked away in a room where the adults are like robots just put there to serve them."

"More conversations. The adults were too quiet."

"Too much talking. The adult could have showed the kids how to handle the conflict rather than just talking about it. I thought she talked the thing to death!"

"It would be better if the adults talked to each other more. That's the way children learn—by being around adult conversations."

"Why didn't they hold the children? They all seemed so lonely to me."

"Why didn't they show the child how to work the puzzle and make those boys go down the slide properly?"

"I saw the caregiver look at her watch to see if it was snack time yet. Why not go by the children's hunger rather than the clock?"

"I like the way the environment is set up so efficiently that it frees the adults to be with the children during play times."

"I didn't like seeing those adults just sitting around doing nothing. I would have liked to see them cooking or cleaning or fixing broken toys or *something*. If they had more to do, the children would learn by watching adults do adult things."

"There was too much 'educational play.' I like watching children indulging in excesses. I love to stir them to hilarity, get them involved in nonsense. That's what they're supposed to do—run around knocking over blocks, yelling. That's what childhood is for! A good game of ring around the rosy sometimes will get them going."

These comments reflect a variety of value judgments about what's good for young children in a play setting.

THEMES REFLECTED BY THE COMMENTS

People versus Object Orientation

Standard early childhood practice emphasizes the importance of the physical environment. Anyone who is setting up an infant-toddler or preschool program will find lists and lists of recommended toys and equipment readily available (often published by manufacturers). Books and articles have been written on how to arrange the environment so it is efficient for the adults, developmentally appropriate for the children, optimally challenging to encourage active exploration, and, above all, safe. If you ask the people who write these books and articles how important objects are for learning, you'd get a long, enthusiastic answer extolling the virtues of an abundance of developmentally appropriate *stuff* available for the children.

If you see the original video of the research behind *Preschool in Three Cultures*, you'll be struck by the abundance of toys, materials, and equipment of the American program compared with both the Japanese and Chinese programs.[2] Depending on your point of view, you might say the Japanese and Chinese programs looked *stark*, or you might say the American program looked *stuffed*. No matter what your point of view, you're bound to notice the difference in the environments. How much do you think this abundance of toys is influenced by the fact that the United States is a consumer society?

POINT TO PONDER 6.2

Object Orientation

As a consumer society, we are surrounded with messages about the importance of owning things. When you combine those messages with a cultural value of objects, children receive a double dose of training toward object orientation. These messages affect the lives of even infants and toddlers.

See *Point to Ponder* 6.2 for thoughts about the affect of consumerism on children in early childhood programs.

Some cultures train their children to be more people oriented than object oriented. They focus on the social world rather than on the physical world.

In some classic research, Young found that African-American families taught their children to pay more attention to person cues. They emphasized the importance of focusing on people rather than on objects by the way they interacted with their children. The styles of interaction motivated the children to learn to judge the moods of people in authority. The interaction styles also included a great deal of touching, especially in the first three years of a child's life.[3] To find out if this research is still valid, try observing parents from a variety of backgrounds to see if they focus babies more on objects or on people. You may have a hard time to see a difference unless you can find parents or other family members who have not been exposed to parenting information or marketing of baby toys and equipment.

When babies did focus on an object, picking up something on their own (it was not usually given to them), they were often redirected to the face of the person holding them. Because babies were held a lot, body contact figured prominently in child-rearing styles. Young believes that this approach to child rearing tends to move the child's interest away from the world of objects and redirects their attention to people. How aware are parents of training their children to focus on the social world rather than on objects? Look at *Point to Ponder* 6.3 to further reflect on this question.

Choice

Part of the reason for all these *things* in the environment in early childhood programs is that many people believe children need enough things to play with readily available so they can make choices. This emphasis on self-selection allows children to experience themselves as decision makers. It is based on a perception that individuals have power over their own lives and children need to learn to make choices from the beginning. It has to do with

POINT TO PONDER 6.3

Are Toys Important?

I asked a number of people from a variety of backgrounds if it is important for babies to have toys to play with. The answer in every case was "yes." I think that this attitude shows the selling job that early childhood professionals and the commercial world have done to convince the public that toys are related to intelligence. I have noticed that some people who claim toys are important still seem to emphasize people contact over playing with toys.

the goals of freedom of choice, self-direction, self-reliance, and independence. The point is to let children have the opportunity to choose from some number of options. The decisions about which options and how many lie in the hands of the adults. The theory is that children will learn to make the connections between their own choices and the consequences of those choices, so they will become skilled decision makers.

Not all adults are enthusiastic about giving children choices. They see a major task of childhood as learning to adapt to what is, to take advantage of what they find in the environment of adults, rather than selecting from a number of options that have been set up for them. They question the value of a child-oriented, developmentally appropriate environment isolated from the real world of adults. According to Jayanthi Mistry:

> In some cultural communities children learn by simply being present as adults go about their jobs and household activities. Adults do not create learning situations to teach their children. Rather, children have the responsibility to learn culturally valued behaviors and practices by observing and being around adults during the course of the day.[4]

There is a definite difference between setting up an environment specifically for children with scaled-down versions of adult implements and appliances (tea sets, miniature refrigerators, child-size carpentry sets, little garden tools, and such) and letting children be part of the adult environment to either observe or use real tools and appliances.

Hsu expands this view from the workaday world to the world of adult recreation and special occasions, saying, "Americans keep their children from the real world of adults—Chinese bring theirs with them to every occasion." He goes further to contrast the birthday parties that are centered on the birthday child, where the adults play the role of assistants or servants, which he has observed in America, to the child birthday parties that are adult occasions like weddings or funeral feasts. Anything that is child centered, in Hsu's opinion, isolates the child from "the real world of adults," which, in his mind, is a valuable environment for learning.[5]

Marta Borbon Ehling says something similar about Mexican-Americans: "Children usually go everywhere that their parents go. They go to parties, weddings, funerals, and church."[6]

Adult Role

The role of the adult is different in a child-centered environment than in an adult-centered environment. In the developmentally appropriate environment, the adult is often present as a learning facilitator rather than as a teacher. After adults set up the environment, they back out of center stage. Their role is one of support as they encourage children's self-initiated explorations. They may also act as a resource, expanding on dramatic play, providing props and materials as needed. They refrain from taking over and directing the action. The idea is self-discovery.

A similar adult role, but with a slightly different goal, is represented by "floor time" which is a play-based therapeutic approach used by teachers to benefit children with special needs as well as some typically developing children. The idea is for the teacher to pay close attention to a single child for a period, being responsive, not directive, while the child explores freely in a safe, interesting environment set up for play. The teacher joins the child on the floor and picks up on the child's interests. During floor time, it's important that the teacher gets out of a teaching role and lets the child direct the direction of the play. Floor time is a way for a teacher to find out what the child is interested in. It's also a time to look for deeper meanings in the child's behavior in order to help the child find new ways to express those meanings.[7] When floor time is used as a response to challenging behavior, it becomes the opposite of time out. Some people even use the term "time in" to label what others call floor time.

In ordinary play situations when the teacher is not engaged in one-on-one floor time, the adult role is more of a facilitator of the teaching-learning process in a free flowing way. The adult may regularly add some questions or words to situations children choose, but straightforward teaching, either with words or through modeling, is usually not emphasized the way self-discovery is. Free play is free play, and the adult is more of a responder than anything else, leaving most goal-oriented inclinations out of his or her role. The role of adults in children's play, even in a child-centered environment, lies on a continuum. On one end, the adult is more observer than anything else; on the other end, the adult may be far more interactive with the children: entering the play, guiding, asking questions, making suggestions, and giving direction. In some programs, the adult takes ideas from the children's

This family brought the baby to the party rather than leaving her home.

play and creates what Betty Jones and John Nimmo call an "emergent curriculum." In other words, some of the content in the plan for learning (including activities and projects) comes from the children rather than from an adult-centered curriculum.

This approach is in contrast to an adult role that emphasizes initiating, teaching, and directing. Some parents prefer that the teacher or caregiver remain in control of everything that happens. Parents understand schooling in terms of their own early experiences and are more comfortable with something familiar to them. A free-play situation in which adults take more of a background role may be unsettling to parents. It may also be too child centered and appear too chaotic for some parents. What are the parents' feelings and ideas about these issues? Discuss them!

School readiness can be a subject of serious disagreement between some preschool teachers and the families they serve. A program that has a play-based curriculum can cause families to feel upset and dissatisfied. It's not unusual for a family or a group of families to push for early academics, for example. Some hope an early start will keep their children up with the others, while others hope that their children will be reading before kindergarten and therefore be ahead of the others. When the professionals argue the perspective of developmental appropriateness, they may convince some families, but others will dig in harder to push their point of view.

Sometimes ideas about teaching academics arises from cultural differences. For example, a Chinese mother's own experience as a child in learning to read in her native language made her want to start her child early because learning characters takes different skills from learning to read in a language that uses an alphabet. Each character has to be memorized. She thinks her child should be sitting down memorizing words instead of playing with play dough and finger paint at preschool. Instead of arguing with this mother, it would be good if her child's teacher could listen to what she has to say, even if the teacher doesn't agree with her about what's best for the child at this stage of development.

Listen and when you're ready to respond, instead of arguing, create a dialogue. There's a big difference between those two modes of communication. The purpose of a dialogue is to understand—not to get your points across. You have to step out of a win-lose mindset. The idea of a dialogue is to expand one's knowledge rather than trying to persuade the other person to accept a different point of view. A first step is to confront your own biases and do some soul searching to get in touch with defensive feelings that can get in the way of good listening. Chapter 2 discussed some ways to do that. An effective dialogue helps people really hear each other—and gain an understanding that gives them a bigger picture than they had originally. Even if the other person is arguing, you can still listen with an open mind and not argue back. It's hard to keep in the dialogue mode in that case, but you can do it if you try. Practice the skill. You can get better at it.

Your program doesn't have to be exactly what the parents feel is ideal for their children. It's okay for children to be exposed to environments and adult roles they aren't used to as long as parents don't believe that it's bad for their child, and as long as children don't react adversely.

It's a give-and-take process. Mistry says, "When a caregiver respects and adapts to a child so too will that child become able to adapt to the caregiver and the child care setting created by that caregiver."[8] The same can be true of parents.

Children are good learners, and most are flexible enough to incorporate what you are adding to their lives. The important thing is if what you are doing is different from what they experience at home, it should be considered as an addition. *It's okay for children to become bicultural. It's not okay to take their home culture away from them.*

Emphasis on Words versus Nonverbal Communication

Put two or more children together to play, and you'll have disputes. It's interesting to watch how adults handle conflicts between children. Some adults depend on words—on spelling things out, getting the cards on the table. Using

POINT TO PONDER 6.4

Early Language Stimulation

When people from high context cultures who don't speak directly to babies come in contact with early childhood professionals, they may feel some pressure to change, even though their methods of nonverbal communication have been passed down from generation to generation and fit their culture well. A general view in early childhood circles is that children must be spoken to from infancy on if they are to become good communicators and eventually gain literacy skills. This brings up the issue that has appeared regularly in this book—Should you try to change parents if you are not of their culture? There is no clear answer to this question, but you must seek to understand their perspective before you make any decisions about what to do.

a lot of words and expecting the children to learn to do that also is a characteristic of what is called a "low context culture."[9] Mainstream Canadian and U.S. cultures are low context cultures. High context cultures (like the Chinese culture) depend less on words than on other kinds of contextual messages. In some ways, two high context people communicate like two twins who know what the other means with minimal words.

Verbal emphasis or de-emphasis starts from the beginning with the way babies are treated. Babies carried around much of the time get good at sending messages nonverbally—through changing body position or tensing up or relaxing muscles, for example. They are encouraged to communicate this way when their caregivers pick up the messages they send. They don't need to depend on words at an early age. *Point to Ponder* 6.4 discusses a controversial language issue in early education circles. Babies who are physically apart from their caregivers learn the benefits of verbal communication. If the babies are on the floor in the infant program or in the other room at home, they need to learn to use their voices to get attention. Changing position or tensing muscles goes unperceived by the distant adult. (Babies at home also learn that silence will get them attention too, as a parent says, "Oh, oh, it's mighty quiet in there. I wonder what's going on!")

Adults who value verbal communication encourage babies to play with language. The "turn taking" in the first scene is an example of an adult and child playing with language. Those who put a high value on verbal communication believe that babies learn through face-to-face "conversations," starting at birth. This is a contrast to a different approach to language learning—that of "eavesdropping" (being around but not involved in adult conversations).[10]

Verbally oriented adults spend a lot of time paying attention to what children say and respond by clarifying and interpreting. They often expand on what the children are saying. They carry on conversations with them. While they are doing all this, they are modeling, without fanfare, correct speech.

Verbally oriented adults place value on words, seeing language development as vitally linked to cognitive development. These adults also see words as critical for social-emotional development. They teach children to use words for problem solving and to express feelings. In a conflict situation, in many programs, you can almost count on some adult saying to the children, "Use your words!" Words are even linked to creativity. For example, when presented with a freshly painted picture, the verbally oriented adult is apt to say, even to the toddler, "Tell me about it."

This approach is very different from expecting the child to learn by being around adults but not being spoken to directly very often. According to Mistry, adults using a nonverbal approach "may model or demonstrate a particular behavior as the child watches . . . the nonverbal style teaches them to watch and pick up appropriate behavior from their caregivers."[11]

DEFUSING A CROSS-CULTURAL ENCOUNTER

Much of this chapter has focused on comparing what have been called "developmentally appropriate" practices with other practices.[12]

After studying how to work most effectively with young children (all of which is culturally based), we carry a standard. When we meet someone who doesn't fit under that standard, we're disappointed because we expect that person to be like us.[13] For example, when we see how a parent seems to ignore her baby or expect his four-year-old to behave in an adult environment, that may trigger a reaction in us. Most of us are conditioned from infancy to think that everyone is like us. Several things can happen when two people with different ideas about the right way to behave meet.

They can both encounter an unpleasant situation or a series of them. Their reaction to the discomfort they feel can be self-protection and withdrawal. This can become a pattern of evasion, which means the two will learn less and less about each other. All this can happen beneath the awareness of either party.

Craig Storti, in *The Art of Crossing Cultures*, suggests a model for changing that pattern. It has to do with first becoming aware of your reaction to behavior that is different from your own. It is important to focus on the feelings as they arise in a cross-cultural encounter and to identify them. Reflect on why you are experiencing these feelings because, according to Storti, the mind can't hold two things at once. When you focus on the awareness you dispel the feeling.[14]

Only when the feelings subside can you truly experience what is going on. The more you react, the less you see and hear. Everything is colored by your reactions. Until you quit reacting, you can't truly *experience* something.

POINT TO PONDER 6.5

The Swing Incident

Look back at the staff's argument over whether to push children in swings or not and apply the individualistic/collectivistic framework to see the situation more clearly. The strong individualistic staff members favored not pushing, but letting children explore the swings on their own, while the more collectivistic staff members felt that pushing a child in a swing built their relationship with that child and was pleasurable for both the adult and the child.

This awareness of reactions is not easy. We've been conditioned over a lifetime to have feelings but not to observe them. If you find it hard to develop instant awareness, you can start with retrospective awareness. Look back on the agitated moment and reflect on it. With enough practice, you can eventually bring your awareness process closer to the critical incident that triggered the feelings.

The point is that your first reaction to a certain behavior colors subsequent reactions. The "count-to-ten" approach to anger works in cross-cultural exchanges. Give yourself time; give the other person time. It is often best to stop talking about a disputed issue until everybody has had time to reflect on their initial reactions.

An Example of a Cross-Cultural Encounter

I remember a significant argument regarding whether or not to push children on swings. The staff was divided. The unofficial spokesperson for the hands-off side made the point that children need to learn to swing by themselves. Until they can, she argued, they aren't old enough to use the swings. She was willing to let children lie on their stomachs on the swing and use their feet to move themselves back and forth. Her response triggered a reaction from the other side, which had strong feelings about the proper way to use a swing. "Swings are for sitting!" See *Point to Ponder* 6.5 for more regarding the hands-off or hands-on argument. As the argument escalated, it became obvious that the instant reactions were not helping one side hear the other. Both parties agreed to resume discussion at a future meeting. The cooling-off period helped. The next time the issue was discussed, both sides were able to be more sensitive listeners. If you can step aside from your own reactions, you can begin to understand and respect the behavior of someone who is different from you. You may never come to approve of that behavior; after all, you probably don't approve of everything in your own culture either. But by

POINT TO PONDER 6.6

Thinking about Power

Naturally, we each think our own cultures and our values are the right ones. If you're in a position of power and you have this attitude, it is imperative that you avoid seeing your job as remediation when you cross cultures. It's important to think about what your purpose is in everything you do with young children and their parents. You have to go beyond the cognitive, psychomotor, affective goals you may be used to conceptualizing, and think about what cultural messages you're sending. To become sensitive to cultural differences it is vital that you become aware of your own culture and how it influences the messages you send. Be open and humble. No matter how much you know, there's always more to learn.

learning to open yourself up more, you broaden your view and have a better chance of getting along with people different from yourself. Most important, *if you are in a power position, you are less likely to wield your power in ways that inhibit the other person.* To take this further, see *Point to Ponder 6.6.*

SUMMARY

Culture has an effect on adults' attitudes toward play. Adults influence children's learning during play by either valuing it or not, by the environment they choose, by the way they interact in this environment, and by the way they expose children to language or not. They also influence children by whether or not they present toys, equipment, and materials and by what kinds of toys, equipment, and materials they present. The diversity regarding ideas about play is great! For example, views on appropriate amounts of stimulation for babies vary. Preferences may be personal, culturally based, or both. In any case, the degree of stimulation enjoyed is different for different people. To organize the many diverse views of play, this chapter showed several play scenes in programs for children and explored adults' reactions to them. A variety of themes emerged including:

- A people-versus-object orientation
- The degree to which giving young children choices is valued
- Varying ideas about what the adult role should be while preschoolers are playing
- An emphasis or deemphasis on verbal communication
- The value of play in a child-centered environment versus the value of keeping children in an adult-centered environment

Even the idea of play as the main way to learn is a cultural phenomenon and not shared by everybody. In some cultures, the idea of children being the center of focus in a carefully set up environment is startlingly strange. Instead children are expected to learn by being part of the adult world and observing adults and/or using real tools. This approach is different from expecting children to manipulate toys and roles by exploring in their own way in a special environment created just for them. Such differing ideas can result in cross-cultural encounters that require skills to work through differences in ways that honor diversity and result in equitable decisions.

FOR FURTHER READING

Bradley, J., and Kibera, P. "Closing the Gap: Culture and the Promotion of Inclusion in Child Care." *Young Children* 61(1), 2006, p. 34–41. Confirms the importance of attending to family culture when working with children with disabilities or challenging behaviors. Based on research findings, the authors stress the importance of adapting practices to cultural differences whenever feasible, particularly in regard to norms of privacy and perceptions of children's development.

Bredekamp, S., and C. Copple. *Developmentally Appropriate Practice in Early Childhood Programs, rev. ed.* Washington, DC: National Association for the Education of Young Children, 1997. Gives the developmentally appropriate perspective on play.

Copple, C., and Bredekamp, S. *Basics of Developmentally Appropriate Practice: An Introduction for Teachers of Children 3 to 6.* Washington, DC: National Association for the Education of Young Children, 2006. Describes the core concepts of developmentally appropriate practice and makes them meaningful to everyday practices. Only when developmentally appropriate practice is understood can cultural variations and departures from it be explored in positive ways. This book helps newcomers to early childhood education understand the basic fundamentals of the field.

Curtis, D., and M. Carter. *The Art of Awareness.* St. Paul, MN: Redleaf, 2000. Provides many tips on how to observe children's play.

Derman-Sparks, L. *The Antibias Curriculum.* Washington, DC: National Association for the Education of Young Children, 1989. Discusses using play and other means to teach young children about equity issues.

Elkind, D. "Work, Chores, and Play: Setting a Healthy Balance." *Exchange*, 39–41. Addresses the developmental issues involved in having children perform household chores.

Fillmore, L. W., "Luck, Fish Seeds, and Second-Language Learning," in *On Becoming a Language Educator*, eds. C. P. Casanave, and S. R. Schecter. Mahwah, NJ: Erlbaum, 1997. A gripping look at how Dr. Fillmore felt upon entering kindergarten and being put at a table at the back of the room with other children who didn't speak English.

Frost, J. L.; S. C. Wortham, and S. Reifel. *Play and Child Development* (2nd ed.). Upper Saddle River, NJ: Merrill/Prentice Hall, 2005. Ties play directly to child development through a seamless blend of research, theory, and practical applications. Examines the role of adults in leading and encouraging children's natural tendencies toward learning by playing.

Gandini, L., and C. Pope, eds. *Bambini: The Italian Approach to Infant/Toddler Care.* New York: Teachers College Press, 2001. An Italian perspective on play and learning.

Jones, E., and Cooper, R. M. *Playing to Get Smart.* New York, NY: Teachers College Press, 2006. Shows the importance of play for children from birth to age 8 and from all ethnic and socioeconomic groups. Furthermore, it's a playful reading experience with jokes, riddles, and stories sprinkled throughout.

Mistry, J. "Culture and Learning in Infancy." in *Infant/Toddler Caregiving: A Guide to Culturally Sensitive Care,* ed. P. Mangione. Sacramento: Far West Laboratory and California Department of Education, 1995. Explains the cultural view that children learn by observing adults, not by playing.

Stegelin, D. A. "Making the Case for Play Policy: Research-Based Reasons to Support Play-Based Environments." *Young Children* 60(2), 76–85. Helps readers become effective advocates for play-based early learning environments. Discusses distinct research areas that support play policy and practice for physical, cognitive, and social and emotional development within diverse childhood settings.

Van Hoorn, J.; Monighan Nourot, P.; Scales, B.; and Rodriquez Alward, K. *Play at the Center of the Curriculum.* Upper Saddle River, New Jersey: Prentice Hall/A Division of Pearson Education, 2007. Explains that play is a primary factor in the development of intelligence, personality, competencies, self-awareness, and social awareness, and demonstrates how to draw from spontaneous play both the methods and the content of a successful curriculum for children from birth to age 8.

Widerstrom, A. H. *Achieving Learning Goals Through Play: Teaching Young Children with Special Needs* (2nd ed.). Baltimore, MD: Brookes Publishing, 2005. Discusses how the typical learning centers in preschool classrooms—blocks, pretend play, music, reading, art, and others—can be adapted for children with special needs.

NOTES

1. J. Costello, and J. Haver, *Zen Parenting*, (Beltsvile, MD: Robins Lane Press, 2004.) A. C. Ross (Ehanamani), *Mitakuye Oyasin: We Are All Related*, (Denver, CO: Wichoni Waste, 1989), pp. 49–50.

   Dorothy Lee compares cultures that have different concepts of space and time and the implications for emphasizing either activity or silence. She says that Western culture believes "space is empty and to be occupied with matter; time is empty and to be filled with activity. Both primitive and civilized non-Western cultures, on the other hand, see space and time as having being and integrity [These cultures have the] conception of nothingness as somethingness. . . . In such societies, children are raised to listen to silence as well as sound. Luther Standing

Bear, describing his childhood as an Oglala Dakota in the eighteen-seventies, wrote: 'Children were taught to sit still and enjoy it. They were taught to use their organs of smell, to look when apparently there was nothing to see, and to listen intently when all seemingly was quiet.'. . . The Wintu Indians have a suffix to refer to alert non-activity, to a silent, non-mobile commitment to awareness. . . . In Japanese traditional culture, free time and space are perceived as the *ma*, the valid interval or meaningful pause." D. Lee, *Freedom and Culture*, (Englewood Cliffs, NJ: Prentice Hall, 1959), p. 55.

According to Thoman and Browder, Chinese Taoist philosophy has a term, "wu wei," which means "nonaction" or "let be." This term implies total passivity, but that's not what it means, because the Chinese have no concept of total passivity. Instead, they believe that people are always engaged in one of two kinds of activity—going with the flow of the true nature of reality or going against it. Those who look passive are not; they are just refraining from activity that is contrary to nature. E. B. Thoman, and S. Browder, *Born Dancing*, (New York: Harper & Row, 1987), p. 75.

2. The video "Preschool in Three Cultures" is available from Yale University Press, 92A Yale Station, New Haven, Conn. 06520. J. J. Tobin, D. Y. H. Wu, and D. H. Davidson, *Preschool in Three Cultures*, (New Haven, CT: Yale University Press, 1989).

3. V. H. Young, "Family and Childhood in a Southern Negro Community," *American Anthropologist* 72 (1970), pp. 269–288.

   V. H. Young, "A Black American Socialization Pattern," *American Ethnologist* 1, (1974), pp. 405–413.

4. J. Mistry, "Culture and Learning in Infancy: Implications for Caregiving," in J. Cortez, and C. L. Young-Holt, eds., *Infant/Toddler Caregiving: A Guide to Culturally Sensitive Care*, (Sacramento, CA: California Department of Education, 1995), p. 21.

5. F. L. K. Hsu, *Americans and Chinese: Purpose and Fulfillment in Great Civilizations*, (Garden City, NY: Natural History Press, 1970), pp. 84–85.

6. M. B. Ehling, "The Mexican American (El Chicano)," in A. L. Clark, ed., *Culture and Childrearing*, (Philadelphia: F. A. Davis, 1981), p. 197.

7. C. Kordt-Thomas, and I. M. Lee. "Floor time: Rethinking play in the classroom." *Young Children* 61(3) March 2006, p. 86–89.

8. Mistry, "Culture and Learning in Infancy," p. 26.

9. E. T. Hall, *Beyond Culture*, (Garden City, NY: Anchor Press/Doubleday, 1981), pp. 104–116.

10. S. B. Heath, *Ways with Words: Language, Life, and Work in Communities and Classrooms.* (Cambridge: Cambridge University Press, 1983).

11. Mistry, "Culture and Learning in Infancy," p. 23.

12. S. Bredekamp, ed., *Developmental Appropriate Practice in Early Childhood Programs Serving Children from Birth Through Age 8*, (Washington, DC: National Association for the Education of Young Children, 1987).

13. According to Storti, "We assume that others are like us for the simple reason that we learned to behave by watching and imitating them. This is the process of conditioning through which we learn how to function in the world: By observing, imitating (for which we are rewarded) and eventually internalizing the behavior of those around us. . . . Thus, while we may not choose to assume that others are like us, while we may even *know* better than to assume that others are like us, and while we may very much wish we could stop expecting everyone to be like us, the force of our conditioning leaves us no alternative." C. Storti, *The Art of Crossing Cultures*, (Yarmouth, ME: Intercultural Press, 1990), pp. 49–50.

14. Ibid.

Focus Questions

Here are some questions to get you thinking about what's in this chapter.

- How would socialization be different if a child was being trained to stand out versus fit in?

- Why would a teacher complain about praising children?

- Doesn't everybody believe in the right to privacy?

- Why would staff members disagree over what to teach children about personal possessions?

- Why do some people believe that it is more important to teach children to respect elders than it

is to teach them to express their feelings openly and honestly?

- Why use the word guidance when discipline works as well?

- What is the difference between internalized and externalized controls?

- What do differences in power and authority have to do with early childhood education?

- What are the differences between direct and indirect communication?

CHAPTER SEVEN

Socialization, Guidance, and Discipline

We are socialized to look at ourselves, the world, and our role in it in certain ways. We socialize our children according to the way we were socialized. I was taught that I am an individual. I feel that I should stand on my own two feet—both literally and figuratively. I see myself as separate and different from other people.

As an individual, it's up to me to make a place for myself in this world. I was taught that I am special and was encouraged to show my specialness. Likewise, I have tried to make each child that I worked with in my early childhood programs feel special.

I know that every culture doesn't stress individuality. Some cultures value a strong interconnectedness that regards the individual as unimportant except as he or she contributes to the welfare of the group. When I read about interconnectedness, I still think of individuals as separate people enmeshed in webs of attachments. But that's not what some people mean. They mean that there's a oneness that isn't made up of separate individuals but of parts of a whole. This view is a very different way to perceive the world and people in general—a view I'm just beginning to understand.[1]

DIFFERING GOALS OF SOCIALIZATION: STAND OUT OR FIT IN

The idea of standing out from the crowd is undesirable for some who see people as part of something bigger. The separateness and flaunting of one's individuality is frowned on by these people. Look at how these themes play out in the following child care setting:

> You're a teacher in a child care program. You're the only staff member of your culture, but more than half of the families the program serves are of the same culture as you. One day you find yourself confronting the whole staff at an in-service training on self-esteem when the hired consultant who is conducting the training uses the phrase "stand out as a unique individual" once too often. Suddenly you find yourself rising out of your seat and speaking passionately to the group. You say, "I'm sick of hearing our children called unique individuals, and I don't think they should stand out!"
>
> The other staff members turn in their seats and stare at you, surprised to hear you express your opinion in this bold manner. You suddenly sit back down and lower your eyes.
>
> The consultant, who is looking at you with all the rest, says quietly, "Go on. Tell us what you mean."
>
> "Well," you start hesitantly, "in my family, we don't keep telling the children that they are special and unique all by themselves. We tell them that they are a member of our family—of our people. Of course they are unique, but their uniqueness makes them fit in—not stand out. They each have something to contribute—not for themselves, but for us all."[2]
>
> "I see you have some strong feelings about this." The consultant leads you on, allowing you to discover where you are going with it.
>
> "I sure do," you find yourself saying. "In this program, we're constantly hammering in the message that it's good to find your identity by standing alone—being an individual. Take all this business about the names in children's clothes and making a big fuss about what belongs to whom. I get sick of that. You're teaching the children the importance of private possessions—ownership. I see sharing as much more important. Otherwise the children grow up to be selfish and too attached to their own things, and eventually they tend to view their possessions as special and unique just like they are—a further way to make them stand out."
>
> You think you're finished until the consultant shushes a staff member who is about to argue with you, turns to you again, and says, "Anything else on your mind?"
>
> You suddenly realize you're not through as another torrent of words comes pouring out, and you find yourself saying, "I hate the way we're told to praise the children for each little accomplishment. It's like putting a spotlight on them for their individualism. Personally, I detest being in a spotlight."[3] Suddenly you're quiet as you realize how uncomfortable you feel about what's happening right now. You're not only in the spotlight, but you're expressing a personal opinion— just like the unique individuals you've been criticizing. You feel torn apart until you remember that you're not doing it for yourself; you're doing it for all the parents of the children in your center who either don't know about the cultural differences their little ones are experiencing or know about them but haven't felt comfortable questioning the "experts."
>
> "You don't believe in pride?" One staff member overrides the silence the consultant has put on the rest of the group.

Without thinking, you jump back in again. "Sure I believe in pride—but not personal pride. I can't stand to see children go around oozing out the message, 'I'm so great, look at me, pay attention to how wonderful and special I am.'"

"Tell us more about your ideas on pride," the consultant urges.

"Well, we should help the children feel proud of being a member of the group, praise them when they care about each other. We could do a lot more to get them to help one another than we do. We're all so busy getting them to be unique individuals that they're turning into selfish little brats."

"Why didn't you ever say any of this before?" The director breaks in, again overriding the silence the consultant has imposed on the group so you could get your say in.

"Because one time I did—not here, at another program. I was told that I was wrong. I was told that this is America, and people who live here should think and act like Americans—when in Rome and all that stuff. I was so mad I couldn't even answer. I'm an American. Some people in my family were here a long time ago—even before the English-speakers came. Others in my family have come more recently, but most people in America have come from somewhere else anyway. What makes them more American than me?"

Once the flood gates were opened, the water stayed stirred up for quite a while. Eventually, a number of sensitively led discussions brought everyone's feelings and views out into the open. At the staff meetings, a greater number of voices began to express a wider diversity of opinions than had been heard before. As a result, most of the staff gained a larger perspective. The staff continued to work on being more sensitive to cultural and individual differences in the center where this scene occurred. It took a lot of arguments and difficult feelings to get to the place where the staff agreed to disagree. Most finally came to believe that because one person disagrees with another doesn't mean one is right and the other wrong, only that they have different perspectives.

Table 7.1 shows how socialization goals differ for collectivists as represented by the teacher in the scene, who found herself in an individualistic early care and education setting. She was raised to be more group oriented, but the program focused on a socialization process with an individual orientation.

THE SOCIALIZATION PROCESS

The socialization process through which children learn to get along with others starts at birth. Through it, children come to see themselves in relationship to those around them and eventually to the wider society. The goals parents have for the socialization of their children depend on their backgrounds, cultures, and their value systems (individual, familial, and cultural). Check out *Point to Ponder* 7.1 for more about the interplay of background and culture. Understanding the goals of parents is important, especially when the goals of

TABLE 7-1 Contrasts in Socialization Goals (Represented by the teacher in the opening scenario)	
Individual Orientation	**Group Orientation**
Individuals stand out from the group. Being special and unique is emphasized for its own sake.	Individuals fit into the group. Uniqueness is only emphasized as it serves the group.
Children are taught about ownership and taking care of their private possessions. Statements like "me" and "mine" are tolerated and even encouraged.	Children are taught to share and taught that it isn't about "me" and "mine" but rather "ours." Private ownership is downplayed.
Children are praised for personal achievement.	If praise is used, it's for helpful behavior and being part of group achievement.
Expressions of personal pride are encouraged.	Humility is valued and only expressions of group pride are encouraged.
Helping one's self is a focus of developing skills.	Helping others is a focus of developing skills.

the program may not mesh with the parents' goals. This chapter explores the clashes that may occur when the goals and values of one group differ from the goals and values of another group and what to do about these differences.

Sample Conflicts

The conflict illustrated by the previous scene deals with the concept of a person as an individual. The white, European-based, Canadian and U.S. cultures look at a child, starting at birth, as a person who must be helped to recognize that he or she is separate and distinct from any other human being. The child is perceived to have an identity, rights, and needs starting at the moment of birth. Because the child is not born with the concept of being a separate individual, one of the goals of the early months is to shatter the newcomer's belief that he or she and the universe are one.

One of the rights of an individual is the right to privacy (also called a need), which is a big issue for members of "individualistic" cultures. Parents go to some trouble to arrange for their privacy. They carry this over to the infant, sending the message that privacy is important. One problem many see with typical child care arrangements in this country is that babies and toddlers lack privacy due to the numbers of children and the need for all to be under close supervision. Provision is sometimes made for nooks and crannies to serve as "hideaways" for children in day care.

POINT TO PONDER 7.1

The Interplay between Background and Culture

Sometimes oppression and culture get mixed-up together. A family's child rearing practices may reflect that they have been a target of oppression, not only in the present generation but also in the past. For example, an African-American family may have a whole set of socialization practices designed to protect their children against racism. They not only have to socialize their children to see themselves as worthy people in spite of societal messages to the contrary, but they also have to teach them to protect themselves when discriminatory practices threaten their health, safety, or lives. The practices of families who are not targets for racism can be less intensely focused on these particular areas of socialization. Some families, however, are beginning to see their jobs as socializing their children to stand up against racism, even when they themselves are not targets. Part of this socialization includes looking clearly at the many messages that put one group in a position of superiority over another. This means that adults must look at unconscious attitudes of superiority within themselves and their children and work to change them.

There is also some worry about children in child care coming to see themselves as individuals with possessions because what they use at the center belongs to the program, not to individual children.[4]

Not all cultures are individualistic. In fact, in some, the "self" is not conceived as something apart or separate from others. The smallest unit is the group, of which individuals are a part, rather than wholes in themselves.[5] Children in these cultures are taught to see themselves as part of something larger than themselves: their family, their people.

Of course, independence as an individual and the ability to function as a group member are not mutually exclusive; every culture depends on both. But in some cultures, the former has the greater priority, and in other cultures, the latter does.

When these two systems—an individual-oriented system and a group-oriented system—bump up against each other, sparks may fly. One of the most important sentences people who find themselves in an argument over perceptions, beliefs, concepts, or values can learn to use is this one: *"I'm not saying you're wrong; I'm just saying I disagree with you."*

Other Areas of Conflict

Language　　Missing from this scenario was a controversy about using languages other than English in early childhood settings. Keeping in the spirit of this book, I strongly urge that anyone working with young children and their families realize the value of children maintaining their home language. Language is part of socialization and if children stop speaking, growing, and learning in the language of their family, the socialization process is stunted.

Some families have strong feelings about home language remaining at home and English being the language of the school. Some of those families are clear about their role in maintaining home language and are strongly motivated to work at it. They also have enough time with their children to be able to accomplish the feat. However, many families just assume that if they speak to their children in the language of the family, the children will continue to understand and use it. That doesn't always happen. In fact, the tendency is for children to switch to English once they learn it and their growth and development in their home language is slowed or even stopped. Those children end up being monolingual, though some try to recapture what they once had by taking language courses in high school and college. Most never regain what they lost in childhood.

Maybe you don't realize the extent of language loss in this country. I do. I've done a little informal research when I give presentations. I have asked countless audiences to raise their hands if their ancestors spoke a language other than English. Lots of hands go up. Then I ask them to raise their hands if their great-grandparents spoke a language other than English. Often there are still many hands up. Then I ask how many had grandparents who spoke or speak a language other than English. Sometimes—depending on the community—there are still quite a few hands up, but usually a lot have gone down. When I ask about parents who speak a language other than English, there are almost always far fewer hands, unless most of the audience is made up of recent immigrants. Then I ask how many speak the language of their parents, grandparents, or ancestors. It's amazing how few hands stay up. It is easy for everyone in the audience to see that the tendency is for English to replace home languages unless a great effort is made to stop that process. We must be on our way to becoming the most monolingual country in the world as every year more and more children come into all English-speaking programs and their home language starts to diminish. Do your own research. Just keep asking people whose families came from another country a generation or two ago about their original home language.

Of course, the ultimate is to become bi- or tri- or multilingual. We know that babies are born with a huge capacity to learn language—many languages. I know people who learned more than one language from birth on. But I know many, many more people who are monolingual English-speakers, even though their ancestors, even their parents, were native speakers of languages other than English. It's important to recognize the risk factors involved when children enter English-only programs.

I imagine a country where not only do children keep their home language and add English to it, but English-speaking children from monolingual homes become bilingual and even trilingual from attending early childhood programs. That happens almost automatically in many countries around the world. We need to catch up with those countries.

Possessions   Just as babies must learn to differentiate themselves from others in cultures that place importance on the individual, toddlers must differentiate between what is theirs and what is not. One of the primary tasks of toddlerhood is learning to think in terms of private property.

Some cultures have a different view of private possessions. Francis Hsu says of the Chinese culture:

> Not only do parents have freedom of action with reference to the children's belongings, but the youngsters can also use the possessions of the parents if they can lay their hands on them. If children damage their parents' possessions they are scolded, not because they touched things that were not theirs but because they are too young to handle them with proper care.[6]

Some cultures put little emphasis on possession and ownership, indeed, on objects in general. They have other priorities. The lessons they teach about touching or not touching, respecting the property of others, are different from those of parents whose possessions are important to them, are part of their identity. Parents who are not object oriented do not teach pride in ownership or consumerism. Of course, any children who watch television get constant messages about consumerism whether their parents believe in it or not. Here are some sample conflicts between adults that can result from differing attitudes about possessions:

1. Arguments regarding what happens to things that are brought from home. Are they to be distinguished from what belongs to the program? Do they stay in a cubby all day? Do they get used or played with but the owner is in charge? Do they get thrown in with everything else?
2. Issues about respecting the property of others. (For example, one child taking another child's lunch.)
3. Attitudes about lost items. (One adult may be very concerned if clothing, toys, or shoes are missing but another adult may not be as concerned.)
4. Children learning consumerism from other children (highlighted when a program has "show and tell," during which time children brag about their possessions).

5. Issues about taking care of things. (For example, children using puzzle pieces as treasure, putting them in purses, and taking them outside to bury them in the sandbox.)

6. Storing things. An object-oriented person may be more concerned about putting things away with all their parts neatly sorted and stored.

Comparing Children   One aspect of socializing children is to teach them to compare themselves with other children. Perhaps most adults don't teach this lesson outright, but because they constantly do it themselves, they model comparison as a way of looking at people. Very often when two adults are discussing a child and one begins to talk of gross motor milestones achieved, the other asks how old the child was or is. This constant comparison of children with each other or with "the charts" develops a certain mind-set in the children, and they pick up the message that comparison means something is better than something else. They learn early that some parents and early childhood educators think that "faster is better."

Not every culture is so comparison minded. Dorothy Lee talks of several cultures that don't stress achievement or indulge in comparisons:

> Navajo adults and children are valued for their sheer being, just because they *are*. There is no urge toward achievement; no one has to strive for success. . . . The Wintu [native Californians] are people who do not compare individuals with one another, or against a standard. . . . For the Lovedue of South Africa . . . there was no expectation of achievement to be met. Children grew at their own pace, and were allowed to differ as they pleased; they were not assessed against an average. The freedom to follow one's own bent was not endangered by comparison of one child to another as to attainments, physical size, or abilities.[7]

Expressing Feelings   When children are regarded as individuals, they may be encouraged to express their feelings. Good early childhood practice says that adults are to accept all feelings as valid and teach appropriate expression of those feelings to children.

Some practitioners see the importance of a child completely exploring a feeling, such as rage. They allow the child to "work it through," regarding what is happening as a process that should not be interrupted until it is finished. Otherwise the unexpressed feelings may remain unfelt and go underground, popping up again and again as leftovers rather than feelings that are entirely connected to the situation that arises. These early childhood practitioners want to reassure the child that expression of feelings won't result in abandonment.

Other cultures don't have the same view of feelings and their expression. They are more concerned about group harmony than about individual expression of, say, anger or fear.

POINT TO PONDER 7.2

Expressing Feelings versus Respecting Elders

"I don't like it and I don't want to!" is heard regularly in early care and education programs. Children who are encouraged to express their feelings sometimes make statements like that. For staff or parents who were socialized to always respect elders, these two statements can be shocking. Understanding that perspective and working together to figure out what to do about the discrepancy in socialization practices requires good communication skills, which have been discussed in previous chapters. Go back and review if you aren't sure how to handle this situation. A hint: Start by communicating with the aim of seeing a perspective other than your own.

Jerome Kagan says:

> Americans place greater value on sincerity and personal honesty than on social harmony. But in many cultures—Java, Japan, and China, for example—the importance of maintaining harmonious social relationships, and of adopting a posture of respect for the feelings of elders and of authority, demands that each person not only suppress anger but, in addition, be ready to withhold complete honesty about personal feelings in order to avoid hurting another. This pragmatic view of honesty is regarded as a quality characteristic of the most mature adult and is given not the derogatory labels of insincerity or hypocrisy.[8]

Dorothy Lee says of the Hopi, "It is his duty to be happy, for the sake of the group, and a mind in conflict and full of anxiety brings disruption, ill-being, to the social unit."[9] See *Point to Ponder* 7. 2 for a common example of when ideas about expressing feelings clash with diverse views.

Dung Trinh Ngoc says that in Vietnamese families, "Children are taught at an early age to control their emotions."[10]

It sounds as though the mandate is to repress feelings, a situation that is regarded as unhealthy in white, northern European–derived Canadian and U.S. cultures. But there are other views, like that of Francis Hsu, who compares the

> prominence of emotions in the American way of life . . . with the tendency of the Chinese to underplay all matters of the heart. . . . Being individual-centered, the American moves toward social and psychological isolation. His happiness tends to be unqualified ecstasy just as his sorrow is likely to mean unbearable misery. A strong emotionality is inevitable since the emotions are concentrated in one individual.
>
> Being more situation-centered, the Chinese is inclined to be socially or psychologically dependent on others, for this situation-centered individual is tied closer to his world and his fellow men. His happiness and his sorrow tend to be mild since they are shared."[11]

POINT TO PONDER 7.3

Guidance and Discipline—Why Two Different Words?

Discipline is the more common term, but in the minds of many it means punishment. Many early childhood educators and some parents prefer the word *guidance* because it is broader and has more positive associations connected with it. Some of those who haven't had training in parenting or early childhood education use the same kind of discipline that their families used on them— punishment. People who learn and use guidance principles have many alternatives to punishment and less often rely simply on doing to young children what was done to them.

GUIDANCE AND DISCIPLINE

The part of the socialization process that receives the most attention is called guidance or discipline. Why are both these words—guidance and discipline— used? Check out *Point to Ponder* 7.3 to see. Discipline (guidance) is a much talked about subject among parents and early childhood practitioners. There is great potential for conflict when one adult disciplines or "guides" the child of another, as happens in child care. What follows is an example of a major area of disagreement.

Internalized versus Externalized Controls

Good early childhood practice, much of which is influenced by the value systems of white Canadians and Americans with northern European backgrounds, dictates that any guidance has behind it a goal of self-discipline. In other words, the adult starts, sometime in toddlerhood, guiding and controlling behavior using methods that will lead eventually to the child guiding and controlling his or her own behavior. Though the adult starts with externalized controls, the idea is that they will lead to "inner controls," a term often used by early childhood practitioners.

In some cultures, however, externalized controls are not expected to lead to inner controls.[12] Children are always watched—not just by their parents, but by the whole community. A misbehaving child away from home will be guided and directed by whoever is around. The responsibility for child rearing is shared among the group, and everyone becomes a substitute parent when the occasion arises.[13] According to Lonnie R. Snowden:

> [T]he Black community invests effective responsibility for control of children's behavior in an extensive network of adults. . . . Because of this extended parenting,

children's behavior receives proper monitoring and more immediate sanctions than is the norm in American society. Children may be expected to develop more active exploratory tendencies and assertive styles, since respected external agencies can be counted on to reliably check excess. The school, however, exercises less direct and legitimate control, while expecting a relatively docile, immobile pattern of behavior. The cultural conflict is clearly drawn.[14]

How difficult it is when adults expect children to behave as if the locus of control lies within them. Not many adults expect this of infants or toddlers, but they expect it of preschoolers. If they discipline with the idea of eventual inner controls in mind, the methods they use may be quite different from those used by adults who see the locus of control as something external to the child. Gone is the kind of cultural consistency that empowers the child.

Sandoval and De La Roza describe the way extended family and interdependent network orientation work to provide external controls in the Hispanic community:

> In grocery stores and other public places the mother is not inhibited from shouting directives to the young children to constantly remind them—even when engaged in no mischief—that her inquiring but protective eyes are on them. . . . By loudly verbalizing their directives they also mean to engage others in the social control of their children, seeking a sort of consensus protection. [If I (the mother) were to see other children getting into trouble I would tend to them as if they were my own.][15]

It's not too hard to see what kinds of problems might arise for children who are disciplined one way at home and another way in child care. When no one gives children directives, as in the previous example, do they wonder if no one cares what they do? That would be a strange feeling indeed. If teachers become dedicated to the idea that being fair doesn't mean treating all children the same, they will be able to expand their notions of guidance. Once they know that a child is more used to external control messages, teachers can pay attention to what those messages are and learn to watch closely, use eye contact, and send various signals more like the kind of authority the child is used to.

Cynthia Ballenger, in her article "Because You Like Us: The Language of Control," discusses a contrast between the mainstream North American early childhood educators' ways of guiding behavior and Haitian ways. "The North American teachers are concerned with making a connection with the individual child, with articulating his or her feelings and problems." North Americans use consequences as an explanation of why not to do something. Nothing is good or bad in itself, but behavior has consequences. The child must learn about each situation. Consequences are the issue, not shared morals and values.

Instead of referring to feelings or consequences, Haitian teachers "emphasize the group in their control talk, articulating the values and responsibilities of group membership." They don't differentiate specific behaviors, but lump everything into "bad behavior." Haitian adults are clear about good and bad, and so are their children. The children know why they need to be good: So they don't bring shame on their families. It's a system of shared values. The lessons are taught in a question-and-answer format. "Do your parents let you kick?" The children understand their role and repeat the expected answers. The sequence often ends with a statement like, "When an adult talks to you, you're supposed to listen so you will become a good person. The adults here like you, they want you to become good children."

Ballenger uses the example of herself helping children cross a parking lot to show "Haitian control talk."

> CINDY: "Did I tell you to go?"
>
> CHILDREN: "No."
>
> CINDY: "Can you cross this parking lot by yourselves?"
>
> CHILDREN: "No."
>
> CINDY: "That's right. There are cars here. They're dangerous. I don't want you to go alone. Why do I want you to wait for me?"
>
> CLAUDETTE: "Because you like us."

Even though Ballenger was using the cultural style familiar to the children, she expected a response about consequences. Instead, she got an answer more like Haitian ways. Ballenger says that, in the Haitian way, a reprimand defines and strengthens relationships.

This statement really hit home with me. I learned long ago in my early childhood training not to scold or reprimand children in any way. I approach disciplinary matters in a positive way. I avoid words like good and bad. I never use love as a reason for doing something. I can get through a whole day in preschool without ever saying "No." I'm not criticizing myself; I'm proud of my skills. However, I admit that my approach may be misinterpreted by children who are used to a more stringent, controlling, and therefore, to them, a more loving approach.[16]

Time-Out

I had some whole new insights about time-out as a way of responding to inappropriate behavior once I began exploring cultural differences in ideas about privacy. I am a person who values privacy. I think everybody needs space and time alone sometimes. I was surprised to find out that not everyone agrees with me. I have met people who hate being alone and whose goal it is never to spend an hour or even a minute alone—people who hate being in an empty house or even an empty room. I come from a culture and a family that values individualism. People who grow up to be more group oriented have different needs than I do.

Time-out can be a hot topic for some people.

I don't use time-out with children very often, but when I do, I use it to meet what I perceive as a need. When a child gets out of control and can't seem to settle down, it seems to me that I am doing him a favor by taking him off by himself. Privacy helps me pull myself back together when I'm distraught. I've seen it work that way for some children, too. I don't use time-out as a punishment; I use it as a device to meet a need. I have known children who weren't able to use time-out as a way to reintegrate and gain control of themselves. I didn't use it for them. I understand that time-out doesn't have the same meaning for everyone.

I brought this subject up at a workshop in the Southwest where there were people from a number of diverse cultures, including some Native Americans. My comments about views on privacy and time-out started a lively and emotional discussion that lasted for a long time. It became clear that even though I might not think of time-out as punishment, for children used to a group orientation, time-out can be very harsh. For those who identify as a group member more strongly than as an individual, the ultimate punishment is shunning. Being removed from the group is no small thing! The workshop participants eventually divided on the issue of whether to use time-out or not. One group of people had outlawed it in their programs and thought everyone should outlaw it. Another group loudly defended time-out as a humane approach to getting children to behave acceptably. Neither group wanted to listen to the other.

A third group sat quietly listening to the other two argue it out. The time was too short to reach a conclusion, but it was clear to all in the room that time-out is a hot topic and seems to relate to cultural differences.

Alan Pence, in a 2004 *Interaction* article, writes about a similar discussion of time-out among a group of education students in Canada. He describes discussions that highlighted the fact that the students had a different idea about the relationship of the individual to the broader community. He contrasts Western practice which recommends children be separated from the group when they are misbehaving to the Aboriginal students in his group who saw this approach as counterproductive. They thought a misbehaving child needed additional engagement with the group rather than being placed in time out.[17] "While Western practice recommends separating children who are misbehaving (giving them a 'time-out'), a number of the Aboriginal students felt this was counterproductive and that additional engagement with the group ('time-in') made more sense" (p. 32).

Discipline is a subject that many adults have strong feelings and ideas about. For that reason, it's common for discussions to turn into arguments. Talking about discipline taps into sensitive areas of personal histories as well as cultural differences. One way to end the argument is when someone in power points out the program's policy and says it has to be enforced. Sometimes that's enough to silence the diverse voices. However, if someone insists that the diverse voices must be heard, there's a better chance that the group can switch to problem solving and figure out what to do. Instead of focusing on the problem and its solution and short-circuiting understanding, it helps to focus on how to include opposing views in the discussion. When people disagree they should not attempt a resolution until they understand all the perspectives. Then the situation can become an opportunity to gain a broader view and learn something new. Changing the goal from outcome to process changes everything.

In the face of different perspectives, it isn't the answer of what to do or the resolution of the problem, but the perspectives themselves that are important. According to Chodron, in her book *When Things Fall Apart*, "the path is the goal" (2000, 143). When we just seek solutions, we miss the opportunity to notice what's going on in the moment. The conversation is what counts, the living in the present instead of seeking an answer for the future.

Betty Jones and Renatta Cooper[18] have a game to play when you are dealing with contrasting perspectives. Try using the tensions you are feeling in a creative manner. They suggest to try playing what they call the "believing game" in which you *pretend* you can take the other person's perspective. To do this you have to suspend reality—the way children do when they use their imaginations. You can do it too—imagine that you believe what the other person believes. You're almost sure to gain some insights if you are able to play the believing game.

Physical Punishment

Another difference in disciplinary approaches may be the use of physical punishment as opposed to explaining, showing disapproval, redirecting, using time-out, and a host of other techniques. Ugly conflicts can arise over this issue, especially when some adults believe firmly in nonviolence and others believe in the benefits of a good spanking and have never experienced any other way of handling children's behavior.

If, however, you work in an early childhood program of any sort, no matter what your culture, you don't have the choice to use physical punishment, because the law forbids it. Further, you're bound by law to report suspected physical abuse (physical punishment that leaves marks on a child). Be sure parents know this from the start so they won't feel betrayed if you have to report suspected abuse.[19] In cases where parents disagree with approaches that avoid physical punishment, it's important to start a dialogue. Be respectful of their differing beliefs, but be clear about the law.

Conflicts are bound to arise when children get together. How you handle them reflects your values (which relate to your culture). Here's the typical white, European-American, early childhood practitioner's view: Although a reasonable number of conflicts between children provides valuable learning experiences, it's worthwhile to prevent excessive conflicts. Conflict prevention comes through careful arrangement of the environment so that one child is less likely to encroach upon another. Plenty of toys and things to do help prevent fights.

When children do get into a conflict, tussling or struggling with each other, the adult comes immediately to the scene to prevent anyone from getting hurt. He or she either settles the problem or gets down on the children's level and talks them through it so they can settle it themselves. Keeping one child from hurting another, even slightly, is an important value for the typical white, European-American, early childhood practitioner.

That value is not universal. A Japanese teacher says, "As the year progresses we put fewer and fewer toys out during free-play time to give children additional opportunities to learn to share and to deal with the conflicts which arise." Then the teacher stays back and lets the children work out the problem. In fact, one child who continually provoked fights and hurt children was considered to "serve the function of giving other children a chance to experience a range of emotions and to rehearse a variety of strategies both for resolving their own disagreements as well as for mediating conflicts among others."[20]

This approach in the Japanese program provided quite a contrast to Chinese ideas about discipline:

> According to Chinese theories of child development, children are not born knowing how to behave correctly and they are unlikely to come to know correct behavior through unsupervised play with peers or through a process of self-discovery

and self-actualization . . . teachers bear the responsibility of teaching students self-restraint and correct behavior.[21]

POWER AND AUTHORITY

Carol Phillips advises that when you're working across cultures, it is important to know how parents want their children to relate to authority figures.[22]

How the authority figures themselves behave is also an issue that can be of importance. When authority figures—teachers or caregivers in a program—behave differently from the way children are used to, those children can experience cultural dissonance. Janice Hale-Benson says, "Black mothers tend to be more firm and physical in their discipline than white mothers, consequently, when the child encounters a white teacher in school practicing all the techniques she learned in college, the children 'run all over her' and are labeled discipline problems."[23]

Related to authority is power. A word heard more and more in early childhood programs these days is *empowerment*. Early childhood practitioners are busy trying to empower children, parents, and each other as they work day-to-day in centers and family day care homes across the nation. What does this word mean, and how can it cause cultural conflicts?

To empower means to bring out the power of the individual or group. Empowerment is based on the idea that power, like love, comes from within and exists in an unlimited supply. In fact, the more you empower others, the more you can experience your own personal power. It's not like commodities where you give away what you have and the other person has not only what he had before but also yours, and you have nothing. Empowering does not mean giving power up, but rather bringing power out. Empowering has to do with personal power, not with overpowering or controlling others.

Everyone doesn't see power in this way. Imagine the conflicts that can arise when adults have differing views of power and its uses. What does that mean in terms of interacting with children? Will one adult understand when another is using her own power either *with* the child or *for* the child rather than *over* the child?

Here is an example of two different ways that adults might react to a child when they have differing views of power and the adult role in relationship to power.

Picture a two-year-old girl trying to solve a problem—she's working to get a toy on a shelf just out of her reach. The adult sitting on the floor nearby is trying to empower her by supporting her in solving this problem without handing her a solution. She waits to see what the child will do. The child continues straining and reaching until she gives up, angry and discouraged. As she moves away from the shelf, she passes by the seated adult, who pushes a large plastic block toward her, seeing the block was all she needed. Immediately, the child starts shoving it over to the shelf and is about to climb up on it to reach the toy when another caregiver comes over, takes the block away, says, "No, don't climb on that," and walks over to put the block back where it belongs.

You can see the potential for conflict here as one adult defeats the other's purpose and relates to the child in an entirely different way.

When two people or two groups have opposing ways of doing things, one way is not necessarily right and the other way necessarily wrong. The two ways are different, and differences should be respected. One way, especially if it is your own, may feel more correct to you. Can you suspend judgment, shift reference frames, and accept that there's another way?

Just because you know something about a person's culture doesn't mean you can predict that person's behavior. Individuals are guided by their individual values, inclinations, behavior styles, and cultural and religious backgrounds. Knowing a person's culture tells you something about the probability that he or she will behave in a certain way; it doesn't tell you that he or she *will* behave in that way.

LEARNING TO READ INDIRECT COMMUNICATION

This chapter started with a scene of a teacher expressing herself directly from the heart about her disagreements with socialization practices that conflicted with her values. Was there a slightly fictional tone to that scene? If you felt the tone, it was because it's very unlikely that people from a culture with that particular set of values would stand up to a crowd and express themselves in that manner.

To get feedback from someone who doesn't believe in the "spotlight," who avoids direct confrontation, who feels it's rude to argue, you have to learn to read subtle messages. If you ask directly, the person's more likely to tell you what you want to hear than to criticize you or the situation. The primary issue is not honesty, but manners and harmony. You may feel irritated that you seem to be expected to read minds. But if you educate yourself a bit, you'll find others who are accustomed to this kind of communication are able to pick up on the subtle verbal and nonverbal messages. It isn't really a matter of reading minds; it's a matter of picking up clues. If you are interested in seeing contrasting features of direct and indirect styles of communication illustrated here and at the beginning of the chapter, check out Table 7.2.

Let's go back to the teacher at the beginning of this chapter and look at all the clues she sent out before she reached the point of direct verbal

TABLE 7-2 Contrasts between Direct and Indirect Communication Styles	
Direct Communication	**Indirect Communication**
Asks direct questions	Avoids asking or answering direct questions
States problems clearly in words	Hints at problems subtly without stating them directly
Depends on words to communicate and understand the communication of others	Depends on nonverbal clues and the context of the situation to convey meaning
Involves direct confrontation with the person	Goes to a third party and explains the problem
Discounts what is reported by a third party because it is gossip and doesn't seem important	Expects that the third party will convey both the importance and the urgency of the problem
Gives feedback in a direct way	Gives feedback in a roundabout way
Emphasizes what is important, stating a strong opinion	Understates what is important, voicing a mild opinion
Values straightforwardness and honesty	Values subtleness and manners

communication. It's important to realize that she acted out of character by directly confronting the entire staff. She reached that point only because she was seeing a European-American therapist who taught her this type of personal expression. Even though she learned to do it, she felt very uncomfortable because such bold criticism went against everything she believed in. (It's more realistic to assume she never would have spoken out so directly, no matter how unhappy or uncomfortable she felt.) But this teacher gave clues to the director long before the staff meeting brought everything to a head.

The first clue came when the teacher complained to a third party about the program, expecting her to deliver the message to the director. She was unhappy about what she considered the cultural inappropriateness of the program's approach to socialization. But the message delivered to the director wasn't stated in those terms. What the third party reported was the teacher's discomfort with a particular incident. This incident wasn't very important in the mind of the director, and the director's reaction to getting the message secondhand was anger. She discounted the whole situation because the teacher hadn't approached her directly. She decided it wasn't worth putting any energy into what she termed "hearsay" and "gossip."

If the director had been more culturally sensitive, she might have seen that the third-party communication was a means of avoiding direct confrontation that is perfectly acceptable and even expected by many people.

Another series of clues came when, every once in a while, the teacher criticized the director's culture in general, but then always exempted anyone of that culture within hearing distance. "But you aren't like that . . ." she had said more than once to the director. What the director didn't know was that on each of these occasions, the teacher had given her a bit of personal feedback about her own behavior. It was roundabout, but that's the accepted way in the teacher's culture.

The director decided to educate herself, so she asked the teacher to teach her about her culture. Although the director's attitude brought the two closer, unfortunately, it was too big a request. It was hard for the teacher to go beyond the outward, easily recognized elements of her culture. She began educating the director about its art, music, and food. She avoided any direct reference to the nitty-gritty of what was bothering her.

While they were establishing their relationship around manifestations of culture, avoiding important cultural conflicts, the teacher continued giving out subtle messages. The director missed every one of them. During one staff meeting, for example, when they were talking about labeling the children's belongings, the teacher brought up a very feeble objection. No one even understood what she was saying; and when the conversation wandered to another subject, she remained silent. The director went back to pick up on her objection, but by then, the teacher just went along with the majority. The director decided that she had changed her mind. What the director didn't realize was that even just voicing a mild opinion was hard for the teacher. The fact that she spoke up at all indicated she had very strong feelings. But the director, because of her own background, where speaking your mind was the ordinary approach, didn't regard the teacher's mild objection as very important.

Many people, when placed in the director's position, feel frustrated at the least and perhaps quite angry and even lied to when told that messages have been sent but have not been picked up. The indirect means of communication so common among some people are very upsetting to someone of a culture that values straightforwardness and honesty.

It's important if you're in the director's position to try to look at indirect communication not as wrong, bad, or dysfunctional, but as simply *another way* of communicating. You can try to teach your way, but realize that it will be no easier for the other person to change than it is for you to change. Perhaps the most you can hope for is mutual respect and understanding.

To socialize children across cultures, you need to open up communication and get all adults involved to observe what's going on and try to understand how the others feel about it. Maybe you can get things out in the open; but even if you do, it's important to realize that, though you can talk about goals and values, it's how you treat the children, how they react to you, and how you respond back that makes the difference. Only through actions and interactions will differences in goals and values have meaning—otherwise it all remains in the realm of theory.

SUMMARY

This chapter started with a scene showing a teacher trying to explain how socialization goals differ, teaching children either that it is good to stand out or to fit in. This scene sets the stage for a number of other conflicts that can occur when early childhood educators and/or parents have diverse ideas about socializing children. Some of those areas of conflict include:

- Issues around teaching children about ownership and private possessions
- Comparing children to each other or to a standard
- Encouraging children to express their feelings honestly and openly without regard to the effects on others

The chapter started with a discussion of the differences between teaching children internalized and externalized behavior controls. Guidance and discipline as important aspects of socialization were also discussed. The topic of physical punishment was covered, but the chapter emphasized that physical punishment is not allowed in early care and education settings. Children's different perceptions of power and authority can cause problems when the authority doesn't act in familiar ways. Teachers who use gentle guidance strategies need to pay attention to how they are received by children whose culture uses more direct confrontive means of guiding behavior. The chapter closed by returning to the opening scene of the teacher who feels her culture is being trampled on by the program policies and staff behavior. The communication difficulties between this teacher and the director are discussed, and the reader is encouraged to think beyond terms of right and wrong when it comes to communication styles. It may be a challenge to understand diverse styles, but honoring them is all important.

FOR FURTHER READING

Ballenger, C. *Teaching Other People's Children*. New York: Teachers College Press, 1999. Classroom research that shows a European-American teacher working with and learning from a community of young Haitian-American learners.

Curtis, D., and M. Carter. *Designs for Living and Learning*. St. Paul, MN: Redleaf, 2003. Shows how planning for effective environments can influence socialization.

Day, M., and R. Parlakian. *How Culture Shapes Social-Emotional Development: Implications for Practice in Infant-Family Programs*. Washington, DC: Zero to Three, 2004. Examines how culture shapes children's fundamental learning about themselves, their emotions, and their way of interacting and relating to others. Recommendations for providing culturally responsive services and resolving cultural dilemmas.

Deloria, V., Jr., and D. R. Wildcat. *Power and Place: Indian Education in America*. Golden, CO: American Indian Graduate Center and Fulcrum Resources, 2001.

Gonzalez-Mena, J. "Lessons from My Mother-in-Law: A Story about Discipline." *Exchange*, January 1997, pp. 44–46.

Gonzalez-Mena, J., and I. Shareef. (2005). Discussing Diverse Perspectives on Guidance. *Young Children* 60(6), 34–38. Looks at a variety of differences when it comes to discipline and guidance. Discusses how to work out the differences in a care and education setting.

hooks, b. *Rock My Soul, Black People and Self-Esteem*. New York: Atria, 2003. Discusses the impact of low self-esteem and the political and cultural barriers that affect the socialization of African-Americans.

Huntsinger, C. S.; P. R. Huntsinger; W-D. Ching; and C-B. Lee. "Understanding cultural contexts fosters sensitive caregiving of Chinese-American children." *Young Children* 55(6), 7–12, 14–15. 2000. Gives brief looks at Chinese history, language, culture, and family tradition and values. Four short profiles of Chinese American families enlighten and pose questions for educators.

Jones, E., and R. M. Cooper. *Playing to Get Smart*. New York, NY: Teachers College Press, 2006. Shows the importance of play for children from birth to age 8 and from all ethnic and socioeconomic groups. Furthermore, it's a playful reading experience with jokes, riddles, and stories sprinkled throughout.

Klein, M. D., and D. Chen, *Working with Children from Culturally Diverse Backgrounds*. New York: Delmar, 2001. Looks at cultural differences in the socialization of children and how to make educational settings more sensitive to diversity.

MacNaughton, G. *Rethinking Gender in Early Childhood Education*. St. Leonards, NSW, Australia: Allen and Unwin, 2000. Through play, children show that they are aware of gender roles. Everyday teaching practices influence the gendering of young children's identities and move them away from gender equity.

Nee-Benham, M. K. P. A., and J. E. Cooper. *Indigenous Educational Models for Contemporary Practice: In Our Mother's Voice*. Mahwah, NJ: Erlbaum, 2000.

Rodriguez, R. *The Hunger of Memory: The Education of Richard Rodriguez*. New York: Bantam Books, 1983. A firsthand account of one child's socialization.

Rogoff, B. *The Cultural Nature of Human Development*. Oxford and New York: Oxford University Press, 2003. Demonstrates that human development and socialization is a product of each individual's participation in the routine activities of the communities in which they live—as seen through the eyes of a wise anthropologist.

Sanchez, S. *Does Your House Have Lions?* Boston: Beacon, 1997. The story of a young man who immersed himself in New York's gay subculture and became a victim of AIDS.

Sandall, S., and M. Ostrosky, eds. *Young Exceptional Children: Practical Ideas for Addressing Challenging Behaviors*. Denver: The Division for Early Childhood of the Council for Exceptional Children, 1999. Most challenging behaviors can be addressed without removing young children from inclusive settings. This book suggests ways to socialize by preventing, identifying, and addressing disruptive behaviors.

Some, S. *The Spirit of Intimacy: Ancient African Teachings in the Ways of Relationships.* New York: HarperCollins/Quill, 2000. Presents knowledge from the author's West African culture about community.

Stonehouse, A., and J. Gonzalez-Mena. *Making Links: A Collaborative Approach to Planning and Practice in Early Childhood Services.* Sydney, Australia: Pademelon Press, 2004. Looks at collaborative planning for play and other meaningful authentic experiences.

Tan, A. L. *Chinese American Children and Families: A Guide for Educators and Service Providers.* Olney, MD: Association for Childhood Education International, 2004. While the information presented in this book is pertinent to Chinese Americans, with relevant applications to East Asian Americans and Southeast Asian Americans, it helps the reader understand the socialization process in all cultures.

NOTES

1. Leslie Willams writes about the Native American perspective that the group is central: "The development of the individual is not seen to be as worthy of attention as is the relationship of that individual to the group. The growth of any one person is seen as integrally tied with the health and integrity of the group as a whole. Thus, the focus is not so much on the internal dynamic as on the relationship of the self to others—and others can include human beings, other beings (including spiritual entities), and the external, material world. The highlighting of relationship may sometimes mean the subsuming of self for the good and enhancement of others." L. R. Williams, "Developmentally Appropriate Practice and Cultural Values: A Case in Point," in B. L. Mallory, and R. S. New, eds., *Diversity and Developmentally Appropriate Practices: Challenges for Early Childhood Education,* (New York: Teachers College Press, 1994), p. 160.

   Elleni Tedla writes of the notion of interconnection among African people: "The bondedness of everyone in creation is recognized. This awareness of the interconnectedness of fittouran (people) is well expressed in the concepts of diginnet (kindness, generosity, caring). E. Tedla, *Sankofa: African Thought and Education,* (New York: Peter Lang, 1995).

   The title of A. C. Ross's book, *Mitakuye Oyasin (We Are All Related),* shows his emphasis on the subject in the Lakota tradition. A. C. Ross, (Ehanamani), *Mitakuye Oyasin: We Are All Related,* (Denver, CO: Wichoni Waste, 1989).

2. Many writers and researchers discuss the contrasting concepts of a person as an individual versus a person as a part of a group. Hall speaks of those Americans who, like himself, regard the individual as a meaningful concept: "We draw a line around the individual and say this is our basic entity—the building block of all social relations and institutions. . . . None of this can be applied to the Pueblo Indian for something akin to lineages in the Pueblo are the viable unit. No human being outside of these groups has significance independent and distinct from the group. The Pueblo view of the group as the basic unit is difficult if not impossible

for the average European to comprehend, because he lacks the experience of having grown up in such a group." E. T. Hall, *Beyond Culture*, (Garden City, NY: Anchor Press/Doubleday, 1981), p. 231.

Tobin et al., in discussing the research done through comparing videotapes of early childhood programs in three countries, say, "Virtually all the Japanese preschool teachers who viewed our tape of an American preschool contrasted the individualism they perceive as characterizing preschool in America with the groupism they believe characterizes their own society and schools." But according to the teachers who commented on the tapes, the goal wasn't to get everybody doing the same thing at the same time. "That isn't the same as real group life. . . . We just try to show them, to teach them the fun and sense of belonging one can get only by being part of a group." No longer are duty and sacrifice foremost values. The teachers' stated goals involved achieving a balance between individualism and groupism: "integrate the individual and group dimensions of self." J. J. Tobin, D. Y. H. Wu, and D. H. Davidson, *Preschool in Three Cultures*, (New Haven, CT: Yale University Press, 1989), pp. 38–40, 71.

Hsu says, "In the American way of life the emphasis is placed upon the predilections of the individual, a characteristic we shall call *individual-centered*. This is in contrast to the emphasis the Chinese put upon an individual's appropriate place and behavior among his fellow men, a characteristic we shall term *situation-centered*." F. L. K. Hsu, *Americans and Chinese: Purpose and Fulfillment in Great Civilizations*, (Garden City, NY: Natural History Press, 1970), p. 10.

Lubeck discusses two distinct cultural patterns: "A collective orientation is apparent when enculturation occurs in a shared function environment where the focus is on social relations, stressing 'kinship,' interdependency, and cooperation, a holistic world view, relational thinking, and the importance of non-verbal communication. An individualistic orientation predominates when enculturation occurs in a nucleated family structure, focusing on manipulatory experience and stressing self-achievement, competition, the ability to abstract parts from wholes, abstract thinking and the importance of verbal communication." S. Lubeck, *Sandbox Society: Early Education in Black and White America*, (Philadelphia: Falmer Press, 1985), p. 110.

Holtzman says, "Mexicans tend to be more family-centered, while Americans are more individual-centered." W. H. Holtzman, R. Diaz-Guerrero, and J. D. Swartz, *Personality Development in Two Cultures: A Cross-Cultural Longitudinal Study of School Children in Mexico and the United States*, (Austin: University of Texas Press, 1975), p. 359.

Suzuki laments the deculturalization of Asian-American life. He argues that the institutions of education and mental health have mistakenly failed to realize the successes of Asian-American child rearing in inculcating family values that may run counter to the accepted norm in terms of individualism and aggressiveness. B. H. Suzuki, "The Asian-American Family," in M. D. Fantini, and R. Cardenas, eds., *Parenting in a Multicultural Society*, (New York: Longman, 1980), pp. 97–98.

3. A number of cultures shy away from spotlighting children for their individual accomplishments. Dorothy Lee has this to say about the Hopis on this subject: "The Hopis have a reluctance to stand out, to be singled out from the group.

Teachers in Hopi schools have reported discomfort and even tears as a reaction to praise in public. It appears that what is in fact disturbing is the comparative evaluation that results in singling out and praising. Hopi do not compare their achievement, nor the importance of their work." D. Lee, *Freedom and Culture*, (Englewood Cliffs, NJ: Prentice Hall, 1959), p. 20.

"Southeast Asian cultural attitudes toward 'singling out' any individual in their society as being 'different' in any way . . . are literally worlds apart from expectations prevalent in the United States." R. D. Morrow, "Cultural Differences—Be Aware!" *Academic Therapy* 23, no. 2 (November 1987), p. 143.

"Modesty and humility for Vietnamese are important social graces, and deeply ingrained into their identity." D. T. Binh, *A Handbook for Teachers of Vietnamese Students: Hints for Dealing with Cultural Differences in Schools*, (Arlington, VA: Center for Applied Linguistics, 1975), p. 16.

Amy Tan points out that an issue in Chinese character development is "how to know your own worth and polish it, never flashing it around like a cheap ring." A. Tan, *The Joy Luck Club*, (New York: Putnam, 1989), p. 254.

4. Dorothy Lee discusses the relationship of freedom, possessions, and privacy in "individualistic" cultures. "The child grows up needing time to himself, a room of his own, freedom of choice, freedom to plan his own time and his own life. He will brook no interference and no encroachment. He will spend his wealth installing private bathrooms in his house, buying a private car, a private yacht, private woods, and a private beach, which he will then people with his privately chosen society. The need for privacy is an imperative one in our society, recognized by official bodies of our government. And it is part of a system which stems from and expresses our basic value." Lee, *Freedom and Culture*, p. 74.

5. Barbara Rogoff writes about this subject and gives examples in her book, *The Cultural Nature of Human Development*, (Oxford and New York: Oxford University Press, 2003).

"Traditional Asian American–Pacific American culture differs from western cultures in that Asians tend to place great emphasis on the family as the central unit rather than the individual." M. Root, C. Ho, and S. Sue, "Issues in the Training of Counselors for Asian Americans," in H. Lefley and P. Pedersen, eds., *Cross-Cultural Training for Mental Health Professionals*, (Springfield, IL: Thomas, 1986), p. 202.

Research by Caudill and his associates showed that the Caucasian-American mother was more "individual oriented and independent. . . . She saw her infant from birth as a separate and autonomous individual with his own needs and desires. . . . In contrast, the motherland Japanese mother was observed to be more group oriented and interdependent in her relations. . . . The Japanese-American mothers . . . appeared to be somewhere in between." S. Shibata and A. Emiko, "The Japanese American," in A. L. Clark, ed., *Culture and Childrearing*, (Philadelphia: F. A. Davis, 1981), p. 121.

Hmong society is extremely group oriented, with the family being the most important social unit. N. Matthiessen, *The Hmong: A Multicultural Study*, (Fairfield, CA: Fairfield-Suisun Unified School District, 1987).

Children "are taught to be loyal first to their family, to consider the wishes of the family over their own." D. T. Ngoc, "Understanding Asian Families: A Vietnamese Perspective," *Children Today*, March–April 1984, p. 12.

"In the U.S. we begin early to groom our children to become independent. We stress early weaning, dressing and feeding oneself at the preschool level, thinking for yourself, being your 'own person,' and becoming self-sufficient children and adults. Almost as soon as an American child is born, he sleeps by himself, often in his own bedroom. Toys and other possessions are identified as 'mine' or 'yours.' American parents foster self-reliance, assertiveness, speaking one's mind, and looking out for 'number one.'

"With Southeast Asians, the opposite is true . . . in contrast to the American emphasis on egocentric, independent behavior, the Southeast Asian child is trained to think of the family first and must learn to subjugate his own personal desires and concerns." Morrow, "Cultural Differences," p. 144.

6. Hsu, *Americans and Chinese*, pp. 75, 84–85.

7. Lee, *Freedom and Culture*, pp. 10, 51.

8. J. Kagan, *The Nature of the Child*, (New York: Basic Books, 1984), pp. 244–245.

9. Lee, *Freedom and Culture*, p. 21.

10. D. T. Ngoc, "Understanding Asian Families," p. 12.

11. Hsu, *Americans and Chinese*, p. 10.

12. External controls aren't just a way to guide behavior in childhood. Even in adulthood, for some cultures, the expectation is that external controls are still needed. Hall gives us an example: "in the northern European tradition until very recently, sexual controls were vested in the woman for the most part; i.e., internalized. In southern Europe this was not so. The controls were in the situation (people) and in physical structures (doors and locks). For years, people in middle- and upper-class Latin America believed that the sexual drive was so strong in men and the capacity of women to resist was so weak, that if a man and a woman were alone together behind closed doors neither could be expected to be able to resist the overwhelming power of the man's drive. Walls, doors, and locks were a physical extension of morality—externalizations of process handled internally by middle-class North Americans." Hall, *Beyond Culture*, p. 27.

13. Janice Hale-Benson reports that "adults in the Black community play substantially different roles as social control agents than do adults in the school . . . a network of significant adults firmly corrects undesirable behavior whenever it occurs and reports such behavior to the parent. Therefore, parents are at the center of this social control network. For the child, this means that he is always under the surveillance of adults. The significant feature of the control system is that it seems to operate external to the child. Therefore, the child seems to develop external locus of control.

"In the school situation, adults seem to behave as if locus of social control exists within the child. They do not function in ways that are consistent with the child's expectations of how adults should behave toward them in situations that require the enforcement of social controls." J. E. Hale-Benson, *Black Children: Their Roots, Culture, and Learning Styles*, (Baltimore, MD: Johns Hopkins University Press, 1986), p. 85.

14. L. R. Snowden, "Toward Evaluation of Black Psycho-Social Competence," in S. Sue and T. Moore, eds., *The Pluralistic Society*, (New York: Human Sciences Press, 1984), p. 188.

15. M. Sandoval, and M. De La Roza, "A Cultural Perspective for Serving the Hispanic Client," in H. Lefley, and P. Pedersen, eds., *Cross-Cultural Training for Mental Health Professionals*, (Springfield, IL: Thomas, 1986), p. 167.

16. C. Ballenger, "Because You Like Us: The Language of Control," *Harvard Educational Review* 62, no. 2 (Summer 1992), pp. 199–208.

17. A. Pence, "Finding a Niche in Building ECE Capacity." *Interaction* 18(1):31–33, 2004.

18. E. Jones, and R. Cooper. *Playing to Get Smart*. New York: Teachers College Press, 2005.

19. You may run into some real cultural conflicts over the definitions of child abuse. According to Shwartz: "In the Chinese culture to not physically discipline one's children, using what may be fairly severe means and methods, is seen within the cultural context as deviant. . . . Black and Hispanic parents and professionals likewise site [sic] the use of spanking and other forms of physical discipline as being part of their child-rearing practices for generations . . . many lower class white families share similar values around authority and discipline. Hispanic families, especially recent immigrants, are truly shocked at the idea of an agency or the state intervening in their private family life and telling them anything about how they discipline their children. Jorge Santiz, a consultant formerly with the San Francisco Child Abuse council, says, 'Child abuse doesn't exist as a legal concept in most Latin countries.' That a child has legal rights separate from the family that are protected by law is a particularly Western notion, rooted in individualism. In many Asian, Latin, and non-western cultures, filial piety is of much more fundamental value than individualism. The individual is expected to comply with familial authority, to the point of sacrificing one's desires. The already gray area between where a parent's rights end and a child's begins is made all the more murky when value systems as different as these are operating." D. Shwartz, *The Children's Advocate*, January–February 1983, p. 6.

20. Tobin, Wu, and Davidson, *Preschool in Three Cultures*, p. 33.

21. Ibid., p. 96.

22. C. B. Phillips, "Culture: A Process That Empowers," in J. Cortez, and C. L. Young-Holt, eds., *Infant/Toddler Caregiving: A Guide to Culturally Sensitive Care*, (Sacramento: California Department of Education, 1995), p. 7.

23. Hale-Benson, *Black Children*, p. 68.

Bibliography

Akbar, N. *The Community of Self.* Tallahassee, FL: Mind Productions, 1985.

Akbar, N. *Light from Ancient Africa.* Tallahassee, FL: Mind Productions, 1994.

Akbar, N. *Breaking the Chains of Psychological Slavery.* Tallahassee, FL: Mind Productions, 1996.

Akcan, S. "Puppet Theater Time in a First Grade French-Immersion Class." *Young Children* 60(2), 2005, pp. 38–41.

Alati, S. "What About Our Passions as Teachers?" *Young Children* 60(6), 2005, pp. 86–89.

Alderete-Baker, E. "Internalized Achievement-Related Motives of Native American Women," Unpublished Ph.D. dissertation, 1998.

Allen, P. G. *Off the Reservation.* Boston: Beacon Press, 1998.

American Academy of Pediatrics. *Children with Special Needs: Applicable Standards from Caring for Our Children: National Health and Safety Performance Standards: Guidelines for Out-of-Home Child Care Programs* (2nd ed.). Chicago, IL: American Academy of Pediatrics, 2002.

American Academy of Pediatrics. *Exclusion and Inclusion of Ill Children in Child Care Facilities and Care of Ill Children in Child Care. Standards from Caring for Our Children: National Health and Safety Performance Standards: Guidelines for Out-of-Home Child Care Programs* (2nd ed.). Chicago, IL: American Academy of Pediatrics, 2003.

American Psychological Assocation Online. *What is Sexual Orientation?* http://www.apa.org/pubinfo/answers.html, 2004.

Anderson, P., "Explaining Intercultural Differences in Nonverbal Communication." In *Intercultural Communication: A Reader,* eds. L. Samovar, and R. Porter. Belmont, CA: Wadsworth, 1994.

Anderson, P., and E. S. Fenichel. *Serving Culturally Diverse Families of Infants and Toddlers with Disabilities.* Washington, DC: National Center for Clinical Infant Programs, 1989, ED 318174.

Baker, Amy C., and L. A. Manfredi/Petitt. *Relationships, the Heart of Quality Care: Creating Community Among Adults in Early Care Settings.* Washington, DC: National Association for the Education of Young Children, 2004.

Balaban, N. *Everyday Goodbyes Starting School and Early Care: A Guide to the Separation Process.* New York: Teachers College Press, 2006.

Ball, J. *Early Childhood Care and Development Program as Hook and Hub for Community Development: Promising Practices in First Nations.* Victoria, BC, Canada: University of Victoria, 2004.

Ballenger, C. "Because You Like Us: The Language of Control." *Harvard Educational Review* 62, no. 2 (Summer 1992), pp. 191–208.

Ballenger, C. *Teaching Other People's Children.* New York: Teachers College Press, 1999.

Bandtec Network for Diversity Training. *Reaching for Answers: A Workbook on Diversity in Early Childhood Education.* Oakland, CA: Bandtec Network for Diversity Training, 2003.

Banks, J. A. "Multicultural Education: Development, Dimensions, and Challenges." *Phi Delta Kappan* 22 (September 1993), p. 20.

Banks, J. A. *Cultural Diversity and Education.* 4th ed. Boston: Allyn and Bacon, 2001.

Barrera, I., and R. Corso. *Skilled Dialogue.* Baltimore: Brookes, 2003.

Bell, D. *Faces at the Bottom of the Well: The Permanence of Racism.* New York: Basic Books, 1992.

Bell, D.; M. Whitebook; and P. Hnatiuk. *The Early Childhood Mentoring Curriculum.* Washington, DC: National Center for Early Childhood Workforce, 1997.

Bell, S. H.; V. W. Carr; D. Denno; and L. J. Johnson. *Challenging Behaviors in Early Childhood Settings: Creating a Place for All Children.* Baltimore, MD: Brookes Publishing, 2004.

Bender, W. N. *Learning Disabilities: Characteristics, Identification, and Teaching Strategies.* 3rd ed. Boston: Allyn and Bacon, 1998.

Benjet, C., and A. E. Kazdin. "Spanking Children: The Controversies, Findings and New Directions." *Clinical Psychology Review* 23, 2003, pp. 197–224.

Bennett, C. I. *Comprehensive Multicultural Education: Theory and Practice.* 4th ed. Boston: Allyn and Bacon, 1999.

Bennett, T. "Future Teachers Forge Family Connections." *Young Children* 61(1), 2006, pp. 22–27.

Bergen, D., ed. *Play as a Medium for Learning and Development.* Portsmouth, NH: Heinemann, 1988.

Bergen, D.; R. Reid; L. Torelli. *Educating and Caring for Very Young Children.* New York: Teachers College Press, 2001.

Bernard, B., and D. Quiett. *Nurturing the Nurturer: The Importance of Sound Relationships in Early Childhood Intervention.* San Francisco: WestEd., 2002.

Bernhard, J. K.; M. Freire; F. Torres; and S. Nirdosh. "Latin Americans in a Canadian Primary School: Perspectives of Parents, Teachers, and Children on Cultural Identity and Academic Achievement." *Canadian Journal of Regional Science,* Spring/Summer 1997, pp. 117–137.

Bernhard, J.; M. L. Lefebvre; G. Chud; and R. Lange. *Paths to Equity: Cultural, Linguistic, and Racial Diversity in Canadian Early Childhood Education.* Toronto: York Lanes Press, 1995.

Bernheimer, S. *New Possibilities for Early Childhood Education: Stories from Our Nontraditional Students.* New York: Peter Lang, 2003.

Bhavnagri, N. P., and J. Gonzalez-Mena. "The Cultural Context of Caregiving." *Childhood Education* 74, no. 1 (Fall 1997), pp. 2–8.

Bialystok, E. *Bilingualism in Development: Language, Literacy, and Cognition.* Cambridge, UK: Cambridge University Press, 2001.

Biggar, H. NAEYC Recommendations on Screening and Assessment of Young English-Language Learners. *Young Children* 60(6), 2005, pp. 44–46.

Billman, J. "The Native American Curriculum: Attempting Alternatives to Teepees and Headbands." *Young Children,* September 1992.

Block, M. N.; B. R. Tabachnick; and M. Espinosa-Dulanto. "Teacher Perspectives on the Strengths and Achievements of Young Children: Relationship to Ethnicity, Language, Gender, and Class." In *Diversity and Developmentally Appropriate Practices: Challenges for Early Childhood Education,* eds. B. L. Mallory, and R. S. New. New York: Teachers College Press, 1994, pp. 223–249.

Bloom, P. J.; P. Eisenberg; and E. Eisenberg. "Reshaping Early Childhood Programs to Be More Family Responsive." *America's Family Support Magazine,* 2003, Spring/Summer, pp. 36–38.

Bowlby, J. *Attachment and Loss: Vol. 1: Attachment.* New York: Basic Books, 1969.

Bowman, B. T., and F. M. Stott. "Understanding Development in a Cultural Context: The Challenge for Teachers." In *Diversity and Developmentally Appropriate Practices: Challenges for Early Childhood Education,* eds. B. L. Mallory and R. S. New. New York: Teachers College Press, 1994, pp. 119–133.

Bradley, J., and P. Kibera. "Closing the Gap: Culture and the Promotion of Inclusion in Child Care." *Young Children* 61(1), 2006, pp. 34–41.

Brault, L., and T. Brault. *Children with Challenging Behavior.* Phoenix, AZ: CPG Publishing, 2005.

Brazelton, T. B. "A Child Oriented Approach to Toilet Training." *Pediatrics* 29, no. 1 (January 1962).

Brazelton, T. B., and S. I. Greenspan. *The Irreducible Needs of Children.* Cambridge, MA: Perseus, 2000.

Bredekamp, S., ed. *Developmental Appropriate Practice in Early Childhood Programs Serving Children from Birth Through Age 8.* Washington, DC: National Association for the Education of Young Children, 1997.

Bredekamp, S. "Resolving Contradictions Between Cultural Practices," in *A World of Difference*, ed. C. Copple. Washington, DC: National Association for the Education of Young Children, 2003.

Bredekamp, S., and Copple, C. *Developmentally Appropriate Practice in Early Childhood Programs*, revised ed. Washington, DC: National Association for the Education of Young Children, 1997.

Breslin, D. "Children's Capacity to Develop Resiliency: How to Nurture It. "*Young Children* 60(1), 2005, pp. 47–52.

Briody, J., and K. McGarry. "Using Social Stories to Ease Children's Transitions." *Young Children* 60(5), 2005, pp. 38–42.

Brody, H. *The Other Side of Eden: Hunters, Farmers, and the Shaping of the World.* New York: North Point Press, 2001.

Bronfenbrenner, U. *Making Human Beings Human: Bioecological Perspectives on Human Development.* London: SAGE Publications, 2004.

Bronfenbrenner, U. *The Ecology of Human Development: Experiments by Nature and Design.* Cambridge, MA: Harvard University Press, 1979.

Brooks-Gunn, J.; A. S. Fuligni; and L. J. Berlin, eds. *Early Child Development in the 21st Century.* New York: Teachers College Press, 2003.

Brown, J. E., *The Spiritual Legacy of the American Indian.* New York: Crossroad, 1982.

Bruno, H. E. "Hearing Parents in Every Language: An Invitation to ECE Professionals." *Child Care Information Exchange* 153 (September/October), 2003 pp. 58–60.

Bruno, H. E. "At the End of the Day: Policies, Procedures and Practices to Ensure Smooth Transitions." *Exchange*, September 2005 pp. 66–69.

Butterfield, P.; C. Martin; A. Prairie; and C. A. Martin. *Emotional Connections: Teaching How Relationships Guide Early Learning* (Teacher ed.). Washington, DC: Zero to Three, 2003.

Buysse, V.; D. C. Castro; T. West; and M. L. Skinner. *Addressing the Needs of Latino Children: A National Survey of State Administrators of Early Childhood Programs* (Executive summary). Chapel Hill: The University of North Carolina: FPG Child Development Institute, 2004.

Buysse, V.; P. Wesley; M. R. Coleman; P. Snyder; and P. Winton, eds. *Evidence-Based Practice in the Early Childhood Field.* Washington, DC: Zero to Three, 2006.

Cajete, G. *Look to the Mountain: An Ecology of Indigenous Education.* Durango, CO: Kivaki Press, 1994.

Caldwell, B. "Advocacy is Everybody's Business." In Neugebauer, B. and R. Neugebauer, eds. *The Art of Leadership.* Redmond, WA: Exchange Press, 2003.

Caldwell, L. B. *Bringing Learning to Life: A Reggio Approach to Early Childhood Education.* New York: Teachers College Press, 2003.

Campbell, K. "Energy Program Helps Refugees Make Transition to Life in the U.S." *PG&E Progress,* April 1985.

Cannella, G. S. *Deconstructing Early Childhood Education: Social Justice and Revolution.* New York: Peter Lang, 1997.

Carlson, V. J., and R. L. Harwood. "Understanding and Negotiating Cultural Differences Concerning Early Developmental Competence: The Six Raisin Solution." *Zero to Three* 20(3): 19–23.

Carlsson-Paige, N., and D. E. Levin. "When Push Comes to Shove: Reconsidering Children's Conflicts." In B. Neugebauer, ed., *Behavior: A Beginnings Workshop Book* (pp. 39–41). Redmond, WA: Exchange, 2005.

Carr, M. *Assessment in Early Childhood Settings: Learning Stories.* Thousand Oaks, CA: Sage, 2001.

Carroll, R. *Cultural Misunderstandings: The French-American Experience.* Chicago: University of Chicago Press, 1988.

Casper, V. "Very Young Children in Lesbian- and Gay-Headed Families: Moving Beyond Acceptance." Zero to Three, January, 2003, pp. 18–26.

Caudill, W., and H. Winstein. "Maternal Care and Infant Behavior in Japan and America." *Psychiatry* 1969, 32, pp. 12–43.

Chan, I. *The Hmong in America: Their Cultural Continuities and Discontinuities.* St. Paul, MN: University of Minnesota, 1981, ERIC, ED 217 105.

Chan, J. "Chinese Intelligence." In *The Handbook of Chinese Psychology,* ed. M. H. Bond. Hong Kong: Oxford University Press, 1996.

Chang, H. *Affirming Children's Roots: Cultural and Linguistic Diversity in Early Care and Education.* San Francisco: California Tomorrow, 1993.

Chang, H. *Getting Ready for Quality: The Critical Importance of Developing and Supporting a Skilled, Ethnically and Linguistically Diverse Early Childhood Workforce.* Oakland, CA: California Tomorrow, 2005.

Chang, H. N.; A. Muckelroy; and D. Pulido-Tobiassen. *Looking In, Looking Out: Redefining Child Care and Education in a Diverse Society.* Oakland, California: California Tomorrow, 1996.

Chang, I. *The Chinese in America: A Narrative History.* New York: Viking, 2003.

Chao, R. "Beyond Parental Control and Authoritarian Parenting Style: Understanding Chinese Parenting Through the Cultural Notion of Training." *Child Development* 65, 1994, pp. 1111–1119.

Chen, X.; K. Rubin; G. Gen; P. Hastings; H. Chen; and S. Stewart. "Child-Rearing Attitudes and Behavioral Inhibition in Chinese and Canadian Toddlers: A Cross-Cultural Study." *Developmental Psychology* 34, no. 4, 1998, pp. 677–686.

Cheng, L-R. L. "Sociocultural Adjustment of Chinese-American Students." In C.C. Park and M. M. Chi, eds., *Asian American Education: Prospects and Challenges,* 1999 (pp. 1–17).

Child Care Health Program. *Serving Biracial and Multiethnic Children and Their Families.* Berkeley, CA: The Child Care Health Program, 2003.

Children's Defense Fund. *The State of America's Children.* Washington, DC: Children's Defense Fund, 2004.

Chodron, P. *When Things Fall Apart.* Boston: Shambhala, 2000.

Christian, L. G. "Understanding Families: Applying Family Systems Theory to Early Childhood Practice." *Young Children* 61(1), 12–21.

Chu, G. "The Changing Concept of Self in Contemporary China." In *Culture and Self: Asian and Western Perspectives,* eds. A. J. Marsella, G. GeVos, and F. L. K. Hsu. New York: Tavistock, 1985, pp. 252–277.

Chud, G., and R. Fahlman. *Early Childhood Education for a Multicultural Society: A Handbook for Educators.* Vancouver: Pacific Educational Press, 1990.

Clarke-Stewart, A., and V. D. Alhusen. *What We Know About Childcare.* New Haven, CT: Harvard University Press, 2005.

Clay, J., "Creating Safe, Just Places to Learn for Children of Lesbian and Gay Parents: The NAEYC Code of Ethics in Action." *Young Children* 59(6). 2004, pp. 34–38.

Colker, L. J. *The Cooking Book: Fostering Young Children's Learning and Delight.* Washington, DC: National Association for the Education of Young Children, 2005.

Coll, C, G.; G. Lamberty; R. Jenkins; H. P. McAdoo; K. Crnic; B. Wasik; G. Hanna; and H. Vazquez. "An Integrative Model for the Study of Developmental Competencies in Minority Children." *Child Development* 67, 1996, pp. 1891–1914.

Columbo, M. "Reflections From Teachers of Culturally Diverse Children." *Young Children* 60(6) November, 2005.

Comer, J. "Research and the Black Backlash." *American Journal of Orthopsychiatry* 40, 1970, pp. 8–11.

Comer, J. P., and A. F. Poussaint. *Black Child Care.* New York: Simon & Schuster, 1975.

Cook, C., and C. Porter. *Babies and Toddlers: Considering Multicultural Perspectives.* Richmond, Victoria, Australia: Free Kindergarten Association Multicultural Resource Centre, 1996.

Cook, R. E.; A. Tessier; M. D. Klein. *Adapting Early Childhood Curricula for Children in Inclusive Settings, 5th edition.* Columbus, OH: Merrill, 2000.

Cooper, R., and E. Jones. "Enjoying Diversity." *Exchange,* October 2005, pp. 6–9.

Copple, C., ed. *A World of Difference: Readings on Teaching Children in a Diverse Society.* Washington, DC: National Association for the Education of Young Children, 2003.

Copple, C., S. Bredekamp. *Basics of Developmentally Appropriate Practice: An Introduction for Teachers of Children 3 to 6.* Washington, DC: National Association for the Education of Young Children, 2006.

Corsaro, W. A. *We're Friends, Right?: Inside Kids' Cultures.* Washington, DC: Joseph Henry Press, 2003.

Corsaro, W. A., and L. Molinari. *I Compagni: Understanding Children's Transition from Preschool to Elementary School.* New York: Teachers College Press, 2005.

Costello, J. and J. Haver. *Zen Parenting*. Beltsville, MD: Robins Lane Press, 2004.

Covey, Stephan R. *Foreword*. In K. Patterson, J. Grenny, R. McMillan, and A. Switzler. *Crucial Conversations*. New York: McGraw-Hill, 2002.

Crawford, J. *Bilingual Education: History, Politics, Theory and Practice*. Trenton, NJ: Crane, 1989.

Cronin, S.; L. Derman-Sparks; S. Henry; C. Olatunji; and S. York. *Future Vision, Present Work: Learning from the Culturally Relevant Anti-Bias Leadership Project*. St. Paul, MN: Redleaf, 1998.

Cummins, J. *Negotiating Identities: Education for Empowerment in a Diverse Society*. Ontario, CA: California Association for Bilingual Education, 1996.

Cummins, J. "Alternative Paradigms in Bilingual Education Research." *Educational Researcher* 28, no. 7 (1999), pp. 26–32, 41.

Curtis, D., and M. Carter. *Designs for Living and Learning*, St. Paul, MN: Redleaf, 2003.

Curtis, D., and M. Carter. *The Art of Awareness*. St. Paul, MN: Redleaf, 2000.

Cushner, K.; A. McClelland; and P. Stafford. *Human Diversity in Education: An Integrative Approach*, 4th ed. Boston: McGraw-Hill, 2003.

D'Addesio; J., B. Grob; and L. Furman. "Social Studies: Learning About the World Around Us. *Young Children* 60(5), 2005, pp. 50–57.

Dahlberg, G.; P. Moss; and A. Pence. *Beyond Quality in Early Childhood Education and Care*. London: Falmer Press, 1999.

Daniel, J., and S. Friedman. "Preparing Teachers to Work With Culturally and Linguistically Diverse Children." *Young Children* 60(6), 2005.

Daper, L., and B. Duffy. "Working with Parents." In G. Pugh, ed. *Contemporary Issues in the Early Years: Working Collaboratively for Children*. London: Paul Chapman Publishing, 2001.

Darling-Hammond, L.; J. French; and S. P. Garcia-Lopez. *Learning to Teach for Social Justice*. New York: Teachers College Press, 2002.

David, J.; O. Onchonga; R. Drew; R. Grass; R. Stechuk; and M. S. Burns. "Head Start Embraces Language Diversity." *Young Children* 60(6), 2005, pp. 40–43.

David, M., and G. Appell. (2001). "Lóczy: An Unusual Approach to Mothering." In J. M. Clark: revised translation by J. Falk, ed., *Lóczy ou Le Maternage Insolite*. Budapest: Association Pikler-Lóczy for Young Children, 2001.

Davis, C., and A. Yang. *Parents and Teachers Working Together*. Turners Falls, MA: Northeast Foundation for Children, 2005.

Day, M., and R. Parlakian. *How Culture Shapes Social-Emotional Development: Implications for Practice in Infant-Family Programs*. Washington, DC: Zero to Three, 2004.

DeLoache, J. and A. Gottlieb. *A World of Babies: Imagined Childcare Guides for Seven Societies*. New York: Cambridge University Press, 2000.

Deloria, V., Jr., and D. R. Wildcat. *Power and Place: Indian Education in America*. Golden, CO: American Indian Graduate Center and Fulcrum Resources, 2001.

Delpit, L. "The Silenced Dialogue: Power and Pedagogy in Educating Other People's Children." *Harvard Educational Review* 58, no. 3, 1988, pp. 280–298.

Delpit, L. *Other People's Children: Cultural Conflict in the Classroom.* New York: New Press, 1995.

Delpit, L., and J. K. Dowdy, eds. *The Skin That We Speak.* New York: The New Press, 2002.

Derman-Sparks, L. *The Antibias Curriculum.* Washington, DC: National Association for the Education of Young Children, 1989.

Derman-Sparks, L. "The Process of Culturally Sensitive Care." In *Infant/Toddler Caregiving: A Guide to Culturally Sensitive Care,* ed. P. Mangione. Sacramento: Far West Laboratory and California Department of Education, 1995.

Derman-Sparks, L. and the ABC Task Force. *Antibias Curriculum: Tools for Empowering Young Children.* Washington, DC: National Association for the Education of Young Children, 1989.

Derman-Sparks, L., and C. B. Phillips. *Teaching/Learning Anti-Racism.* New York: Teachers College Press, 1997.

Derman-Sparks, L., and P. G. Ramsey. "What If All the Children in My Class Are White?" *Young Children* 60(6), 2005, pp. 20–27.

Derman-Sparks, L., and P. G. Ramsey. *What If All the Kids Are White: Antibias Multicultural Education with Young Children and Families.* New York: Teachers College Press, 2006.

DiNatale, L. "Developing High-Quality Family Involvement Programs in Early Childhood Settings." *Young Children* 57(5), 2002, pp. 90–95.

Dirk, P. "The Power of Feelings: Emotions, Imagination, and the Construction of Meaning in Adult Learning." In S. Merriam, ed. *The New Update on Adult Learning Theory,* pp. 63–72. San Francisco: Jossey-Bass, 2001.

Dombro, A. L., and C. Lerner. "Sharing the Care of Infants and Toddlers." *Young Children* 61(1), 2006, pp. 29–33.

Donaldson, G. A. *Cultivating Leadership in Schools: Connecting People, Purpose and Practice.* New York: Teachers College Press, 2001.

Dorris, M. *Paper Trail.* New York: HarperCollins, 1994.

Dragon, P. B. *A How-To Guide for Teaching English Language Learners in the Primary Classroom.* Washington, DC: National Association for the Education of Young Children, 2004.

Dreikurs, R., and L. Grey. *Logical Consequences: A New Approach to Discipline.* New York: Dutton, 1990.

Dung, T. N. "Understanding Asian Families: A Vietnamese Perspective." *Children Today,* March–April 1984.

Duong, T. B. *A Handbook for Teachers of Vietnamese Students: Hints for Dealing with Cultural Differences in Schools.* Arlington, VA: Center for Applied Linguistics, 1975.

Eberly, J. L., and S. L. Golbeck. "Blocks, Building and Mathematics: Influences of Task Format and Gender of Play Partners Among Preschoolers." In S. Reifel and M. H. Brown, ed., *Advances in Early Education and Day Care: Social Contexts of Early Education, and Reconceptualizing Play (II)* (2nd ed., vol. 13, pp. 39–54). Greenwich, CT: Jai Press, 2004.

Edelman, M. W. "Children in America: A Report Card." Interview in *Parade Magazine*, p. 13, October 19, 2003.

Edelman, L. "A Relationship Based Approach to Early Intervention." *Resources and Connections* 3(2), 2004, pp. 2–10.

Edwards, C. P., and L. Gandini. "Teachers' Expectations About the Timing of Developmental Skills: A Cross-Cultural Study." *Young Children*, May 1989, pp. 15–19.

Edwards, C. P.; L. Gandini; and D. Giovaninni. "The Contrasting Developmental Timetables of Parents and Preschool Teachers in Two Cultural Communities," In *Parents' Cultural Belief Systems*, eds. S. Harkness and C. M. Super. New York: Guiliford Press, 1996, pp. 270–288.

Edwards, P.; K. L. Fear; and M. A. Gallego. "Role of Parents in Responding to Issues of Linguistic and Cultural Diversity," In *Meeting the Challenge of Linguistic and Cultural Diversity in Early Childhood Education*, eds. E. E. Garcia, and B. McLaughlin, with B. Spokek, and O. N. Saracho. New York: Teachers College Press, 1995, pp. 141–153.

Eggers-Pierola, C. *Connections and Commitments: A Latino-Based Framework for Early Childhood Educators.* Newton, MA: Educational Development Center, 2002.

Eggers-Pierola, C. *Connections and Commitments: Reflecting Latino Values in Early Childhood Programs.* Portsmouth, NH: Heinemann, 2005.

Ehling, M. B. "The Mexican American (El Chicano)," In *Culture and Childrearing*, ed. A. L. Clark. Philadelphia: F. A. Davis, 1981.

Elkind, D. "Work, Chores, and Play: Setting a Healthy Balance." *Exchange*, 2006, pp. 39–41.

Ellison, S. *Don't Be So Defensive!* Kansas City, MO: Andrews McMeel, 1998.

Epstein, J. L. "Families, Schools, and Community Partnerships." *Young Children* 61(1), 2006, pp. 40.

Fadiman, A. *The Spirit Catches You and You Fall Down: A Hmong Child, Her American Doctors, and the Collision of Two Cultures.* New York: Noonday Press, 1997.

Fantini, M. D., and R. Cardenas, eds. *Parenting in a Multicultural Society.* New York: Longman, 1980.

Fasoli, L., and J. Gonzalez-Mena. "Let's Be Real: Authenticity in Child Care." *Exchange*, March 1997, pp. 35–40.

Feeney, S., and N. K. Freeman. *Ethics and the Early Childhood Educator: 2005 Code Edition.* Washington, DC: National Association for the Education of Young Children, 2005.

Fenichel, E. S., and L. Eggbeer. *Preparing Practitioners to Work with Infants, Toddlers, and Their Families: Issues and Recommendations for the Professions.* Arlington, VA: National Center for Clinical Infant Programs, 1990.

Fenion, A. "Collaborative Steps: Paving the Way to Kindergarten for Young Children with Disabilities." *Young Children* 60(2), 2005, pp. 32–37.

Fernandez, M. T., and K. Marfo. "Enhancing Infant-Toddler Adjustment During Transitions to Care." *Zero to Three* 26, 2005, pp. 41–48.

Fernea, E. W. *Children in the Muslim Middle East.* Austin: University of Texas Press, 1995.

Fillmore, L. W. "Luck, Fish Seeds, and Second-Language Learning." In *On Becoming a Language Educator,* eds. C. P. Casanave, and S. R. Schecter. Mahwah, NJ: Erlbaum, 1997.

Fisher, R., and W. Ury. *Getting to Yes: Negotiating Agreement Without Giving In.* New York: Penguin Books, 1991.

Fitzgerald, D. *Parent Partnership in the Early Years,* London: Continuum, 2004.

France, P. "Working with Young Bilingual Children." *Early Child Development and Care* 10, 1980, pp. 283–292.

Freeman, D. E., and Y. S. Freeman. *Between Worlds: Access to Second Language Acquisition.* Portsmouth, NH: Heinemann, 1994.

Freeman, N. K., and S. Feeney. "The NAEYC Code is a Living Document." *Young Children* 59(6), 2004, pp. 12–16.

French, K. "Supporting a Child with Special Health Care Needs." *Young Children* 59(2), 2004, pp. 62–63.

French, K., and H. M. Cain. "Including a Young Child with Spina Bifida." *Young Children* 61(3), 2006, pp. 78–85.

Friedman, S. "Social Studies in Action." *Young Children* 60(5), 2005, pp. 44–47.

Fromberg, D. P. *Play and Meaning in Early Childhood Education.* Boston: Allyn and Bacon, 2002.

Frost, J. L.; S. C. Worthams; and S. Reifel. *Play and Child Development* (2nd ed.). Upper Saddle River, NJ: Merrill/Prentice Hall, 2005.

Gaines, P. *Laughing in the Dark.* New York: Anchor, 1994.

Galinsky, E. "From Our President: Why Are Some Parent/Teacher Partnerships Clouded with Difficulties?" *Young Children* 45, no. 5 (July 1990), pp. 2–3, 38–39.

Gandini, L., and C. Pope, eds. *Bambini: The Italian Approach to Infant/Toddler Care.* New York: Teachers College Press, 2001.

Gandini, L.; L. Hill; and C. Schwall, eds. *In the Spirit of the Studio: Learning from the Atelier of Reggio Emilia.* New York: Teachers College Press, 2005.

Gantner, M. "Lessons Learned from My Students in the Barrio." *Educational Leadership* 54, no. 97 (1997), pp. 44–45.

Gao, G.; S. Ting-Toomey; and W. Gudykunst. "Chinese Communication Processes." In *The Handbook of Chinese Psychology,* ed. M. H. Bond. Hong Kong: Oxford University Press, 1996, pp. 280–293.

Garcia, E. *Understanding and Meeting the Challenge of Student Cultural Diversity.* Boston: Houghton Mifflin, 1994.

Garcia, E. *Student Cultural Diversity: Understanding and Meeting the Challenge,* 2nd ed. New York: Houghton Mifflin, 1999.

Garcia, E. E., and B. McLaughlin, eds., with B. Spokek, and O. N. Saracho. *Meeting the Challenge of Linguistic and Cultural Diversity in Early Childhood Education.* New York: Teachers College Press, 1995.

Gardner, H. *Frames of Mind.* New York: Basic Books, 1983.

Gardner, H. *To Open Minds, Chinese Clues to the Dilemma of Contemporary Education.* New York: Basic Books, 1989.

Garner, A. *Families Like Mine: Children of Gay Parents Tell it Like it Is.* New York: HarperCollins Publishers, 2004.

Garrett, W. E. "The Hmong of Laos: No Place to Run." *National Geographic* 141 (January 1974), pp. 78–111.

Garrett, W. E., "Thailand: Refuge from Terror." *National Geographic* 157, (May 1980), pp. 633–642.

Gartrell, D. "Guidance Matters." *Young Children* 60(6), 2005, pp. 84–85.

Gartrell, D. "Guidance Matters: Boys and Men Teachers." *Young Children* 61(3), 2006, pp. 92–93.

Gelnaw, A. "Belonging: Including Children of Gay and Lesbian Parents—and All Children—in Your Program." *Exchange,* 2005, pp. 42–44.

Gelnaw, A.; M. Brickley; H. Marsh; and D. Ryan. *Opening Doors: Lesbian and Gay Parents and Schools.* Washington, DC: Family Pride Coalition, 2004.

Genishi, C., and M. B. Brainard. "Assessment of Bilingual Children: A Dilemma Seeking Solutions." In *Meeting the Challenge of Linguistic and Cultural Diversity in Early Childhood Education,* eds. E. E. Garcia, and B. McLaughlin, with B. Spokek, and O. N. Saracho. New York: Teachers College Press, 1995, pp. 49–62.

Genishi, C., and A. Haas Dyson. "Ways of Talking: Respecting Differences." In B. Neugebauer, ed., *Literacy: A Beginnings Workshop Book* (pp. 32–25). Redmond, WA: Exchange, 2005.

Gerber, M., ed. *Manual for Resources for Infant Educators.* Los Angeles: Resources for Infant Educators, 1988.

Gerber, M. "RIE Principles and Practices." In S. Petrie and S. Owen, eds., *Authentic Relationships in Group Care for Infants and Toddlers: Resources for Infant Educarers (RIE) Principles into Practice* (pp. 35–49). London and Philadelphia: Jessica Kingsley Publishers, 2005.

Gerber, M., and A. Johnson. *Your Self-Confident Baby.* New York: Wiley, 1998.

Gestwicki, C. *Home, School, and Community Relations: A Guide to Working with Parents.* Albany, New York: Thompson Delmar, 2004.

Getch, Y. Q., and S. Neuharth-Pritchett. "Asthma Management in Early Care and Education Settings." *Young Children* 59(2),2004, pp. 34–41.

Golbeck, S. L. "Building Foundations for Spatial Literacy in Early Childhood." *Young Children* 60(6), 2005, pp. 72–83.

Gomez, M. L. "Breaking Silences: Building New Stories of Classroom Life Through Teacher Transformation." In *Reconceptualizing the Early Childhood Curriculum: Beginning the Dialogue*, eds. S. A. Kessler, and B. B. Swadener. New York: Teachers College Press, 1992, pp. 165–188.

Gonzalez, D. *Hablemos de Ninos.* Caguas, Puerto Rico: Impresos Taino, 2001.

Gonzalez, M.; L. C. Moll; and C. Amanti. *Funds of Knowledge: Theorizing Practices in Households, Communities, and Classrooms.* Mahwah, NJ: Erlbaum, 2005.

Gonzalez, N.; L. C. Moll; and C. Amanti. *Funds of Knowledge: Theorizing Practices In Households, Communities, and Classrooms.* Mahwah, NJ: Erlbaum, 2005.

Gonzalez-Mena, J. "English as a Second Language for Preschool Children." In *Language in Early Childhood Education*, rev. ed., ed. C. B. Cazden. Washington, DC: NAEYC, 1981, pp. 127–132.

Gonzalez-Mena, J. "Do You Have Cultural Tunnel Vision?" *Child Care Information Exchange*, July–August 1991, pp. 29–31.

Gonzalez-Mena, J. "Taking a Culturally Sensitive Approach in Infant-Toddler Programs." *Young Children* 47, no. 2 (January 1992), pp. 4–9.

Gonzalez-Mena, J. *The Child in the Family and the Community.* New York: Merrill, 1993.

Gonzalez-Mena, J. "The Man Who Ordered a Tortilla and Got an Omelette." In *Family Information Services.* Minneapolis, MN: Family Information Services, 1995, pp. M & O, 5–6.

Gonzalez-Mena, J. "Cultural Sensitivity in Routine Caregiving Tasks." In *Infant/Toddler Caregiving: A Guide to Culturally Sensitive Care*, ed. P. Mangione. Sacramento: Far West Laboratory and California Department of Education, 1995.

Gonzalez-Mena, J. "When Values Collide." *Exchange*, March 1996, pp. 30–32.

Gonzalez-Mena, J. "Lessons from My Mother-in-Law: A Story about Discipline." *Exchange*, January 1997, pp. 44–46.

Gonzalez-Mena, J. "Cross-Cultural Conferences." *Exchange*, July 1997, pp. 55–57.

Gonzalez-Mena, J. "Understanding the Parent's Perspective: Independence or Interdependence?" *Exchange*, September 1997, pp. 61–63.

Gonzalez-Mena, J. "Dialogue to Understanding Across Cultures." *Exchange*, July 1999, pp. 6–8.

Gonzalez-Mena, J. "In the Spirit of Partnership: High Maintenance Parent or Cultural Difference?" *Exchange*, July 2000.

Gonzalez-Mena, J. "Personal Power: Creating New Realities." *Child Care Information Exchange*, January 2001, pp. 59–61.

Gonzalez-Mena, J. "Making Meaning of Separation: Contrasting Pictures of the First Good-Bye." *The First Years, Nga Tau Tuatahi* (New Zealand Journal of Infant and Toddler Education) 3, no. 2 (September 2001).

Gonzalez-Mena, J. "Culture, Identity, and Caregiving Practices." *Every Child* (Journal of Australian Early Childhood Association) 7, no. 3 (Winter 2001), pp. 2–3.

Gonzalez-Mena, J. "Cross-Cultural Infant Care and Issues of Equity and Social Justice." *Contemporary Issues in Early Childhood* online journal at www.triangle.co.uk/ciec 2, no. 3, 2001.

Gonzalez-Mena, J. "Personal Power: Creating new realties." *Child Care Information Exchange*, (2002, January/February) pp. 59–62.

Gonzalez-Mena, J. "Working with Cultural Differences: Individualism and Collectivism," *The First Years: Nga TauTuatahi* (New Zealand Journal of Infant and Toddler Education) 3, no. 2 (September 2002).

Gonzalez-Mena, J. "What Can an Orphanage Teach Us? Lessons from Budapest." *Young Children* 59(5), 2004, pp. 26–30.

Gonzalez-Mena, J. *Foundations of Early Childhood Education in a Diverse Society.* New York: McGraw-Hill, 2005.

Gonzalez-Mena, J. *The Child in the Family and the Community* 4th edition. Upper Saddle River, NJ: Merrill Prentice Hall, 2006.

Gonzalez-Mena, J. *50 Strategies for Working and Communicating with Parents.* Columbus, OH: Merrill, 2006.

Gonzalez-Mena, J. "Caregiving Routines and Literacy." In S. E. Rosenkoetter and J. Knapp-Philo, eds., *Learning to Read the World: Language and Literacy in the First Three Years.* Washington, DC: Zero to Three (forthcoming).

Gonzalez-Mena, J., and J. K. Bernhard, "Out-of-Home Care of Infants and Toddlers: A Call for Cultural and Linguistic Continuity." *Interaction* 12(2), Summer 1998, pp. 14–15.

Gonzalez-Mena, J., and N. P. Bhavnagri. "Diversity and Infant-Toddler Caregiving," *Young Children*, September 2000.

Gonzalez-Mena, J., and N. P. Bhavnagri. "Cultural Differences in Sleeping Practices." *Exchange*, March 2001, pp. 91–93.

Gonzalez-Mena, J.; E. Chahin; and L. Briley. "The Pikler Institute: A Unique Approach to Caring for Children." *Exchange*, November/December 2005, pp. 49–51.

Gonzalez-Mena, J., and D. W. Eyer. *Infants, Toddlers, and Caregivers.* Mountain View, CA: Mayfield, 2001.

Gonzalez-Mena, J., and D. Eyer. *Infants, Toddlers, and Caregivers.* New York: McGraw-Hill, 2006.

Gonzalez-Mena, J., and I. Shareef. "Discussing Diverse Perspectives on Guidance." *Young Children* 60(6), 2005, pp. 34–38.

Gonzalez-Mena, J., and A. Stonehouse. "In the Child's Best Interests." *Child Care Information Exchange*, November 1995, pp. 17–20.

Gonzalez-Mena, J., and A. Stonehouse. "High-Maintenance Parent or Parent Partner? Working with a Parent's Concern." *Child Care Information Exchange*, 16–18, 2003, July/August.

Gould, P., and J. Sullivan. *The Inclusive Early Childhood Classroom.* Beltsville, MD: Gryphon House, 1999.

Gray, H. "You Go Away and You Come Back." *Young Children* 59(5), 2004, pp. 100–107.

Greenberg, P. "Teaching About Native Americans or Teaching About People, Including Native Americans?" *Young Children,* September 1992.

Greenfield, P. M. "Independence and Interdependence as Developmental Scripts: Implications for Theory, Research, and Practice." In *Cross-Cultural Roots of Minority Child Development* (pp. 1–37) eds. P. M. Greenfield, and R. R. Cocking. Mahwah, NJ: Lawrence Erlbaum, 1994.

Greenfield, P. M., and R. R. Cocking. *Cross-Cultural Roots of Minority Child Development.* Hillsdale, NJ: Erlbaum, 1994.

Greenfield, P. M., Quiroz, B., and Raeff, C. "Cross-Cultural Conflict and Harmony in the Social Construction of the Child." In *New Directions for Child and Adolescent Development* 87 (pp. 93–108), eds. S. Harkness, C. Raeff, and C. M. Super. San Francisco: Jossey-Bass, 2000.

Greenman, J. "Living in the Real World: Diversity and Conflict." *Exchange,* October 1989, p. 11.

Greenman, J. "Parent Partnerships: What They Don't Teach You Can Hurt." *Child Care Information Exchange,* 78–82, (1998, November/December).

Greenman, J. "Places for Childhood Include Parents, Too." In *The Art of Leadership,* eds. B. Neugebauer, and R. Neugebauer. Redmond, WA: Child Care Information Exchange, 2003.

Greenman, J. *What Happened to My World? Helping Children Cope with Natural Disasters and Castastrophe.* Washington, DC: National Association for the Education of Young Children, 2006.

Greenspan, S. I. *Building Healthy Minds.* Cambridge, MA: Perseus, 1999.

Greenspan, S. I. *The First Idea: How Symbols, Language, and Intelligence Evolved from Our Primate Ancestors to Modern Humans.* Cambridge, MA: Da Capo Press, 2004.

Greenspan, S. I., and S. Wieder. *The Child with Special Needs.* Reading, MA: Perseus Books, 1998.

Grieshaber, S., and G. S. Cannella. *Embracing Identities in Early Childhood Education: Diversity and Possibilities.* New York: Teachers College Press, 2001.

Grisham-Brown, J.; M. L. Hemmeter; and K. Pretti-Frontczak. *Blended Practices for Teaching Young Children in Inclusive Settings.* Baltimore, MD: Brookes Publishing, 2005.

Gudykunst, W. B., ed. *Intercultural Communication Theory: Current Perspectives.* Beverly Hills, CA: Sage, 1983.

Guralnick, M. J., ed. *Early Childhood Inclusion: Focus on Change.* Baltimore, MD: Brookes Publishing, 2001.

Hakuta, K. *Mirror of Language.* New York: Basic Books, 1986.

Hale, J. E. "An African-American Early Childhood Education Program: Visions for Children." In *Reconceptualizing the Early Childhood Curriculum: Beginning the Dialogue*, eds. S. A. Kessler, and B. B. Swadener. New York: Teachers College Press, 1992, pp. 205–224.

Hale, J. E. *Black Children: Their Roots, Culture, and Learning Styles.* Baltimore, MD: Johns Hopkins University Press, 1986.

Hale, J. E. "The Transmission of Cultural Values to Young African American Children." *Young Children* 46, no. 6 (September 1991), pp. 7–15.

Hall, E. T. *Beyond Culture.* Garden City, NY: Anchor Books, 1977.

Hanson, M. J., and E. W. Lynch. *Understanding Families: Approaches to Diversity, Disability, and Risk.* Baltimore, MD: Brookes Publishing, 2004.

Harkness, S., and C. M. Super, eds. *Parents' Cultural Belief Systems.* New York: Guiliford Press, 1996.

Harwood, R. L.; J. G. Miller; and N. L. Irizarry. *Culture and Attachment: Perceptions of the Child in Context.* New York, Guilford Press, 1995.

Hatch, J. A. *Teaching in the New Kindergarten.* Clifton Park, NY: Thomson Delmar Learning, 2005.

Hayden, J., ed. *Landscapes in Early Childhood Education: Cross-National Perspectives on Empowerment.* New York: Peter Lang, 2000.

Heath, S. B. *Ways with Words: Language, Life and Work in Communities and Classrooms.* Cambridge: Cambridge University Press, 1983.

Heffron, M. C.; B. Ivins; and D. Weston. "Finding an Authentic Voice. Use of Self: Essential Learning Process for Relationship-based Work." *Infants and Young Children* 18(4), 2005, pp. 323–336.

Hildebrand, V.; L. A. Phenice; M. M. Gray; and R. P. Hines. *Knowing and Serving Diverse Families.* Englewood Cliffs, NJ: Prentice Hall, 1996.

Hofstede, G. "National Cultures Revisited." *Behavior Science Research* 18, no. 4 (1983), pp. 285–305.

Hofstede, G. *Culture's Consequences: Comparing Values, Behaviors, Institutions, and Organizations Across Nations.* 2nd ed. Thousand Oaks, CA: Sage, 2001.

Hollowell, E. *When You Worry about the Child You Love.* New York: Fireside, 1996.

Holman, L. J. "Meeting the Needs of Hispanic Immigrants." *Educational Leadership* 54, no. 7 (1997), pp. 37–38.

Holtzman, W. H.; R. Diaz-Guerrero; and J. D. Swartz. *Personality Development in Two Cultures: A Cross-Cultural Longitudinal Study of School Children in Mexico and the United States.* Austin: University of Texas Press, 1975, p. 359.

hooks, b. *Killing Rage: Ending Racism.* New York: Henry Holt, 1995.

hooks, b. *Rock My Soul: Black People and Self-Esteem.* New York: Atria, 2003.

Hopson, D. P., and D. S. Hopson. *Different and Wonderful: Raising Black Children in a Race-Conscious Society.* Englewood Cliffs, NJ: Prentice Hall, 1990.

Howard, G. R. "Whites in Multicultural Education: Rethinking Our Role." *Phi Delta Kappan*, September 1993, pp. 36–41.

Howard, G. R. *We Can't Teach What We Don't Know*. New York: Teachers College Press, 1999.

Howes, C., and S. Ritchie. *A Matter of Trust*. New York: Teachers College Press, 2002.

Hsu, F. L. K. *Americans and Chinese: Purpose and Fulfillment in Great Civilizations*. Garden City, NY: Natural History Press, 1970.

Hsu, F. *Americans and Chinese: Passage to Differences*, 3rd ed. Honolulu: University Press of Hawaii, 1981.

Hsu, J. "The Chinese Family: Relations, Problems, and Therapy." in *Chinese Culture and Mental Health*, eds. W. S. Tseng, and D. Y. H. Wu. Orlando, FL: Academic Press, 1985.

Huntsinger, C. S.; P. R. Huntsinger; W-D. Ching; and C-B. Lee. "Understanding Cultural Contexts Fosters Sensitive Caregiving of Chinese-American Children." *Young Children* 55(6), 2000, pp. 7–12, 14–15.

Hyson, M. *The Emotional Development of Young Children*, 2nd ed. New York: Teachers College Press, 2004.

Hyun, E. *Making Sense of Developmentally and Culturally Appropriate Practice (DCAP) in Early Childhood Education*. New York, Peter Lang, 1998.

Jacobson, T. *Confronting Our Discomfort: Clearing the Way for Anti-Bias in Early Childhood*. Portsmouth, NH: Heinemann, 2003.

Jamblon, J. R.; A. L. Dombro; and M. L. Dichtelmiller. *The Power of Observation*. Washington, DC: Teaching Strategies, 1999.

Jipson, J. "Extending the Discourse on Developmental Appropriateness: A Developmental Perspective." *Early Education and Development* 2, no. 2 (1991), pp. 95–108.

Johnson, D., and R. Johnson. "Cultural Diversity and Cooperative Learning." ed. J. W. Putname. In *Cooperative Learning and Strategies for Inclusion*. 2nd ed. Baltimore: Brookes, 1998.

Johnson-Powell, G., and J. Yamamoto, eds. *Transcultural Child Development*. New York: Wiley, 1997.

Johnston, P. H. *Choice Words: How Our Language Affects Children's Learning*. Portland, ME: Stenhouse, 2004.

Jones, E. *Teaching Adults: An Active Learning Approach*. Washington, DC: National Association for the Education of Young Children, 1987.

Jones, E., and R. Cooper. *Playing to Get Smart*. New York: Teachers College Press, 2006.

Jones, E., and L. Derman-Sparks. "Meeting the Challenge of Diversity." *Young Children* 47, no. 2 (January 1992), pp.12–18.

Jones, E., and J. Nimmo. *Emergent Curriculum*. Washington, DC: National Association for Education of Young Children, 1994.

Kagan, J. *The Nature of the Child.* New York: Basic Books, 1984.

Kagiticibasi, C. *Family and Human Development Across Cultures.* Mahwah, NJ: Erlbaum, 1996.

Kaiser, B., and J. S. Rasminsky. *Challenging Behavior in Young Children: Understanding, Preventing, and Responding Effectively.* Boston: Allyn and Bacon, 2003.

Kaiser, B., and J. S. Rasminsky. "Including Children with Challenging Behavior in Your Child Care Community." *Exchange,* 2005, July, pp. 32–34.

Kals, E., and H. Ittner. "Children's Environmental Identity, Indicators and Behavior Impacts." In S. Clayton, and S. Opotow, eds. *Identity and the Natural Environment— the Psychological Significance of Nature.* Cambridge, MA: The MIT Press, 2003.

Katz, L. "Child Development Knowledge and Teacher Preparation: Confronting Assumptions." *Early Childhood Research Quarterly* 11, no. 2 (1996), pp. 135–146.

Katz, L., and T. K. Schery. "Including Children with Hearing Loss in Early Childhood Programs." *Young Children* 61(1), 2004, pp. 86–95.

Kawagley, A. O. *A Yupiaz Worldview: A Pathway to Ecology and Spirit.* Prospect Heights, IL: Waveland Press, 1995.

Kendall, F. *Diversity in the Classroom.* New York: Teachers College Press, 1983.

Kennedy, G., ed. *From the Center of the Earth: Stories Out of the Peace Corps.* Santa Monica, CA: Clover Park Press, 1991.

Kersey, K., and C. R. Malley. "Helping Children Develop Resiliency: Providing Supportive Relationships." *Young Children* 60(1), 2005, pp. 53–58.

Kessler, S., and B. Swaderner. *Reconceptualizing the Early Childhood Curriculum, Beginning the Dialogue.* New York: Teachers College Press, 1992.

Keyser, J. "Creating Partnerships with Families: Problem-solving Through Communication." *Child Care Information Exchange,* no. 138, 2001, pp. 4–7.

Kincheloe, J. L.; S. R. Steinberg; N. M. Rodriguez; and R. E. Chennault, eds. *White Reign: Deploying Whiteness in America.* New York: St. Martin's Press, 1998.

King, A., and M. Bong. "The Confucian Paradigm of Man: A Sociological View." In *Chinese Culture and Mental Health,* eds. W. S. Tseng, and D. Y. H. Wu. Orlando, FL: Academic Press, 1985, pp. 29–45.

Kitano, M. K. "Early Childhood Education for Asian American Children." *Young Children,* January 1980, pp. 13–26.

Kitayama, S.; H. Markus; and H. Matsumoto. "Culture, Self, and Emotion: A Cultural Perspective on 'Self-Conscious' Emotions." In *Self-Conscious Emotions: The Psychology of Shame, Guilt, Embarrassment, and Pride,* eds. J. P. Tangeny, and K. W. Fischer. New York: Guiliford Press, 1995.

Klass, C. S. *The Child Care Provider.* Baltimore: Brookes, 1999.

Klein, M. D., and D. Chen. *Working with Children from Culturally Diverse Backgrounds.* New York: Delmar 2001.

Knight, G. P.; M. E. Bernal; and G. Carlo. "Socialization and the Development of Cooperative, Competitive, and Individualistic Behaviors Among Mexican American Children," In *Meeting the Challenge of Linguistic and Cultural Diversity in Early Childhood Education*, eds. E. E. Garcia, and B. McLaughlin, with B. Spokek, and O. N. Saracho. New York: Teachers College Press, 1995, pp. 85–102.

Kordt-Thomas, C., and I. M. Lee. "Floor Time: Rethinking Play in the Classroom." *Young Children* 61(3), March 2006, pp. 86–89.

Kottak, C. P., and K. A. Kozaitis. *On Being Different*. Boston: McGraw-Hill College, 1999.

Koulouras, K.; M. L. Porter; and S. A. Senter. "Making the Most of Parent Conferences," In *The Art of Leadership*, eds. B. Neugebauer and R. Neugebauer. Redmond, WA: Child Care Information Exchange, 2003.

Kranowitz, C. S. *The Out of Sync Child: Recognizing and Coping with Sensory Integration Dysfunction*. New York: Paragee, 1998.

Kreidler, W. J., and S. Whitall. "Resolving Conflict." In C. Copple, ed., *A World of Difference: Readings on Teaching Children in a Diverse Society*. Washington, DC: National Association for the Education of Young Children, 2003, pp. 52–56.

Kristal, J. *The Temperament Perspective: Working with Children's Behavioral Styles*. Baltimore, MD: Brookes Publishing, 2005.

Kusserow, A. S. *American Individualisms: Child Rearing and Social Class in Three Neighborhoods*. New York: Palgrave McMillan, 2004.

Kyttä, M. "The Extent of Children's Independent Mobility and the Number of Actualized Affordances as Criteria for Child-Friendly Environments" *Journal of Environmental Psychology* 24(2), 2004, pp. 179–198.

Ladson-Billings, G. *The Dreamkeepers: Successful Teachers of African American Children*. San Francisco: Jossey-Bass, 1994.

Ladson-Billings, G. "What We can Learn from Multicultural Education Research." *Educational Leadership* 51, no. 8 (1994), pp. 22–26.

Lally, J. R. "The Impact of Child Care Policies and Practices on Infant/Toddler Identity Formation," *Young Children*, 1995, November, pp. 58–67.

Laurion, J., and C. Schmiedicke. *Creating Connection: How to Lead Family Child Care Support Groups*. St. Paul, MN: Redleaf Press, 2005.

Lawrence-Lightfoot, S. *Respect: An Exploration*. Cambridge, MA: Perseus, 2000.

Leach, P. *Your Baby and Child from Birth to Age Five*. New York: Knopf, 1987.

Lee, D. *Freedom and Culture*. Englewood Cliffs, NJ: Prentice Hall, 1959.

Lee, F. Y. "Asian Parents as Partners." *Young Children*, March 1995, pp. 4–8.

Lee, J. *Asian Americans*. New York: New Press, 1992.

Lee K.; C. Cameron; F. Xu; G. Fu; and J. Board. "Chinese and Canadian Children's Evaluations of Lying and Truth Telling: Similarities and Differences in the Context of Pro- and Antisocial Behaviors." *Child Development* 68, no. 5 (1997), pp. 924–934.

Lee, L. "Working with Non-English-Speaking Families." *Exchange*, July 1997, pp. 57–58.

Lee, L. *Serving Families: A Handbook on the Principles and Strategies of the Parent Services Project Approach*. San Rafael, CA: Parent Services Project, 2002.

Lee, L., and E. Seiderman. "The Parent Services Project." *Families Matter Series*. Cambridge, MA: Harvard Research Project, 1998.

Lefley, H., and P. Pedersen, eds. *Cross-Cultural Training for Mental Health Professionals*. Springfield, IL: Thomas, 1986.

Lesser, L. K.; T. Burt; and G. Aimee. *Making Room in the Circle: Lesbian, Gay, Bisexual and Transgender Families in Early Childhood Settings*. San Rafael, CA: Parent Services Project, 2005.

Lessow-Hurley, J. *The Foundations of Dual Language Instruction*. New York: Longman, 2000.

Leven, D. E., and N. Carlsson-Paige. *The War Play Dilemma*. New York: Teachers College Press, 2005.

LeVine, R. A. "Child Rearing as Cultural Adaptation," In *Culture and Infancy: Variations in the Human Experience*, eds. P. H. Leiderman, S. R. Tulkin, and A. Rosenfeld. New York and San Francisco: Academic Press, 1977.

LeVine, R. A. "A Cross-Cultural Perspective on Parenting," In *Parenting in a Multicultural Society*, eds. M. D. Fantini, and R. Cardenas. New York: Longman, 1980, pp. 17–26.

LeVine, R.A.; S. LeVine; P. H. Leiderman; T. B. Brazelton; S. Dixon; A. Richan; and C. H. Keefer. *Child Care and Culture: Lessons from Africa*. New York: Cambridge University Press, 1994.

Lewin-Benham, A. *Possible Schools: The Reggio Approach to Urban Education*. New York: Teachers College Press, 2004.

Lewis, C. C. *Educating Hearts and Minds: Reflections on Japanese Preschool and Elementary Education*. New York: Cambridge University Press, 1995.

Lieberman, A. F. "Concerns of Immigrant Families." In *Infant/Toddler Caregiving: A Guide to Culturally Sensitive Care*, ed. P. Mangione. Sacramento: Far West Laboratory and California Department of Education, 1995.

Liederman, P. H., et al. *Culture and Infancy: Variations in Human Experience*. New York: Academic Press, 1977.

Lin, C. Y., and V. Fu. "A Comparison of Child-Rearing Practices among Chinese, Immigrant Chinese, and Caucasian-American Parents." *Child Development* 61, 1990, pp. 429–433.

Little Soldier, L. "Working with Native American Children." *Young Children* 47, no. 6 (September 1992), pp. 15–17.

Little Soldier, L. "Is There an 'Indian' in Your Classroom? Working Successfully with Urban Native American Students." *Phi Delta Kappan* 78, no. 8 (1997), pp. 650–653.

Logue, M. E. "Teachers Observe to Learn—Differences in Social Behavior of Toddlers and Preschoolers in Same-Age and Multiage Groupings. *Young Children* 61(3), 2006, pp. 70–77.

Lombardi, J., and M. M. Bogle. (Eds.). *Beacon of Hope: The Promise of Early Head Start for America's Youngest Children.* Washington, DC: Zero to Three, 2004.

Loomis, C., and J. Wagner. "A Different Look at Challenging Behavior." *Young Children* 60(2), 2005, pp. 94–99.

Lopez, E. J.; L. Salas; and J. P. Flores. "Hispanic Preschool Children: What About Assessment and Intervention? *Young Children* 60(6), 2005, pp. 48–54.

Louv, R. *Last Child in the Woods: Saving Our Children from Nature Deficit Disorder.* New York: Workman, 2005.

Lubeck, S. *The Sandbox Society: Early Education in Black and White America.* Philadelphia: Falmer Press, 1985.

Lubeck, S. "Deconstructing 'Child Development Knowledge' and 'Teacher Preparation.'" *Early Childhood Research Quarterly* 11, no. 2 (1996), pp. 147–168.

Lynch, E. W., and M. J. Hanson. *Developing Cross-Cultural Competence: A Guide for Working with Young Children and Their Families.* Baltimore, MD: Brookes, 1992.

MacDonald, B. "Purposeful Work: A Montessori Approach to Everyday Challenging Behaviors." *Exchange,* 2005, pp. 51–54.

MacNaughton, G. *Rethinking Gender in Early Childhood Education.* St. Leonards, NSW, Australia: Allen and Unwin, 2000.

Mah, A. Y. *Falling Leaves: The Memoir of an Unwanted Chinese Daughter.* New York: Wiley, 1997.

Makin, L., J. Campbell, and C. J. Diaz. *One Childhood, Many Languages.* Pymble, NSW, Australia: HarperEducational, 1995.

Malcomson, S. L. *One Drop of Blood: The American Misadventure of Race.* New York: Farrar Straus Giroux, 2000.

Mallory, B. L., and R. S. New, eds. *Diversity and Developmentally Appropriate Practices: Challenges for Early Childhood Education.* New York: Teachers College Press, 1994.

Mandarin Asian Pacific Lesbian/Bisexual Network. *Beloved Daughter, Family Letter Project.* San Francisco: API Family Pride, 2002.

Mander, J. *In the Absence of the Sacred.* San Francisco: Sierra Club Books, 1991.

Mangione, P., ed. *Infant/Toddler Caregiving: A Guide to Culturally Sensitive Care.* Sacramento: Far West Laboratory and California Department of Education, 1995.

Marulanda, A. *Sigamos Creciendo con Nuestros Hijos.* Bogata, Columbia: Grupo Editorial Norma, 2001.

Mastretta, A. *Tear This Heart Out.* New York: Riverhead Books, 1997.

Matthiessen, N. *The Hmong: A Multicultural Study.* Fairfield, CA: Fairfield-Suisun Unified School District, 1987.

McCall, N. *Makes Me Wanna Holler.* New York: Vintage Books, 1994.

McCracken, J. B. *Valuing Diversity: The Primary Years.* Washington, DC: National Association for the Education of Young Children, 1993.

McGoldrick, M.; J. Giordano; and J. K. Pearce, eds. *Ethnicity and Family Therapy,* 2nd ed. New York: Guiliford Press, 1996.

McIntosh, P. *White Privilege and Male Privilege: A Personal Account of Coming to See Correspondences Through Work in Women's Studies.* Working Paper No. 189. Wellesley, MA: Wellesley College Center for Research on Women, 1988.

McLoyd, V. "The Impact of Economic Hardship on Black Families and Children: Psychological Distress, Parenting, and Socioemotional Development. *Child Development* 61, 1990, pp. 311–346.

McLoyd, V. "Socioeconomic Disadvantage and Child Development." *American Psychologist* 53, no. 2 (1998), pp. 185–204.

Means, R. *Where White Men Fear to Tread.* New York: St. Martin's Press, 1995.

Medicine, B. "Child Socialization Among Native Americans: The Lakota (Sioux) in Cultural Context." *Wicazo Sa Review* 1, no. 2 (Fall 1985), pp. 23–28.

Meisels, S. J., and S. Atkins-Burnett. *Developmental Screening in Early Childhood.* Washington, DC: National Association for the Education of Young Children, 2005.

Meyer, J. *Kids Talking: Learning Relationships and Culture With Children.* Lanham, MD: Rowman & Littlefield Publishers, Inc., 2003.

Miller. D. F. *First Steps Toward Cultural Difference: Socialization in Infant/Toddler Day Care.* Washington, DC: Child Welfare League of America, 1989.

Miller, K. "Developmental Issues that Affect Behavior." In B. Neugebauer, ed., *Behavior: A Beginnings Workshop Book* (pp. 12–13). Redmond, WA: Exchange, 2005.

Miller, P.; A. Wiley; H. Gung; and C. H. Liang. "Personal Storytelling as a Medium of Socialization in Chinese and American Families." *Child Development* 68, no. 3 (1997), pp. 557–567.

Miner, B. "Teachers, Culture, and Power: An Interview with African-American Educator Lisa Delpit." *Rethinking Schools,* March/April 1992, pp. 14–16.

Mistry, J. "Culture and Learning in Infancy." In *Infant/Toddler Caregiving: A Guide to Culturally Sensitive Care,* ed. P. Mangione. Sacramento: Far West Laboratory and California Department of Education, 1995.

Modigliani, K. *Parents Speak About Child Care.* Boston: Wheelock College Family Child Care Project, 1997.

Mooney, C. G. *Theories of Childhood: An Introduction to Dewey, Montessori, Erikson, Piaget, and Vygotsky.* St. Paul, MN: Redleaf, 2000.

Morelli, G.; B. Rogoff; and D. Oppenheim. "Cultural Variation in Infants' Sleeping Arrangements: Questions of Independence." *Developmental Psychology* 28, no. 4 (July 1992), pp. 604–619.

Morgan, G. "Is Education Separate from Care?" *Exchange*, 2005, pp. 6–10.

Morrow, R. D. "Cultural Differences—Be Aware!" *Academic Therapy* 23, no. 2 (November 1987), p. 2.

Morrow, R. D. "What's in a Name? In Particular, a Southeast Asian Name?" *Young Children*, September 1989, pp. 20–23.

Morse, A. *Language Access: Helping Non-English Speakers Navigate Health and Human Services.* Washington, DC: National Conference of State Legislature Children's Policy Initiative, 2003.

Native American Parent Preschool Curriculum Guide. Oakland, CA: Office of Native American Programs, Division of Educational Development and Services, 1986.

NAEYC Code of Ethical Conduct. Position Statement of the National Association for the Education of Young Children. In *NAEYC Early Childhood Program Standards and Accreditation Criteria* (p. 119). Washington, DC: National Association for the Education of Young Children, 2005.

National Association for the Education of Young Children. *NAEYC Early Childhood Program Standards and Accreditation Criteria.* Washington, DC: National Association for the Education of Young Children, 2005.

Nee-Benham, M. K. P. A., and J. E. Cooper. *Indigenous Educational Models for Contemporary Practice: In Our Mother's Voice.* Mahwah, NJ: Erlbaum, 2000.

Neihardt, J. G., *Black Elk Speaks.* New York: Pocket Books, 1972.

Neugebauer, B., ed. *Alike and Different: Exploring Our Humanity with Young Children.* Washington, DC: National Association for the Education of Young Children, 1992.

Neugebauer, B., ed. *Behavior: A Beginnings Workshop Book.* Redmond, WA: Exchange Press, Inc., 2005.

New, R. S., and A. L. Richman. "Maternal Beliefs and Infant Care Practices in Italy and the United States." In *Parents' Cultural Belief Systems*, eds., S. Harkness, and C. M. Super. New York: Guiliford Press, 1996, pp. 385–404.

New Zealand Ministry of Education, *Te Whariki: Early Childhood Curriculum.* Wellington, New Zealand: Ministry of Education, 1996.

Nieto, S. S. *Affirming Diversity: The Sociopolitical Context of Multicultural Education.* 3rd ed. New York: Addison Wesley, Longman, 2000.

Nieto, S., ed. *Why We Teach.* New York: Teachers College Press, 2005.

Nourot, P. M.; B. Scales; J. Van Horn; and M. Almy. *Looking at Children's Play:A Bridge Between Theory and Practice.* New York: Teachers College Press, 1987.

Nugent, J. K. "Cross-Cultural Studies of Child Development: Implications for Clinicians." *Zero to Three* 15, no. 2 (October/November 1994), pp. 1–7.

Nyman, S. I. "Mentoring Advocates in the Context of Early Childhood Education." In Neugebauer, B. and R. Neugebauer, eds. *The Art of Leadership.* Redmond, WA: Exchange Press, 2003.

O'Brien, M. *Inclusive Child Care for Infants and Toddlers: Meeting Individual and Special Needs.* Baltimore: Brookes, 1997.

Odom, S. L.; T. Teferra; and S. Kaul. "An Overview of International Approaches to Early Intervention for Young Children with Special Needs and Their Families." *Young Children* 59(5), 2004, pp. 38–43.

Ogbu, J. U. "Understanding Cultural Diversity and Learning." *Educational Researcher,* November 1992, pp. 5–14.

Olsen, L.; J. Bhattacharya; and A. Scharf. *Ready or Not: School Readiness and Immigrant Communities.* Oakland, CA: California Tomorrow, 2005.

Olson, M., and M. Hyson. "Supporting Teachers, Strengthening Families Initiative Adds a National Leadership Program for Early Childhood Professionals." *Young Children* 60(1), 2005, pp. 44–45.

Ordonez-Jasis, R., and R. W. Ortiz. "Reading Their Worlds: Working with Diverse Families to Enhance Children's Early Literacy Development. *Young Children* 61(1), 2006, pp. 42–49.

Ortiz, A. A., and J. R. Yaters. "Consideration in the Assessment of English Language Learners Referred to Special Education." In A. J. Artiles and A. A. Ortiz, eds., *English Language Learners with Special Education Needs: Identification, Assessment and Instruction* (pp. 65–85). McHenry, IL: Center for Applied Linguistics and Delta, 2002.

Outsama, K. *Laotian Themes.* Philadelphia: Temple University Press, 1977.

Parent Services Project (PS). "Working Together for Children and Families." Brochure. San Rafael, CA: Author, 2001.

Parlakian, R. The Power of Questions: Building Quality Relationships with Families." Brochure. Washington, DC: Zero to Three, 2001.

Pate, R. R.; K. A. Pfeiffer; S. G. Trost; and P. Ziegler; and M. Dowda. "Physical Activity Among Children Attending Preschools." *Pediatrics* 114(5), 2004, pp. 1258–1263.

Patterson, K.; J. Grenny; R. McMillan; and A. Switzler. *Crucial Conversations: Tools for Talking When Stakes Are High.* New York: McGraw-Hill, 2002.

Patterson, M. B. D. "America's Racial Unconscious: The Invisibility of Whiteness." In *White Reign: Deploying Whiteness in America,* eds., J. L. Kincheloe, S. R. Steinberg, N. M. Rodriguez, and R. E. Chennault. New York: St. Martin's Press, 1998, pp. 103–122.

Payne, R. *A Framework for Understanding Poverty.* Highlands TX: Aha! Process, Inc., 2003.

Pence, A. "Finding a Niche in Building ECE Capacity. *Interaction* 18(1), 2004, pp. 31–33.

Pence, A. R. "Reconceptualizing ECCD in the Majority World: One Minority World Perspective." *International Journal of Early Childhood* 30, no. 2 (1998), pp. 19–30.

Penn, H., and Moss, P. "The Five Per Cent Phenomenon." (Monograph), 1998.

Petrie, S., and S. Owen, eds. *Authentic Relationships in Group Care for Infants and Toddlers: Resources for Infant Educarers (RIE) Principles into Practice.* London and Philadelphia: Jessica Kingsley Publishers, 2005.

Phillips, C. B. "Nurturing Diversity for Today's Children and Tomorrow's Leaders." *Young Children* 43, no. 2 (1988), pp. 42–47.

Phillips, C. B. "The Movement of African-American Children Through Sociocultural Contexts: A Case of Conflict Resolution," In *Diversity and Developmentally Appropriate Practices: Challenges for Early Childhood Education,* eds. B. L. Malloy, and R. S. New. New York: Teachers College Press, 1994, pp. 137–154.

Phillips, C. B. "Culture: A Process That Empowers." In *Infant/Toddler Caregiving: A Guide to Culturally Sensitive Care,* ed. P. Mangione. Sacramento: Far West Laboratory and California Department of Education, 1995.

Phillips, C. B., and R. M. Cooper. "Cultural Dimensions of Feeding Relationships." *Zero to Three* 12, no. 5 (June 1992), pp. 10–13.

Phipps, P. A. "Working with Angry Parents—Taking a Customer Service Approach," In *The Art of Leadership,* eds. B. Neugebauer, and R. Neugebauer. Redmond, WA: Child Care Information Exchange, 2003.

Pikler, E. "Learning of Motor Skills on the Basis of Self-Induced Movements." In J. Hellmuth, ed., *Exceptional Infant* (vol. 2, pp. 54–89). New York: Bruner/Mazel, 1971.

Pikler, E. "Some Contributions to the Study of Gross Motor Development of Children." In A. Sandovsky, ed., *Child and Adolescent Development* (pp. 52–64). New York: Free Press, 1973.

Pikler, E. "Can Infant-Child Care Centers Promote Optimal Development?" In M. Gerber, ed., *RIE Manual* (pp. 93–102). Los Angeles: Resources for Infant Educarers, 1979.

Pikler, E. "A Quarter of a Century of Observing Infants in a Residential Center." In M. Gerber, ed., *RIE Manual* (pp. 90–92). Los Angeles: Resources for Infant Educarers, 1979.

Pikler, E., and A. Tardos. "Some Contributions to the Study of Infants' Gross Motor Activities." In *Proceedings of the 16th International Congress of Applied Psychology.* Amsterdam: ICAP, 1968.

Pipher, M. *In the Middle of Everywhere: Helping Refugees Enter the American Community.* New York: Harcourt, 2002.

Poussaint, A. F. "Understanding and Involving African American Parents." *Young Children* 61(1), 2006, p. 48.

Powers, J. *Parent-Friendly Early Learning: Tips and Stategies for Working Well with Families.* St. Paul, MN: Redleaf, 2005.

Powers, J. "Six Fundamentals for Creating Relationships with Families." *Young Children* 61(1), 2006, p. 28.

Price, W. F., and R. H. Crapo. *Cross-Cultural Perspectives in Introductory Psychology.* Belmont, CA: Wadsworth, 1999.

Procidano, M. E., and C. B. Fisher. *Contemporary Families: A Handbook for School Professionals.* New York: Teachers College Press, 1992.

Quintero, E. P. "Multicultural Literature: A Source of Meaningful Content for Kindergartners." *Young Children* 60(6), 2005, pp. 28–32.

Quiroz, B.; P. Greenfield; and M. Altchech. "Bridging Cultures with a Parent-Teacher Conference." In *Readings for Bridging Cultures,* ed. C. Rothstein-Fisch. Mahwah, NJ: Lawrence Erlbaum, 2003.

Raeff, C.; P. M. Greenfield; and B. Quiroz. "Conceptualizing Interpersonal Relationships in the Cultural Contexts of Individualism and Collectivism." In *New Directions For Child and Adolescent Development* 87 (pp. 59–74), eds. S. Harkness, C. Raeff, and C. M. Super. San Francisco: Jossey-Bass. 2000.

Rael, J. *Being and Vibration,* Tulsa, OK: Council Oak Books, 1993.

Ramirez, M., and A. Castenada. *Cultural Democracy, Bicognitive Development and Education.* New York: Academic Press, 1974.

Ramsey, P. G. *Teaching and Learning in a Diverse World* (3rd ed.). New York: Teachers College Press, 2004.

Ramsey, P., and L. Derman-Sparks. "Viewpoint: Multicultural Education Reaffirmed." *Young Children* 39, no. 2 (January 1992), pp. 10–11.

Ranson Jacobs, L. "The Value of Real Work with Children Exhibiting Challenging Behavior." *Exchange,* 2006, January, pp. 36–38.

Rashid, H. B. "Promoting Biculturalism in Young African-American Children." *Young Children* 39, no. 2 (1984), pp. 12–23.

Raver, S. A. *Intervention Strategies for Infants and Toddlers with Special Needs.* 2nd ed. Columbus, OH: Merrill, 1999.

Rinehart, N. M. "The Curriculum Belongs to the Community: Curriculum Planning and Development for Tlingit and Haida Young Children." *Zero to Three* 26(4), 2006, pp. 46–48.

Rodriguez, R. *The Hunger of Memory: The Education of Richard Rodriguez.* New York: Bantam Books, 1983.

Rogoff, B. *Apprenticeship in Thinking.* New York: Oxford University Press, 1990.

Rogoff, B.; F. Stott; B. Bowman. "Child Development Knowledge: A Slippery Base for Practice." *Early Childhood Research Quarterly* 11, no. 2 (1990), pp. 1169–1184.

Rogoff, B. *The Cultural Nature of Human Development.* New York: Oxford University Press, 2003.

Root, M.; C. Ho; and S. Sue. "Issues in the Training of Counselors for Asian Americans." In *Cross-Cultural Training for Mental Health Professionals,* eds. H. Lefley, and P. Pedersen. Springfield, IL: Thomas, 1986.

Rosenkoetter, S. E., and J. Knapp-Philo, eds. *Learning to Read the World: Language and Literacy in the First Three Years.* Washington, DC: Zero to Three, 2006.

Rosenow, N. "The Impact of Sensory Integration on Behavior: Discovering Our Best Selves." In B. Neugebauer, ed., *Behavior: A Beginnings Workshop Book* (pp. 33–35). Redmond, WA: Exchange, 2005.

Ross, A. C. (Ehanamani). *Mitakuye Oyasin: We Are All Related.* Denver, CO: Wichoni Waste, 1989.

Rothstein-Fisch, C. *Bridging Cultures: Teacher Education Module.* Mahwah, NJ: Lawrence Erlbaum, 2003.

Rothstein-Fisch, C.; Greenfield, P. M.; and Trumbull, E. "Bridging Cultures with Classroom Strategies." *Educational Leadership* 56, no. 7 (1999), pp. 64–67.

Rothstein-Fisch, C.; Trumbull, E.; and Greenfield, P. M. *Classroom Organization and Management: Factoring in Culture.* New York: Sage Foundation, forthcoming.

Rowe, J. "Out of Time." *Yes!,* Winter. www.yesmagazine.org, retrieved August 28, 2006.

Russell, G. M. "Surviving and Thriving in the Midst of Anti-Gay Politics." *The Policy Journal of the Institute for Gay and Lesbian Strategic Studies* 7(2), 2004, p. 1–7.

Russell, J. A., and M. S. M. Yik. "Emotion among the Chinese." In *The Handbook of Chinese Psychology,* ed. M. H. Bond. Hong Kong: Oxford University Press, 1996, pp. 166–188.

Ryan, S., and S. Grieshaber. "It's More than Child Development: Critical Theories, Research, and Teaching Young Children." *Young Children* 59(6), 2004, pp. 44–52.

Sanchez, S. *Does Your House Have Lions?* Boston: Beacon, 1997.

Sandall, S.; M. McClean; and B. Smith. *DEC Recommended Practices in Early Intervention/Early Childhood Special Education.* Arlington, VA: Council for Exceptional Children, 2000.

Sandall, S., and M. Ostrosky, eds. *Young Exceptional Children: Practical Ideas for Addressing Challenging Behaviors.* Denver: The Division for Early Childhood of the Council for Exceptional Children, 1999.

Sandall, S. R., and I. S. Schwartz. *Building Blocks for Teaching Preschoolers with Special Needs.* Baltimore, MD: Brookes Publishing, 2002.

Sandoval, M., and M. De La Roza. "A Cultural Perspective for Serving the Hispanic Client," In *Cross-Cultural Training for Mental Health Professionals,* eds. H. Lefley, and P. Pedersen. Springfield, IL: Thomas, 1986.

Sandoz, M. *Crazy Horse: The Strange Man of the Oglalas.* Lincoln: University of Nebraska Press, 1961.

Saracho, O. N., and B. Spodek. "Preparing Teachers for Early Childhood Programs." In *Meeting the Challenge of Linguistic and Cultural Diversity in Early Childhood Education,* eds. E. E. Garcia, and B. McLaughlin, with B. Spokek, and O. N. Saracho. New York: Teachers College Press, 1995, pp. 154–166.

Saracho, O. N., and B. Spodek, eds. *Understanding the Multicultural Experience in Early Childhood Education.* Washington, DC: National Association for the Education of Young Children, 1983.

Schaef, A. W. *Codependency, Misunderstood, Mistreated.* HarperSanFrancisco, 1986.

Scott, D. M. "The Pathway to Leadership Takes Many Roads: A Personal Journey." *Young Children* 60(1), 2005, p. 42.

Segal, M.; W. Masi; and R. Leiderman. In *Time and With Love: Caring for Infants and Toddlers with Special Needs.* 2nd ed. New York: New Market Press, 2001.

Seiderman, E. "Putting All the Players on the Same Page: Accessing Resources for the Child and Family." In Neugebauer, B. and R. Neugebauer, eds. *The Art of Leadership.* Redmond, WA: Exchange Press, 2003.

Seplocha, H. "Partnerships for Learning: Conferencing with Families." *Young Children* 59(5), 2004, pp. 96–99.

Shareef, I., and J. Gonzalez-Mena. "Beneath the Veneers of Resistance and Professionalism." *Exchange,* May 1997, pp. 6–8.

Shick, L. *Understanding Temperament.* Seattle, WA.: Parenting Press, 1998.

Shirilla, J., and D. J. Weatherston, eds. *Case Studies in Infant Mental Health: Risk, Resiliency, and Relationships.* Washington, DC: Zero to Three, 2002.

Sholtys, K. C. "A New Language, A New Life: Recommendations for Teachers of Non-English-Speaking Children Newly Entering the Program." *Young Children,* March 1989, pp. 76–77.

Shonkoff, J. P., and D. A. Phillips, eds. *From Neurons to Neighborhoods: The Science of Early Childhood Development.* Washington, DC: National Academy Press, 2000.

Sigel, I. E., and K. Myung-In."The Answer Depends on the Question: A Conceptual and Methodological Analysis of a Parent Belief-Behavior Interview Regarding Children's Learning." In *Parents' Cultural Belief Systems,* eds. S. Harkness, and C. M. Super. New York: Guilford Press, 1996, pp. 83–120.

Siraj-Blatchford, I., and P. Clarke. *Supporting Identity: Diversity and Language in the Early Years.* Philadelphia: Open University Press, 2000.

Slapin, B., and D. Seale. *Books without Bias: Through Indian Eyes.* Berkeley, CA: Oyate, 1988.

Sleeter, C., and C. Grant. *Making Choices for Multicultural Education.* 3rd ed. Columbus, OH: Merrill, 1999.

Small, M. *Our Babies, Ourselves: How Biology and Culture Shape the Way We Parent.* New York: Anchor Books, 1998.

Small, M. "Dare to Bare." New York Times, October 11, 2005.

Snowden, L. R. "Toward Evaluation of Black Psycho-Social Competence." In *The Pluralistic Society.* eds. S. Sue, and T. Moore. New York: Human Sciences Press, 1984.

Sodetani-Shibata, A. E. "The Japanese American." In *Culture and Childrearing*, ed. A. L. Clark. Philadelphia: F. A. Davis, 1981.

Some, S. *The Spirit of Intimacy: Ancient African Teachings in the Ways of Relationships.* New York: HarperCollins/Quill, 2000.

Sommers, C. H., and C. Satel. *One Nation Under Therapy: How the Helping Culture is Eroding Self-Reliance.* New York: St. Martins Press, 2005.

Soto, L. D. "Understanding Bicultural/Bilingual Young Children." *Young Children,* January 1991.

Soto, L. D. *Language, Culture, and Power: Bilingual Families and the Struggle for Quality Education.* New York: State College of New York Press, 1997.

Soto, L. D., and J. L. Smrekar. "The Politics of Early Bilingual Education." In *Reconceptualizing the Early Childhood Curriculum: Beginning the Dialogue*, eds. S. A. Kessler, and B. B. Swadener. New York: Teachers College Press, 1992, pp. 189–202.

Spencer, M. B.; G. K. Brookins; and A. W. Recharde, eds. *Beginnings: The Social and Affective Development of Black Children.* Hillsdale, NJ: Lawrence Erlbaum, 1985.

Stegelin, D. A. "Making the Case for Play Policy: Research-Based Reasons to Support Play-Based Environments." *Young Children* 60(2), 2005, pp. 76–85.

Stephens, K. "Meaningful Family Engagement." *Exchange*, 2005, May, pp. 18–25.

Stephens, K. "Responding Professionally and Compassionately to Challenging Behavior." In B. Neugebauer, ed., *Behavior: A Beginning Workshop Book* (pp. 7–11). Redmond, WA: Exchange, 2005.

Stern, D. N. *The Interpersonal World of the Infant.* New York: Basic Books, 1985.

Stewart, E. C. *American Cultural Patterns: A Cross-Cultural Perspective.* Yarmouth, ME: Intercultural Press, 1972.

Stipek, D. "Differences Between Americans and Chinese in the Circumstances Evoking Pride, Shame, and Guilt." *Journal of Cross-Cultural Psychology* 29, no. 5 (1998), pp. 616–629.

Stoecklin, K. L. "Creating Environments That Sustain Children, Staff, and Our Planet." *Exchange*, 2005, July, pp. 39–48.

Stonehouse, A., and J. Gonzalez-Mena. "Responding in the Spirit of Partnership: High Maintenance Parents." *Child Care Information Exchange*, January 2000, pp. 10–12.

Stonehouse, A., and J. Gonzalez-Mena. "Working with a High-Maintenance Parent: Building Trust and Respect Through Communication." *Child Care Information Exchange*, November 2001, pp 57–60.

Stonehouse, A., and J. Gonzalez-Mena. *Making Links: A Collaborative Approach to Planning and Practice in Early Childhood.* Sydney, Australia: Pademelon Press, 2004.

Storti, C. *The Art of Crossing Cultures.* Yarmouth, ME: Intercultural Press, 1990.

Stringfellow, L.; N. D. Liem; and L. Liem. In *Culture and Childrearing*, ed. A. L. Clark. Philadelphia: F. A. Davis, 1981.

Sturm, C. "Intercultural Communication in Child Care: Creating Parent-Teacher Dialogue." Master's thesis, 1995.

Sturm, L. "Temperament in Early Development." *Zero to Three*, March, 2004, p. 56.

Sue, S., and T. Moore, eds. *The Pluralistic Society.* New York: Human Sciences Press, 1984.

Sullivan, D. R. *Learning to Lead.* St. Paul, MN: Redleaf Press, 2003.

Sung, B. L. *Chinese Immigrant Children in New York City: The Experience of Adjustment.* New York: Center for Migration Studies, 1987.

Swick, K. J. *Empowering Parents, Families, Schools and Communities During the Early Childhood Years.* Champaign, IL: Stipes Publishing, 2004.

Takaki, R. *A Different Mirror: A History of Multicultural America.* Boston: Back Bay Books, 1993.

Tan, A.L. *Chinese American Children and Families: A Guide for Educators and Service Providers.* Olney, MD: Association for childhood Education International, 2004.

Tardos, A. "Facilitating the Play of Children at Lóczy." *Educaring* 6(3), 1985, pp. 1–2.

Tardos, A. "Patterns of Play Observed at Lóczy." *Educaring* 7(2), 1986, pp. 1–7.

Tatum, B. D. *Why Are All the Black Kids Sitting Together in the Cafeteria?* New York: Basic Books, 1997.

Tedla, E. *Sankofa: African Thought and Education.* New York: Peter Lang, 1995.

Tee, O. P. "Innovative Use of Local Resources for Children's Play: A Case in Malaysia." *Young Children* 59(5), 2004, pp. 14–18.

Thaxton, S. M. "Grandparents as Parents—Understanding the Issues." In *The Art of Leadership*, eds. B. Neugebauer, and R. Neugebauer. Redmond, WA: Child Care Information Exchange, 2003.

Thompson, N. L., and R. D. Hare. "Early Education for American Indian and Alaska Native Children in Rural America." *Zero to Three* 26(4), 2006, pp. 43–45.

Thorman, E. B., and S. Browder. *Born Dancing.* New York: Harper & Row, 1987.

Thornberg, R. "The Situated Nature of Preschool Children's Conflict Strategies. *Educational Psychology* 26(1), 2006, pp. 109–112.

Tizard, B., and M. Hughes, *Young Children Learning.* Cambridge, MA: Harvard University Press, 1984.

Tobaissen, D. P., and J. Gonzalez-Mena. *A Place to Begin: Working with Parents on Issues of Diversity.* Oakland, CA: California Tomorrow, 1998.

Tobin, J. J.; D. Y. H. Wu; and D. H. Davidson. *Preschool in Three Cultures.* New Haven, CT: Yale University Press, 1989.

Tortora, S. *The Dancing Dialogue: Using the Communicative Power of Movement with Young Children.* Baltimore, MD: Brookes Publishing, 2005.

Trawick-Smith, F. *Early Childhood Development: A Multicultural Perspective.* Columbus, OH: Merrill, 1997.

Triandis, H. C. "Cross-cultural Studies of Individualism and Collectivism." *Nebraska Symposium on Motivation* 37, 1989, pp. 43–133.

Tronick, E. Z.; G. A. Morelli; and S. Winn. "Multiple Caretaking of Efe (Pygmy) Infants." *American Anthropologist* 89, 1987, pp. 96–106.

Trueba, H. T. *Raising Silent Voices.* Boston: Heinle and Heinle, 1989.

Trumbull, E., and B. Farr. *Language and Learning: What Teachers Need to Know.* Norwood, MA: Christopher Gordon Publishers, 2005.

Trumbull, E.; R. Diaz-Meza; A. Hasan; and C. Rothstein-Fisch. *Five-Year Report of the Bridging Cultures Project: 1996–2000.* San Francisco: WestEd, 2001, http://www.WestEd.org/BridgingCultures.

Trumbull, E.; C. Rothstein-Fisch; and P. Greenfield. *Bridging Cultures in Our Schools: New Approaches That Work.* San Francisco: WestEd, 2000.

Turnbull, A., and R. Turnbull. *Families, Professionals, and Exceptionality: Collaborating for Empowerment.* 4th ed. Upper Saddle River, NJ: Merrill Prentice Hall, 2001.

Udell, T., and G. Glasenapp. "Managing Challenging Behaviors: Adult Communication as a Prevention and Teaching Tool." In B. Neugebauer, ed., *Behavior: A Beginnings Workshop Book* (pp. 26–29). Redmond, WA: Exchange, 2005.

Unell, B. C., and J. L. Wyckoff. *The Eight Seasons of Parenthood. How the Stages of Parenting Constantly Reshape Our Adult Identities.* New York: Time Books, 2000.

Uttal, L. *Making Care Work: Employed Mothers in the New Childcare Market.* New Brunswick, New Jersey: Rutgers University Press, 2002.

Valdes, G. *Con Respeto: Bridging the Distances Between Culturally Diverse Families and Schools.* New York: Teachers College Press, 1996.

Van Hoorn, J.; P. M. Nourot; B. Scales; and K. R. Alward. *Play at the Center of the Curriculum*, 3rd ed. Columbus, OH: Merrill, 2003.

Van Hoorn, J., P. M. Nourot; B. Scales; and K. R. Alward. *Play at the Center of the Curriculum.* Upper Saddle River, New Jersey Prentice Hall/A Division of Pearson Education, 2007.

Vandell, D. L. "Early Child Care: The Known and the Unknown." *Merrill-Palmer Quarterly.* 50(3), 2004, pp. 387–414.

Vandenbroeck, M. *Globalization and Privatization: The Impact on Child Care Policy and Practice* (Working Paper No. 38). The Hague, The Netherlands: Bernard van Leer Foundation, 2006.

Vartuli, S. "Beliefs: The Heart of Teaching." *Young Children* 60(5), 2005, pp. 76–86.

Villa, J., and L. Colker. "A Personal Story: Making Inclusions Work." *Young Children* 61(1), 2006, pp. 96–100.

Villarruel, F. A.; D. R. Imig; and M. J. Kostelnik. "Diverse Families." In *Meeting the Challenge of Linguistic and Cultural Diversity in Early Childhood Education*, eds. E. G. Garcia, and B. McLaughlin, with B. Spokek, and O. N. Saracho. New York: Teachers College Press, 1995, pp. 103–124.

Vinson, B. M. "Fishing and Vygotsky's Concept of Effective Education." *Young Children* 56(1), 2001, pp. 88–89.

Volk, D., and S. Long. "Challenging Myths of the Deficit Perspective: Honoring Children's Literacy Resources." *Young Children* 60(6), 2005, pp. 12–19.

Wagner, D. A., and H. W. Stevenson, eds. *Cultural Perspectives on Child Development.* San Francisco: Freeman, 1982.

Wardel, F. "Are You Sensitive to Interracial Children's Special Identity Needs?" *Young Children,* January 1987, pp. 53–59.

Wardel, F. "Endorsing Children's Differences: Meeting the Needs of Adopted Minority Children." *Young Children,* July 1990, pp. 44–46.

Washington, V. "Sharing Leadership: A Case Study of Diversity in Our Profession." *Young Children* 60(1), 2005, pp. 23–31.

Wassermann, S. *This Teaching Life: How I Taught Myself To Teach.* New York: Teachers College Press, 2004.

Werner, E. *Cross-Cultural Child Development: A View from the Planet Earth.* Monterey, CA: Brooks/Cole, 1979.

White, R. "Young Children's Relationship with Nature: Its Importance to Children's Development and the Earth's Future." Retrieved 2004 from www.whitehutchinson .com/children/articles/childrennature.shtml.

Whitebook, M., and L. Sakai. *By a Thread: How Child Care Centers Hold on to Teachers. How Teachers Build Lasting Careers.* Kalamazoo, MI: W. E. Upjohn Institute for Employment Research, 2004.

Whitelaw Drogue, P. "Stop Refereeing and Start Building Communication Skills." *Exchange.* 2006 January/February, pp. 6–8.

Whitin, D. J. "Pairing Books for Children's Mathematical Learning." *Young Children* 60(2), 2005, pp. 42–48.

Whiting, B.; B. Edwards; and C. Pope. *Children of Different Worlds: The Formation of Social Behavior.* Cambridge, MA: Harvard University Press. 1988.

Widerstrom, A. H. *Achieving Learning Goals Through Play: Teaching Young Children with Special Needs* (2nd ed.). Baltimore, MD: Brookes Publishing, 2005.

Wien, C. A. *Negotiating Standards in the Primary Classroom: The Teacher's Dilemma.* New York: Teachers College Press, 2004.

Williams, B.; D. Cunningham; and J. Lubawy. *Preschool Math.* Beltsville, MD: Gryphon House, 2005.

Williams, K. C., and M. H. Cooney. "Young Children and Social Justice." *Young Children* 61(2), 2006, pp. 75–82.

Williams, L. R. "Developmentally Appropriate Practice and Cultural Values: A Case in Point," In *Diversity and Developmentally Appropriate Practices: Challenges for Early Childhood Education,* eds. B. L. Mallory, and R. S. New. New York: Teachers College Press, 1994, pp. 155–165.

Williamson, G. G., and M. Anzalone. *Sensory Integration and Self-Regulation in Infants and Toddlers: Helping Very Young Children Interact With Their Environment.* Washington, DC: Zero to Three, 2001.

Wolf, A. W.; B. Lozoff; S. Latz; and R. Paludetto. "Parental Theories in the Management of Young Children's Sleep in Japan, Italy and the United States." In *Parents' Cultural Belief Systems,* eds. S. Harkness, and C. M. Super. New York: Guilford Press, 1996, pp. 364–384.

Wolpert, E. *Start Seeing Diversity: The Basic Guide to an Anti-Bias Classroom,* St. Paul, MN: Redleaf Press, 2005.

Wong-Fillmore, L. "When Learning a Second Language Means Losing the First." *Early Childhood Research Quarterly* 6, 1991.

Woodard, C.; G. Haskins; G. Schaefer; and L. Smolen. "Let's Talk: A Different Approach to Oral Language Development." *Young Children* 59(4), 2004, pp. 92–95.

Woyke, P. P. "Hopping Frogs and Trail Walks: Connecting Young Children and Nature." *Young Children* 59(1), 2004, pp. 82–85.

Wright, M. A. *I'm Chocolate, You're Vanilla: Raising Healthy Black and White Children in a Race-Conscious World.* San Francisco, Jossey-Bass, 1998.

Wu, D. "Child Training in Chinese Culture." In *Chinese Culture and Mental Health,* eds. W. S. Tseng, and D. Y. H. Wu. Orlando, FL: Academic Press, 1985, pp. 113–134.

Wu, D. "Chinese Childhood Socialization." In *The Handbook of Chinese Psychology,* ed. M. H. Bond. Hong Kong: Oxford University Press, 1996, pp. 143–154.

Wu, D., and W. Tseng. "Family and Child." In *Chinese Culture and Mental Health,* ed. W. S. Tseng, and D. Y. H. Wu. Orlando, FL: Academic Press, 1985, pp. 83–84.

Wurm, J. *Working in the Reggio Way: A Beginner's Guide for American Teachers.* St. Paul, MN: Redleaf Press, 2005.

Yntema, S. *Vegetarian Children.* Ithaca, NY: McBooks Press, 1987.

York, S. *Roots and Wings: Affirming Culture in Early Childhood Programs.* St. Paul, MN: Redleaf Press, 1991.

Young Children. "Resources for Early Childhood Education Around the Globe." *Young Children* 59(5), 2004, pp. 82–83.

Young Children. "Resources for Exploring the Creative Arts with Young Children." *Young Children* 59(4), 2004, pp. 58–59.

Young Children, "Resources for Exploring the Ethical Dimensions of the Early Childhood Profession." *Young Children* 59(6), 2004, pp. 40–42.

Young Children. "Resources on Health and Safety for Early Childhood Educators." *Young Children* 59(2), 2004, pp. 64–66.

Young Children. "Resources on Embracing Diversity in Early Childhood Settings." *Young Children* 60(6), 2005, pp. 55–59.

Young Children, "Resources on Kindergarten and Beyond." *Young Children* 60(2), 2005, pp. 59–62.

Young Children. "Resources on Leadership in Early Childhood Education." *Young Children* 60(1), 2005, p. 46.

Young, V. H. "Family and Childhood in a Southern Negro Community." *American Anthropologist* 72, 1970, pp. 269–288.

Young, V. H. "A Black American Socialization Pattern." *American Ethnologist* 1, 1974, pp. 405–413.

Youngquist, J. "From Medicine to Microbes: A Project Investigation of Health." *Young Children* 59(2), 2004, pp. 28–32.

Zepeda, M.; J. Gonzalez-Mena; C. Rothstein-Fisch; and E. Trumbell. *Bridging Cultures in Early Care and Education.* Mahwah, NJ: Erlbaum, 2006.

Zigler, E. F.; D. G. Singer; and S. J. Bishop-Josef. *Children's Play: The Roots of Reading.* Washington, DC: Zero to Three, 2004.

Credits

CHAPTER 1
Page 8   © image100/PunchStock

CHAPTER 2
Page 30   © Jack Hollingsworth/Getty Images

CHAPTER 3
Page 46   © Digital Vision/Getty Images

CHAPTER 4
Page 66   © The McGraw-Hill Companies, Inc./Lars A. Niki, photographer

CHAPTER 5
Page 86   © Michael Newman/PhotoEdit

CHAPTER 6
Page 102   © Digital Vision/Punchstock/Punchstock
Page 105   © Elizabeth Crews
Page 113   © David Turnley/Corbis

CHAPTER 7
Page 124   © Digital Vision/PunchStock
Page 137   © Bob Daemmrich/The Image Works

Index